Inside the Changing Circus

A Critic's Guide

DAVID LEWIS
HAMMARSTR(

ALSO BY THE AUTHOR

Behind the Big Top

Circus Rings Around Russia

Big Top Boss: John Ringling North and the Circus

Roller Skating for Gold

Broadway Musicals: A Hundred Year History

Flower Drum Songs: The Story of Two Musicals

Fall of the Big Top: The Vanishing American Circus

Table of Contents

About the Photographs 11
Preface 13
Enter, With Luck, the Impresario 19
From Foreign Lands 37
Directing the Impossible 59
To Go or Not to Go? 77
Midways on the Way 91
A Special Place 103
On With the Show! 115
Clowns Are Us 131
Animal Attitudes 149
Ring Spoilers 163
Intermissions Without End 175
The Thrill Might Be Gone 183
Some Big Top Broccoli, Ma'am? 197
Rising Stars, Falling Stars 219
Last Impressions 235
High Wire Critic 247
Ten Years From Now 263
Sources 277
Index 281

*to Ken Dodd
my sharing Sarasota friend*

About the Photographs

In the sea of photo fishing, where one circus company may cooperate and many will not, where one institution may throw up hurdles, the next, treat you like a friend over to borrow pictures, let me acknowledge here the compassionate cooperation of a few sharing souls.

From the Milner library's Special Collections at Illinois State University, what a pleasure it is to be featuring, however few in number, a sampling of the remarkable photography of Sverre O. Braathen. His magnificent color Kodachrome slides have only in recent years come to the embracing acclaim of circus fans and photography critics. I only regret that you will not be viewing them here in glorious color. However, their black-and-white conversions, I believe, convey the man's gift for framing the human figure against the circus panorama. Actually, in some instances, black-and-white can alter our perceptions favorably by casting more attention onto composition; and in this regard, some of Braathen's work may gain. For his, as well as the other excellent Milner images that enrich these pages, I am especially grateful to the Milner's Special Collections librarian, Maureen Brunsdale, and to her valiant library specialist, Mark Schmitt. Mark took my wish list, ran with it "into the vault," and returned with an abundance of options, answering all of my queries with enthusiasm and dispatch.

From Baraboo, Wisconsin, Tim Tegge, likewise, rallied to my cause, digging deep into his Tegge Circus Archives to address some of the more obtuse subjects I cover that cry out for visual evidence. For example, the panda bear that makes a cameo herein comes to you courtesy of Mr. Tim. For another, Cirque du Soleil, which was by far the most elusive subject to illustrate. Yes, it merits images. And surely I'd have some for you, trust me, had Cirque du Soleil responded to my e-mails. Or were the reprint fees charged by newspapers and other media not so prohibitively steep. But thanks to the trouper in Tim, his eyes forever on the pulse of the Now, the great Cirque du Soleil will not go forgotten in these pages. No it won't! Up ahead, in spirit at least, it waits its turn to seduce you with its own quirky magic.

Valuable contributors to the contemporary scene include Phillip Thurston of the Big Apple Circus and its superlative photographer Bertrand Gray; Phil Weyland, at a work on a documentary about trapeze legend Miguel Vazquez; James Royal at Kelly Miller Circus; and my own friend Boyi Yuan, who, during a trip we took last year to China, had the good instincts to record key evidence of how that country's acrobatic troupes are reinventing themselves. Some of Boyi's and my photos, which may lack optimum clarity, are here, nonetheless, in lieu of images from Chinese program magazines I would love to have used, but for which I was unable to obtain reprint permission. Boyi also helped me at the eleventh hour make some critical decisions about last minute choices.

Finally, two other rich sources enrich the visual parade: a few of the many outstanding photographs graciously handed to me by Russian circus officials when I conducted research in the Soviet Union in 1979; and the work of another unsung shutter wiz, the late great Ringling photographer Ted Sato. Answering my request, 20 years ago, to use some his wonderful work in a previous book, Mr. Sato sent me a batch of his black-and-whites, and in essence said, they're yours, take them.

Ah, the joy of the Big Catch when you go photo fishing under the big top!

Preface

So what is your preference at the circus — genuine performance art built on world-class skills, or a feel-good holiday for the family with interactive clowns, animal rides, snow cones, peanuts, and pin the donkey?

Might you be that perennial big top buff who is easily entertained? Or the trendy cynic who derides scary clowns and capering elephants in favor of acrobatic ballet?

Whoever you are, accept, if you will, my premise that we are likely living through the most artistically turbulent times the circus has ever known. You the consumer (I will assume you pay for your tickets) face an abundance of options in circus-going — from high-tech ersatz theatre-ballet troupes to the lower end retro circus-carnival operations. All of which provides the ideal landscape to explore the perpetually changing nature of circus. Please check any rigid definitions at the door.

My aim here is take you on two parallel journeys, the principal one being the story of how circuses are produced and directed, promoted and sold to you, and of how you can sharpen your knowledge of and appreciation for the art of the show itself, even turn out your own reviews; the other, a consideration at intervals of how circus art, spanning thousands of years, has steadily evolved up to the present day and will doubtlessly continue to evolve well into the future. I may not answer all your questions or win you over to my personal passions and/or biases. But maybe, at the end of the tour, you will leave with reason to rethink some of your own.

Beware the potholes of tacky showmanship that also lay ominously ahead. This book is a critical survey, not a valentine. It's a mess out there, I'll grant you, but a fascinating mess, what with so many shows representing so many different takes on circus entertainment competing for your patronage. Be they pretentiously subversive or subversively amusing, "traditional" or "alternative," they all make up the challenging panoply of "circus." And in taking them on, you stand to benefit, if only in the strengthening of your own circusy convictions. Under one big top you may feel wondrously elevated; under another, a wish that you had stayed home instead to watch a rerun of Roller Derby.

I promise you an open mind. And I hope to get, in return, the same from you. I entered the world of sawdust and spangles, as once it was called, over fifty years ago, when some of arguably the greatest circus performers who ever lived were in their prime. Names like Wallenda, Brunn, Colleano, Cristianii, Alzana and Zoppe spoiled me rotten. And in so doing, those ring icons turned me into a very demanding fan. When you are exposed to such mesmerizing artistry at so young and impressionable an age, you grow up haunted with an attitude of grand entitlement — give me more of the same or I'm not going to be happy. In fact, I might write a review that dares to express why I am not happy. Maybe that is why I became a critic at so young an age. In a strange way, I still feel fourteen-years-old — the age when I was first published, ironically, in the *White Tops*, a circus fan's magazine that specializes in putting out rosy notices. My aberrational debut in its pages surely marked a capricious stroke of fate, for which the editor who sent my opinionated prose, warts, rants, and all, to the presses, the late Walter H. Hohenadel, deserves a good share of the credit — or blame. I deeply respect the pivotal role he played in my life.

My opinions and views have been formed and reformed by a lifetime of watching circuses of all ilk, not just in the States, but in the Soviet Union when it was still the Soviet Union; under a few European tents in the mid-sixties, and, more recently, in China. Luckily, I grew up drawing as much satisfaction from a single ring as I did from three. Never for a second did I suffer any anxieties over which was better.

Research never ends, not if you live in the present. This book benefits from a number of discoveries, thanks to sharing archivists, librarians and friends. From the generosity of Ken Dodd in Sarasota, over the years I have received tape and video recordings, more recently, an address by Harold Ronk looking back over his years with the circus as ringmaster. From Erin Foley, formerly archivist at the Circus World Museum in Baraboo, the access she granted me to Ringling Barnum Archives before they were officially opened to the public led to my discovery of an extraordinary John Ringling North note to the creative staff shortly after his taking in the opening night performance of his circus at Madison Square Garden in 1951. Extraordinary, because he left so few written clues behind. Such discoveries can shake our long-held impressions.

Another major find was something that had always been there — Bloomington, Illinois, a bustling circus community in the first half of the last century that produced many, if not most, of the greatest aerialists in the world. I am delighted to bring this little town to your attention. Surely it deserves a far more prominent place in the record.

And yet another big boost to my understanding of world developments was the interview granted to me in Beijing last year by Tin Run Min, a scholar of acrobatic arts, filling me in on ancient Chinese acrobatic traditions and how directors are adapting them into newer, more contemporary programs.

Running my own blog has reaped the insights of others who leave comments, and it has put me on the mailing list of cyber courier Don Covington, who regularly digs up numerous stories and articles about circus developments around the world. Covington's finds add considerably to the record. Others who have pointed me to file cabinets or links include Olive, at the Bill Rose section of the New York Public Library, who handed me an old wood box containing three by five cards, encouraging me to take a look. To my utter surprise, I discovered my name on one of the cards, referencing a copy in *their* collection of my self-published article, printed on a high school mimeograph machine, *1957 Sawdust*.

How far time and technology have advanced since then! Into the fast and fluid digital age of author-publisher communications — e-mails and attachments instead of manuscripts to the post office and snail-mail waits — I have been impressively taken. And what a graceful ride it's been, thanks to Ben Ohmart and Sandy Grabman and the fine and flexible people at Bear Manor Media.

Warmest thanks, also, to my sister Kathy, who lent her proof reading skills to help root out a number of distracting little errors.

Is the circus dying? Might the astoundingly successful Cirque du Soleil itself eventually fade away? I would rue either happening. It is a question asked over and over again, and a recurring theme in movies about the big top. As long as the circus maintains the capacity to thrill, I can't imagine its demise. All you need is the right show, even just the right act, to reignite the public's appetite for more of the same. In China during the spring of 2010, traveling with my friend Boyi Yuan, without whom I could never have made the journey, my eyes were opened to a creative revolution underway among the leading troupes, some brilliantly reinventing their delivery formats through private funding and direction.

In Beijing at the Chaoyang Theatre, Boyi and I shared the thrill you get in the presence of something you can hardly believe is happening, something so original, so seemingly complex as to, yes, take your breath away. We beheld a self-assured young man bearing exotic restraint, working atop a rolla bolla (plank balanced across a cylinder) which itself was supported by a trio of equilibrists perched on yet another rolla bolla beneath. The star at the top, all the while sustaining his balance at one end on the precarious plank, proceeded to place a small ball at the other and then kick it just barely high enough into the air in order for it to land directly on the top of his head!

These are those riveting moments, however few and far between, that keep you coming back for more. And so, in these pages, it is my deepest wish to enhance your understanding of how such moments come about, and, more importantly, of how great performances in the ring are produced.

The goal, of course, is the circus of our dreams. The circus we subconsciously long for every time we step into the next tent and take a chance on the next show, hoping, like a hopeless lover, for the object of infinite desire to magically return…

DLH
August 2011

1.
Enter, With Luck, the Impresario

The *circus* — that most exhilarating of all popular amusements — needs the true impresario to keep it fresh, alive, magical and compelling. To push its spangled heroes to ever more incredible heights, to demand the impossible and to keep us, its fans, gratefully astonished.

It needs the passion of a Paul Binder to remind us that the ring is a sacred thing, the audacity of a Cirque du Soleil to illustrate what a fluid, ever-changing form circus art is. It needs gifted producing mortals driven to infuse the form with gripping showmanship and to expect great performances...

Might his elephants in their pink tutus dancing a ballet composed by Igor Stravinsky and choreographed by George Balanchine bring down the house on opening night at Madison Square Garden? Now was the moment. Standing his solitary distance in the spangled shadows, he studied faces in the house, listened for reactions. Were they smiling? Laughing? Would the critics acclaim? The crowds follow?

In another time and another place, another impresario, this one known for nearly demanding blood from his performers, snuck under the seats with pen and pencil in hand to see if that's what they would give him at the next show. Anything short of the mark — a sloppy entrance, a frown instead of a smile during a parade, worst of all, an omitted trick — would be noted and addressed, not subtly, after the performance when he called in the entire company back to have at them in the ring, note by nit picky note.

And in a day closer to our own time, perhaps the impresario of *all* impresarios slipped behind his infamous "black curtain" to join a few trusted colleagues, ready to give a dubious new six-person aerial number one last chance to convince him that it deserved to remain in the program. The show was about to open. After having watched the act for the first time, he had left in a sulk, calling it "a pile of scrap metal." Now he was back, wanting to see if the struggling artists had salvaged the "scrap." Shape it up, or scrap it out.

Three big top tycoons, each a distinctively different personality exerting his creative influence as producer. "He" is John Ringling North, Cliff Vargas, and Guy Laliberte. He is the unseen force behind the big top, whose particular vision of "circus" is what you get when you decide to buy a ticket and take a chance on his show.

Among other forms of popular culture, invariably one individual calls the shots. The cinema, by fairly common agreement, looks to the director; the theatre, to the playwright; dance to the choreographer; and popular music, to popular composers.

But at the circus, none of these figures casts the deciding spell. He is neither a director nor a writer, a choreographer or composer — even though, to a degree, they all can play a significant part in the creation of a circus performance. Under the big top, where wizards execute a variety of disparate feats merged into a single program, it is the owner himself whose vision rules the day. It is he who engages the acts, who selects the director, decides upon how to approach costume design, lighting and music. He is the one whose tastes and preferences form the showcase in which artist and audience will come together.

We may, deferring to our higher fantasies, call him the impresario. We will more likely I must warn you, call him by a lot of other names, from the very respectable "producer," all the way down to fly-by-night hack promoter.

It is not my aim, however, to dwell anymore than need be in the trenches of mere big top survival, so let us begin at the top.

To whom should go principal credit for Ballet of the Elephants? Its most distinguished contributors were surely famed composer Igor Stravinsky and the Russian dancer George Balanchine. But the ballet was essentially a spectacular stunt, albeit quite amusing, or even thoroughly enchanting to some. The idea had invaded the brain of John Ringling North the previous year while touring through Europe scouting acts for the show. And North's outlandish imagination fired the publicity mills. Even *The New Yorker* took note, producing a whimsical yarn titled "There Goes Igor."

"Walter McClain, the elephant trainer, said that he had been told to say that he liked the music, but speaking for the elephants he said that they didn't give a tinker's damn whether they work to it or not." McClain told the writer that elephants worked best to music "with a strong beat." When rehearsals had commenced in Sarasota, the elephants were belligerently unmoved by Stravinsky's very un-circus like composition. They stood "stock still for a moment, then they began to trumpet fearfully." All of which suggests how close the Garden crowd came on opening night to witnessing a stampede of the elephants.

"It was only after much goading that they could be prevailed upon to go into their dance," reported *The New Yorker*. "Balanchine suggested some new choreography, but the elephants were not amenable."

Nonetheless, en pointe or off, North's thundering ballet was the talk of the town. To some critics, a charm. To others, a question mark. "It was eye filling and it was joyful. It was gay," remembered North's secretary Jane Johnson with a blissful sigh, "It was absolutely the most spectacular thing I ever saw!"

It was such an attention grabber, that Cole Bros. Circus the following season presented its own version of an elephant ballet.

And it would inspire, many years later, a popular children's book by author Leda Schubert, who wrote that Mr. North "was a showman with a vision for a new kind of circus. It would be spectacular."

And so it was.

Circus owners come in all manner and attitudes. The true impresario is an inventive genius, driven by a passion for art, while the producer tends to preserve proven traditions, following rather than leading. And yet a third class are the expedient operators who turn as big a profit as they can on as mediocre a program as they can get away with.

They give themselves away every day. Every season. So, from heaven to hell, under big and little tops we will go, from performances that thrill, astonish, enchant and amuse you through and through (a rarity) clear on down to the bargain basement big tops littered with carnival rides and other revenue-enhancing gimmicks designed to vacuum every last dollar from your wallet. And I have your first bit of advice: Leave your credit cards at home.

Under a circus tent or inside a building, you can see some of best entertainment in the world — and some of the worst. As we go forward on this journey, you will, I hope, learn to become a more discriminating circus fan. Here are a few introductory illustrations of how several different circus owners work:

John Ringling North: In 1951, shortly following the opening night splash of Ringling Bros. and Barnum & Bailey, Mr. North returned to his suite at the Waldorf Astoria Hotel. He took pen to Waldorf stationary and scribbled out, in a forceful hand, instructions to the creative staff concerning parts in the show needing immediate attention: He began, "…for Christ's sake, this is not a free for all and we want the best for our show at all time. This is paramount."

The force of a true impresario: John Ringling North, 1949. COURTESY OF TEGGE CIRCUS ARCHIVES, BARABOO.

Apparently, North was making reference to conflicts or jealousies among certain performers that he had observed playing out in the rings during the show. "From this moment on there are to be no petty bickering, disputes, etc. No politics. No bullshit. No nothing. All should think of this and only this always. We have nothing to sell except tickets, and recalling Gresham's law of diminishing returns. The sale of tickets is dependent at all times on the excellence of the performance."

Later in his notes, he returned to the issue: "As of today, I demand that all acts finish and any feuds as such will engage themselves for mortal combat outside of the circus arena."

He requested better production values for one of his newly imported acts, juggler Veronica Martel. "Sammy Grossman [musical arranger], arrange Veronica Martel so it will be perfection. Doug Morris, give her better lighting. This is a new star with a magnetic personality."

"Throw out Lou Jacobs car gag. He didn't get the idea the opening night. Bob Hope [one of a parade of the celebrities who appeared at the premiere] got over quickly and he stayed there milking and milking and milking. He should have known better."

A sponsor tie-in left the boss unimpressed. "Can't we improve that Buick car and American Airlines deal. It stinks."

He called for cuts to a girl and gorilla comedy bit. "It needs editing, and Sammy Grossman motif. I booked the act and it has possibilities for the circus. Discuss with Pat [Valdo] and Murray [director Murray Anderson]."

Wirewalker Hubert Castle, on his return to the show, left North wanting. "Believe me, he needs that costume. Tell Artie [Concello] to tell Castle that I would wish him to be as good as he was when I first discovered him…rather than as good as he convinced Arthur he was when he wanted to engage him in place of Unus." Unus, the man who "stood on his forefinger," had left at the end of the 1950 tour, apparently Concello considered Castle a viable replacement.

The existence of this revealing note in North's own handwriting sheds remarkable light on how he worked, if only on rare occasions. If we are to consider it exceptional, the reason might be that, at the very moment, moviemaker Cecil B. De Mille was traveling with the show at work on his Academy Award-winning movie *The Greatest Show on Earth*. This may have emboldened North, then riding the crest of his own fame, to exert himself more actively.

For the most part, North was a hands-off producer, and so he left behind precious few clues concerning his thoughts on the composition of the shows he produced. A more accurate account, it seems, of his modus operandi was offered years later by one of his best directors, John Murray Anderson: "A man of great courage...John left me completely unmolested in my work. I introduced many innovations, but all of them, however, within the idiom of the circus. North never interfered but was content to accept most of the credit."

We will never know how many of North's opening night notes were acted upon, largely because there is little evidence to believe that North issued such pointed feedback on a regular basis. And since he almost never watched the circuses he produced beyond opening night, there would have been less incentive among the staff to honor his directives, especially those considered impractical.

On a larger sense, however, everything for which John Ringling North stood invariably infused, shaped and colored the show. The big picture was his. It was he, after all, who conceived "Ballet of the Elephants." It was he who had selected most of the acts imported from abroad; he who had hired revue stager John Murray Anderson to direct; who brought in Balanchine and Stravinsky; who recruited industrial designer Norman Bel Geddes to give the big top itself a glamorous new look (it turned blue), and to refashion the midway.

It should, of course, be of no surprise to us that even the most "hands off" owner will now and then manage with his hands on. And North, as it turns out, was no exception. During a production conference for the 1955 show, while those gathered were discussing how to integrate the horses into the finale, "Rainbow Around the World," the big show boss became animated. According to the notes of director Richard Barstow, "Mr. North wants to use the flash of horses with gold wings that open into rainbows around the track for finish. Weldy is seeing Miles about this."

What Mr. North wanted is what the audience got.

In amusing contrast to North's usual distance, there was the madness of ubiquitously hands-on Cliff Vargas, who produced a few very fine Circus Vargas shows before, tragically, succumbing to cancer in his mid-sixties. "Mr. V," as he was referred to by the staff, would throw himself behind the wheel of one of his trucks, if need be, to get it off yesterday's lot and onto tomorrow's. He would work concessions inside the tent if the mood struck him, other times serve as his own ringmaster. And so suspiciously demanding could Mr. V be, that he'd even sneak under the seats during the show, pen and paper in hand, to watch every act and take notes. Sloppy executions drew blood from his pen. A simple failure of one of the performers to smile during a parade could send him over the top. After the performance, over the top he'd go, ordering the cast back into the tent to have at them. How could he get away with such nit-picking tyranny? Mr. V, they liked to say, paid top dollar and he expected his performers to *perform*.

Vargas left more footprints than North. Another hands-on obsessive is Kenneth Feld, who runs Ringling Bros and Barnum & Bailey with an iron fist. He is one shrewd bottom-line pragmatist, known for obsessing each morning over yesterday's haul at the ticket windows. In some ways, Feld's fastidious attention to detail calls to mind James A. Bailey, the man who worked so well with his flamboyant partner, P.T. Barnum. Bailey's daily presence on the circus grounds was an expected, his face, familiar to all. When P.T. came around, to some, not only did he get no respect, he got the boot!

An old horse handler named Jim Thomas told circus fan Harry "Doc Chapman about the time, around 1885, when Mr. Barnum "was chased from the front when he came on the lot and tried to get inside free. None of the troupers knew who he was."

Clifford Vargas. COURTESY OF TEGGE CIRCUS ARCHIVES, BARABOO.

Whenever Kenneth Feld comes around, and often he does, everybody knows who he is. Mr. Feld once stormed out of a production meeting with his "directors," who apparently were endeavoring to actually direct that day, blasting, "Nobody will tell me how to run a circus!" And nobody did — or has. And they won't. By his own account, what Mr. Feld enjoys the most is sitting out in the seats and observing audience reactions. By sheer coincidence, in 2010, Mr. Feld was seated across the aisle from me at Coney Island when one of his shows was appearing there. And when I glanced his way during the second half of the program, I noticed him to be well composed in his chair, eagerly watching the performance.

He has all but said to the press, "what they want, that's what I give them." This sentiment can reap consistent profits. It can also deny the creativity necessary to keep the show fresh, the crowds coming back. Being too deferential to mob appetites means producers risk pandering their programs down to mediocrity. And yet there are those who argue that the right mix of mediocrity sells. The Ringling circus of today is a reflection, as are all circuses, of the man at the top.

Moving down the ownership chain, after impresario and then producer, near the bottom comes promoter. Did you ever pick up a free or discount coupon to a circus, only to discover, once you got there, you were being stalked by the Tilt-a-Whirl, by pony and elephant rides, slides and bungee bounces? Behind this excessive merchandising looms another sort of show owner, the dispenser of free kiddie tickets en masse. This is a front-end promotion designed to lure boys and girls to the gates, for they will have to be accompanied by adults bearing full price tickets. And, once inside the tent, it's pay back time. Into a concession pit the family will land, surrounded by photo ops with clowns (for a price); clown face paint-ons (for a price), and all the various rides and slides, not to mention cotton candy and snow cones. As of this writing, you can get your child lifted onto the back of a lumbering elephant for six dollars.

Not to hastily dismiss. These shows, too, *can* deliver, albeit sporadically. Rare is the budget-strapped big top without a few redeeming features, which can make circus going an adventure. Certainly, for children new to the world of sawdust and spangles, a circus of average virtues may satisfy.

Who produces such a show? For one, many of today's Shrine Temples. For another, Barbara and Geary Byrd, who operate Carson and Barnes Circus, a true big top survivor of 75 seasons on the road. This form succeeds by an unspoken pact with the public: Your children will get in for free, you, their parents, will pay, and we, the owners, will entertain you as best we can, offering you a variety of acts, some very good. And you will not complain while we spend time before the show and during the intermission endeavoring, in the good American way, to sell you on our refreshments, souvenirs and rides. We, as you probably realize and can, we hope, appreciate, have to make money somehow if we are to stay in the business and be able to hand out so many free tickets. We know that you may not return, but there are plenty of other people out there struggling to make ends meet, wanting to give their little boys and girls a real circus day, who will accept our offer. And we realize, having shrewdly persevered for countless decades, that most young children are not discriminating circus fans but will actually thrill to the most basic acts. We also know they would love to ride an elephant. Okay, so is it a deal?

Finally, to the bottom feeder big tops: One of the most notorious is operated on the fly by Canada's Dick Garden, who simply floods markets with free kids tickets, even hands out free adult passes now and then, just to haul in large enough crowds to make nut (daily expenses) off the rides and concessions. Garden's "circus" from hell goes by many names; one was Sterling and Reid. Don't say you weren't warned.

No American circus is about to revert to the blatant grifting that flourished over fifty years ago when pickpockets and short change artists regularly plied the crowds, and when the likes of a Ben Davenport, who hired these extraction experts to gather additional revenue, gave them their own private car on his circus train. In 1949, while touring Canada, he made hay with his Dailey Bros. Circus. The visit that Davenport made north of the border the following year proved to be pay back time. The public stayed away in droves. By the time the train arrived back in the barn, the show was flat broke. Within a few years, one of the most notoriously corrupt American circus owners was out of business.

But this rather unpleasant chapter in the life of Ben Davenport would not deter a group of circus people in Sarasota from honoring him in 2009, by inducting him into the Circus Ring of Fame. Perhaps, more than anything else, this bears out what I have hinted at — that it takes all kinds of characters to make up — and break up — a circus. Davenport may have swindled the public. He was also loved and respected by many of those whom he employed. Surely, this applied to his late and wonderful daughter Norma Davenport Cristiani, who sat on the panel that voted in circle of fame inductees.

I believe there is an almost odious inbred respect within the circus community for many troupers merely because they stayed, as the old saying goes, "with it and for it."

Even on the Ringling show, which built a reputation on treating the customer with the utmost respect, according to ticket seller Bill Taggart, at least during the last under canvas days, a modest form of short changing was not only condoned but encouraged by some mid-level managers.

American circuses have long since turned away from petty thievery. From there, they deviously advanced to other, less egregious means, beginning with bogus telephone charity solicitations — and then, more ethically, moving on to the free kids ticket angle as bait for drawing customers to the refreshment stands and elephant rides. The shrewdest of circus owners, who can't make it on art, find ways to make it anyway.

Truth be told, rare is the long-time operator who has not, during economic downturns, been forced to cut corners and put out a skimpy product. John Pugh's raggedly uneven Cole Bros. Circus of Stars, as he now calls it, has sadly and slowly drifted downwards into concession pit territory, diminishing the compromised show itself into a blurry, barely visible reflection of its better days when it toured as Clyde Beatty-Cole Bros. Circus.

Cliff Vargas, dead at the age of 66, by then was grappling with a diminishing customer base. The stellar shows he had produced during the mid-1980s were thinning out as he, apparently seeking higher profits on a smaller outlay, tried his hand at the arena market. This he did despite, ironically, having built his name on promising the public "the return to the circus under the big top as it once was in America."

As it *once* was, maybe. But as it "once was" was never a sure thing either. When he died in 1989, his circus was clearly on the wane. So, too, his vision. Vargas at one time mortgaged his home to raise funds for expansion. Today, the revived Circus Vargas, a one-ring shopping mall entity, plays to mere hundreds rather than to the thousands who, during its heyday seasons in the mid-1980s, filled the tent. What a sad cry from the magnificent three-ring glory it reached over twenty-five years ago. That thrill is long gone. This new version of Circus Vargas is run by a couple of former trapeze artists, Nelson and Katya Quiroga. Their motives are admirable. The show they put out is full of promise, but still short of the mark.

A true impresario is loathe to take the lower road. Loathe to hire con men or combine circus and carnival into one package. The true impresario, of course, is a rarity. Paul Binder, the real article, kept his focus on the show itself. So, of course, did John Ringling North, who not only scouted the world's finest performers, but fostered new, sometimes revolutionary ideas to re-energize the performance and keep the customer coming back for more. This I call producing from the top. In 1953, North engaged a child prodigy xylophonist named Mr. Mistin, Jr., whom he alleged, astoundingly, to be only 5-years-old, and gave him a huge ballyhoo. Some of the critics wondered why. A little outside your conventional circus program? The kid charmed audiences with his perky virtuosity at the keyboard. But he did not return the next season, as most crowd pleasers do. North knew when not to overplay a novel attraction of limited shelf life.

The circus under North's direction made a greater impact with compelling features like Unus, whose stunning one-finger stand electrified circus poster art. Such tricks are what sell tickets. In his glory years, Cliff Vargas did a little talent scouting himself, one of his best discoveries being the Ayak Brothers, an aerial duo from South Africa who took terrific risks executing superb partner acrobatics and split-second connections aloft.

Other showmen, now and then, by accident or design, take the higher road by signing outstanding talents. One year, hard scrabble tent showman Dory Miller, who founded Carson & Barnes Circus, had *four* flying

Paul Binder, founder of the Big Apple Circus, brought the European style tent show to America. COURTESY OF BERTRAND GUAY/BIG APPLE CIRCUS.

trapeze troupes working at the same time. The legendary Polack Bros. Circus was born out of the Great Depression, initially touring as just another carnival with a few circus acts thrown in for added appeal. A few years later, co-owner Louis Stern talked his partner, Irving J. Polack into an artistic about face. They shucked the carnival aside, formed a high-class,one-ring show (a fairly daring departure for the era), sold it to Shrine Temples, and soon were touring two units of Polack Bros.

Stern's artistic epiphany did not end there. After Polack passed away in 1949, Stern ascended to an even higher level putting him closer to the impresario class. He veered into creative showmanship by engaging the inventive aerial director Barbette and giving him the freedom and resources to direct the entire show. Through Barbette, Stern revealed an impressive deference to high-end circus. He and Barbette even dared to conclude one of their shows with the questionable placement of a woman's *pipe band* from Scotland, the Dagenham group. A very different ending at that, some found it off putting for a circus to conclude with massed pipers. Others may have thrilled to the wailing beat of the flat Scottish music.

These gallant departures infused Mr. Stern with newfound pride. A 1955 program magazine piece on his producing style, written by publicity

Louis Stern, with performer Valerie Antalek. Stern's Polack Bros. Circus reintroduced Americans to the one-ring format. COURTESY OF TEGGE CIRCUS ARCHIVES, BARABOO.

man Justus Edwards, correctly noted, "Stern has been a leader in bringing about the present high popularity in America of the Continental style circus, wherein one act is presented at a time, with every act superior in merit. In his constant quest for new ideas, he is not averse to breaking with established tradition." The perfect definition, and well earned in this instance, of the true impresario. Unfortunately, Stern's creative charge was short lived. In 1957, Polack lost its Shrine sponsorships owing to a dispute over the sharing of profits from program ads, and was forced to make do with a variety of replacement auspices. Revenues took a dive, forcing Stern back onto a more conventional course.

The man who today commands the gold crown among big top lords is undoubtedly Guy Laliberte. Heard of him? Maybe not. Heard of Cirque du Soleil? You just haven't yet linked the two names. They are infinitely inseparable. Laliberte was among a cocky band of young Canadian street performers (he ate fire, played an accordion) who wanted to start a circus back in the early 1980s. It was this Laliberte who had the savvy to seize upon governmental and corporate funding at the get-go, and this made him de facto CEO, Big Gun in charge of the first Cirque du Soleil, which opened in 1984. Once they developed a credible following, only three years later, down in Hollywoodland during a city-wide arts festival, the fellow who had raised the money and gambled it all on a fateful Los Angeles premiere was now the young tycoon who held the purse strings and thus the power. And this kid was born to wield power.

Guy Laliberte may still not be a household name, although, of late, he has traveled to outer space on one of those contemporary save-the-planet missions (something having to do with water), which may make him, at last, a household name — or a synonym for space plumbing, something he may or may not relish. Most of all, I think, he relishes the power and the money it has made him. In 2009, there were a total of nineteen Cirque du Soleil shows world wide. They are estimated to bring in 90 million customers in over 200 cities on five continents. Permanent Cirque shows light up marquees in Las Vegas, Macau, Florida's Walt Disney World, Tokyo and Hollywood. Dubai and Moscow may soon join the list.

The Laliberte producing process, mostly hands off, is so complex that he himself may not understand it. As complex as the man's imagination. It can involve a number of people contributing from different angles over a long gestation process for each new show. We are talking up to a year if not more. From the little we know of this Laliberte, it appears he is both very intuitive and very intellectual. He seems to have taught himself how to make, usually, the right decisions (there have been a few missteps),

Many mortals have tried to duplicate whatever they may believe is that intangible magic that marks the Cirque way; none to my knowledge has succeeded.

Inside Laliberte's brain, I would guess, reside all of the artistic passions and the creative drive necessary to envision and foster new shows. It is astonishing that he has lasted this long. Twenty five years now and counting. That speaks a lot for his capacity to imagine and reinvent. His spangled empire is by far the largest independently run circus operation that has ever existed. Even were we to factor in the public sector, only would the old Soviet Union juggernaut of jugglers and tumblers and wild animal trainers outrank in size and scope what Laliberte has built up, starting with just that one little tent which he brought to Los Angles in 1987, betting the entire kitty on success, knowing that failure would likely lead to the end of a notable three-year-old youth circus.

What is the Laliberte way, and how will you know it? Most Cirque fans can spot it cities ahead. They can spot it in the look of the tent, the movement of a single performer in the ring. The mood of an act. It is there in nearly every gesture. And even if the shows change, as they do and have to, the Cirque way is virtually unmistakable. Although, more and more, I am spotting good imitations of it in modern dance and alternative performance art troupes.

If you have seen one, have you seen them all? How about my asking you: If you have seen one Balanchine, have you seen them all? If you have heard one Sondheim song, have you heard them all? Or one *Star Wars*, or *Harry Potter*? Or *American Idol*?

No, they vary from one to another, just as do the brilliant Pixar movies. And yet they all bear an unmistakable mystique. Why? Because the same man is still at the top, that's why. Cirque is a style. So was, in its era, a circus produced by John Ringling North; and so is, no matter how much he changes it, a typical Ringling show produced by Kenneth Feld. Beyond the special effects and the intense atmosphere, in fact one Cirque opus can differ significantly from another Cirque opus. Compare the fluffy and cerebral *Corteo* to the red hot *Varekai*, and tell me those two are the same. I would argue they are not; you have taken in two very different animals wearing perhaps similar stripes. Both share impeccably polished productions. Beyond that, the differences can be stark, which is why the impresario in Laliberte is so interesting to observe.

Cirque fans, and there are many passionate ones, may point to Franco Dragone as the real "genius" behind the company's initial success in Canada and the United States. It was, to be sure, Dragone who *directed* the first Cirque show to hit the states, *We Reinvent the Circus*. But working alongside Dragone in the beginning, the company's first artistic director, Guy Caron, was another key force. In my book of speculations, in fact it was Caron more than Dragone who designed how the shows would look and sound. The two gentlemen created what we have come to regard as the show's identity. And yet it was the money man, Guy Laliberte, who

Circus King hosts the first lady: In the backyard of Ringling Bros. and Barnum & Bailey at Washington, D.C., John Ringling, the figure with hat in hand, escorts Mrs. Calvin Coolidge to the circus in 1927. USED WITH PERMISSION FROM ILLINOIS STATE UNIVERSITY'S SPECIAL COLLECTIONS, MILNER LIBRARY.

took that format and image and exploited it globally. A producer's job is to do just that, to join artist and audience.

We need to be clear about this at the outset, lest you fall into the trap of believing that a circus should conform to a set form. No two shows, even those put out by the same producer, can ever be precisely the same. You will, trust me, deprive yourself of a lifetime of prospective pleasure by holding so rigid a view. You will run out of options until everything strikes you as irrelevant. In fact, life is forever changing, as is the circus. And as we go forward, we will consider a number of forms from the three-ring extravaganzas that only a few years ago were *de rigueur* American, to the one-ring paradigm that is now once again the reigning reality. We will venture from the sublime to the shabby. What you must be on the look out for as I take you onto the midway and under the tents, or inside those cold impersonal arenas, are all of the subtle and not so subtle variations between the different circus companies, all of whom have somehow managed to remain on the road.

Circuses have in fact endured because of not just the movers and shakers but those crustier characters who survive by their wits, luring into the tent on a free coupon perhaps the kid who is thrilled at what he sees and decides to see other shows. He may grow up to be a performer. And then, for all we know, the next great impresario.

So, these are an introductory cross-section sample of the faceless giants — or midgets — who pull the producing strings behind the tents, who can make circus day an absolute delight or a damnable drag on your time and patience.

Those who refuse to give Guy Laliberte his due, and there are legions of Laliberte non-fans, fail to understand the critical importance of the man at the top. If Franco Dragone invented Cirque du Soleil as his ardent fans argue, it was the other man who sold Dragone's vision to the world. Who marketed it and who multiplied that vision many times over in many fresh incarnations. *That* is no small feat. In every operation, the man or woman at the top, whether hands on or hands off, has the ultimate say over everything that goes on. They are the personalities whose drive and demands keep the form alive. For when you are swept away at a circus, you are more motivated to see other shows. Same as how a fine film will motivate you to spend more money at the cinema. We need great producers to lead the way, to remind us of what it was in the first place that attracted us to the circus.

On his own, director Franco Dragone has experienced moderate success creating his own shows, among them a successful Vegas showcase for Celine Dion. Mr. Dragone has mostly, it would appear, spent a lot of time not directing. One of his recent projects was a show to be built around a Dr. Seuss tale, "If I Ran the Circus," originally slated to tour under canvas in the spring of 2008. Las Vegas auditions and rehearsals were advertised, then postponed. The economic downturn was blamed. Over a year later, the project was still on hold. The spring to which the new Dragone tent show aspired came and went. And so did another spring, and another. And the show is still, presumably, somewhere in the planning stages.

What Dragone may need to give his passion practical wings is that which he, unfortunately, may never himself be: The impresario.

2.
From Foreign Lands

When American circus producers book plane travel to scout for new acts, they fly well beyond U.S. borders — over the great ocean, and other oceans, where future ring stars are born.

America's long-time love affair with imported talent is rooted in two reliable realities: First, foreign performers usually possess developed skills superior to our own — almost as true today as it was over two hundred years ago when the first circus opened in Philadelphia. Then, as now, headline features came from elsewhere, and elsewhere is not Oshkosh, Wisconsin, or Santa Rosa, California. Not even Philadelphia, PA, or that larger city to the east. A growing list of rare exceptions to the rule will be addressed later. Keep the faith, you who long for an American century.

Secondly, far-flung entertainers bear exotic imprints from distant lands, and so they give our circus programs a beguiling other worldly air. And how American audiences fall for the mystery of foreign faces from foreign places.

We might ponder, at this juncture, an historical lack of such wizardry among the natives who lived on American soil for thousands of years before they were ruthlessly displaced by advancing white settlers from the east. Before manifest destiny raped and plundered the Indians and overturned the landscape, favoring tractors and factories over orchards and land-worshiping rituals. Although native Americans are said to have engaged in "juggling games," along with gambling, there is little if any evidence of their taking to tumbling or rope-walking. No, America remains woefully bereft of the juggling and acrobatic traditions that thrive on the other side of the world. We are still thousands of years behind two major regions, Egypt and China, where skills we associate with circus were invented and perfected. Some point to Egypt as the birthplace of juggling; others argue that the Egyptians, in fact, were taught to juggle by adept visitors from India. Scholars of the sawdust generally trace these ancient arts back nearly two thousand years to Egypt. So, here we are in the year 1781 BC, a time in antiquity when priests and shamans employed juggling to foresee future events, to outwit danger and explore the mysteries of the universe. This was a time when female dancers and acrobats demonstrated "toss juggling." Etchings and engravings of their exploits were discovered in the fifteenth Beni Hassan tomb of an unknown prince. Proof positive is there.

From the Orient: Japanese jugglers Yuka Tsusaka and Otomi Nakanosan entertain in South Bend, Indiana, 1908. USED WITH PERMISSION FROM ILLINOIS STATE UNIVERSITY'S SPECIAL COLLECTIONS, MILNER LIBRARY.

From Egypt to China over a thousand years hence, the magical manipulations of objects through the air continued, both for amusement and for settling disputes. In the state of Song, Lan Zi kept seven swords impressively in motion. In Shinan, the diplomatic juggler Yi Liao settled a conflict between two houses. During a battle between the states of Song and Chu, another wizard of manipulations, Xiong Yiliao kept nine balls

Ancient acrobatic arts were developed throughout Egypt and China. The identity of these contortionists is unknown. USED WITH PERMISSION FROM ILLINOIS STATE UNIVERSITY'S SPECIAL COLLECTIONS, MILNER LIBRARY.

airborne. In war and peace, an art that would endure for centuries into the present played a key role. Perhaps juggling better epitomizes the essence of circus than any other single skill.

Ever since the very first juggler on planet earth dazzled the very first spectator, a myriad of other human skills that followed would expand the burgeoning repertoire of what would one day become the first complete circus show. More intricately developed routines were mastered by Chinese acrobats during the early BC years. Wu of Han hosted a festival of acrobatics for a foreign guest in 108 BC. The term westerners used to describe these feats — "Chinese circus" — had little meaning in the far east. More correctly, I agree, the Chinese called it "Chinese Variety Art." In fact, on Asian television programs today you will see its residual influence on the young, who continue to keep alive ancient forms of plate spinning and body balancing.

BC to AD: The story took a thundering turn into blood, guts and glory at the Roman Colosseum during the first century BC. There, Circus Maximus staged robust chariot and horse races and various other athletic contests, making the event far closer to an Olympic tournament than to our shared definition of circus. Nonetheless, it has and will likely forever be argued that the roots of circus entertainment lie in the ruins of the Colosseum, where once as many as 270,000 spectators gathered to cheer on courageous gladiators, to gawk over fiercely fought races that could end up in blood-splattered mud. There, it has been written, Christians were fed to the lions, though I have yet to find out exactly for what reasons and whether or not the helpless believers were armed.

There, it has also been written, jugglers and tumblers joined the exhibitions to lend levity and harmless relief. Julius Caesar enlarged his giant venue in 50 BC. And if you still couldn't secure a seat or a standing space, you might find a spot on the surrounding hillside. And what a socially progressive operation this was: the first public event not to separate the men from the women.

Inside that dangerously bigoted Colosseum, I must concede, however reluctantly, that perhaps the most enduring single element distinguishing circus for centuries in the public's imagination — peril and risk taking — was first fully exploited. In time, out from the carnage of Rome would rise a more humanely heroic form of daring artistry whose language was immediately physical and universally understood by all. Its distinctive reach would draw crowds far and wide.

Rome had other venues as well: smaller circuses named Flaminius, Neronis (named after Nero, one of its most ardent patrons), and

Maxentius. The word circus is derived from a Greek word, kirkos, which means "circle or ring."

You may still be asking, as I have for years, was Circus Maximus a *real* circus? Even if the bloody Colosseum spectacles threw in circus *type* acts, they were no more a "circus" in my book than are the rodeos of today, which usually include a clown, or two. The central, most consistent feature

From Rome: The blood, guts and glory of Circus Maximus contained the seeds of the modern circus. COURTESY OF TEGGE CIRCUS ARCHIVES, BARABOO.

in any entertainment must be its defining feature. The Colosseum races were just that, races. Hardly a circus as we know it. And yet, our modern circus did pattern itself broadly after the Roman exhibitions of virility and bravado intermingled with daring wild animal interactions. Call what emerged a flamboyantly muscular genre.

After Rome fell, so too the hair-raising thrills of Circus Maximus. Its individual acts of human skill, however, would continue to seek out and win patronage before royalty and common crowds alike. Wandering artists plied their talents throughout Europe at fairgrounds and public gatherings. You will see their spiritual descendants today on street corners and grassy fields tossing three or four clubs for donations.

We could spend pages discussing the erratic evolution of rope walkers, bear trainers, clowns and acrobats into the modern-era circus program that began on the back of a fast moving horse in an open London field in 1769. The rider, 24-year-old Philip Astley, sold his exhibitions to a willing public. Now, had Mr. Astley's audience not vanished in a couple of years, he may never have added buffoons and rope dancers in a gamble to lure it back. His showmanship paid off, and so, in time, more acts were signed. Almost by accident, Astley the showman was inventing truly a distinctive new form of amusement called "circus." Yes, at least for the moment, I've left those ruthlessly hedonistic Romans behind.

Leading up to the advanced Astley moment were staggering developments in circus art. Take juggling: In Greece, there exists a statue of a man across whose limbs are balanced many balls. In Ireland, a hero named Cuchulainn juggled nine apples. Centuries later, King Conaire's royal buffoon Tulchinne kept nine swords, nine silver shields and nine balls of gold all in the air at the same moment. And what followed in the Astley era only added more complexity and pluck to a captivating new diversion. Jugglers jumped aboard horses to perform. Jugglers juggled with their feet. Weight jugglers manipulated cannonballs and other heavy objects. Jugglers worked in groups.

And in America? The laid-back natives who are said to have combined juggling with gambling evidently imbued in their offspring a decided preference for the latter. Or they preferred weaving baskets and worshiping the weather over tossing oranges and apples. America awaited the invasion of touring troupes from abroad.

During the free-wheeling free shows of the Middle Ages, performers were reviled by church hierarchy as agents of witchcraft. But the church could not stop the heretical show-offs from enticing willing street crowds with their irresistible tricks. They found favor among the ruling class, too. So popular had juggling become that bards and jesters believed it necessary to master the basics in order to bolster their stage credentials and marketability. Jugglers cross-mingled with poets, singers and storytellers. These early roots of circus intersected freely with the festive commedia del arte troupes; the same spirit today imbues our more eccentrically creative younger artists, each seeking to spread alternative visions. Out of this experimental zeal came the Pickle Family Circus, now but a charming memory, and, more recently, the promising new Circus Bella from Oakland, California.

The history of the form is wide-ranging and eclectic. And it should force you to acknowledge something you must accept if you are to proceed with any degree of faith: in essence, circus (from Rome to Ringling, Moscow to Montreal) has never been a set, well-defined genre. It is forever changing, and the only question relative to its changing is this: Might it ultimately substitute its most compelling feature — risk taking — for something else as viable, or no where near? Therein lies the Big Question.

You see, returning to the bloody fountains of Rome, the so-called "modern" circus bears unmistakable traces of those rough and rowdy Italian games, whether or not we like to admit this. For, traditionally, circus has taken risks. Can it continue to sustain its natural vitality minus the pursuit of peril? Legendary wire walker Karl Wallenda, who died doing that which he loved best, defined the activity he had spent his life serving in six words: "Look what a man can do."

Yes, look and behold, and believe.

Or might circus be able to perpetuate itself without risk-taking as long as its actors can deliver exhilarating surprises, as long as, in the worlds of Russian dog and cat trainer Svetlana Shamsheeva, it can "show something to the public to *wow*."

Svetlana hit the exact right three-letter word.

Perhaps no other emotion experienced at the circus is as universally appealing as the "wow" factor — that sense of wonder and awe in the living presence of a human being turning a trick we have never seen before, or one that we have seen but are still astonished to behold in real time again. It could be the equestrienne's somersault from horse to horse; the wirewalker's uninhibited tango aloft; the pole-vaulters precise landing.

We witness mortals overcoming tremendous odds. Tumblers trumping gravity. And we feel a rush of adrenalin, a rare life force affirming our own dreams. Under the big top there are a thousand metaphors for the power of the human imagination to inspire great things. Circus takes thrilling shape from this power to achieve. Indeed, circus is a celebration of man's reach for the miraculous.

Now, to keep you coming back for more, that is the job of the owner. The best among them seek out and sign performers who push the envelope in exciting new directions. To my question during the one interview he granted me — Exactly what qualities did you look for when scouting new acts for your show? — answered John Ringling North, needing little time and few words, "something I haven't seen before."

He knew that a circus rises on surprise, fails in stagnation. Surprise is what draws us back to the big tops time and time again, and it is why topline producers are constantly on the look out for artists bearing original feats. The cutting-edge skills, the dazzling displays of creative athleticism that they seek are more likely to be found in the Old World or down in South America where they are passed on from family to family, or in Russia or China where there exist strong institutionalized traditions for perpetuating circus arts.

For a kid to grow up the daughter of a circus star almost guarantees her the same success, if she wants it, and most do. European circus families

From Russia: Circus families and state-funded schools have produced some of the world's best acts. The top mounted horse rider is Mstislav Zapashny. Circa 1979. AUTHOR'S COLLECTION.

that sprang up in the aftermath of Astley's new circus would produce and supply stellar acts for shows around the world for years to come. And many of them would end up as U.S. residents after first being signed to perform with Ringling Bros. and Barnum & Bailey. They accepted, whether they liked it or not, sharing the audience with other acts appearing alongside them at the same time in other rings. They raised families.

The names Wallenda and Zachinni, Codona and Leitzel became household names through the halcyon days of the 1920s. In later years, Francis Brunn and Alberto Zoppe, Rose Gold and Pinito Del Oro, Josephine Berosini, Unus, Alfred Court and Hubert Castle and so many, many more dominated our American programs.

Mr. North sought them out on his annual trips abroad, as had his

From China: Today's acrobatic troupes fairly dominate the world stage. PHOTO BY AUTHOR.

Uncle John. Today, our most artistically ambitious circus companies, from Ringling to Big Apple to UniverSoul, and, of course, Cirque du Soleil, all have scouts on the ground at one time or another in the major capitols from Russia to Beijing, Paris to Peru, on the hunt for tomorrow's headline attractions, checking out festivals and competitions and monitoring circuses around the world for importable attractions.

Aside from the families of Europe, the next biggest suppliers of acts are a few countries with government-funded training programs. The Soviet Union, remember that?, was one. Today, China is probably the leader. Shortly after President Richard M. Nixon's groundbreaking visit to China in 1972, a cultural exchange program was established the same year between the two countries, and the first Chinese contingent to visit the states was the Shenyang Acrobatic troupe. They opened in Chicago on December 18, appearing there and in Indianapolis, New York, and Washington, DC, playing to a total of 45,000 people across 18 performances. An even more significant visit was that made by the Shanghai

Acrobatic Troupe in 1986, when its various acts were fully integrated into a Ringling Bros. Circus program. What a dramatic difference the American production elements wrought, taking the troupe off of a stage and into the swirling spectacle of three rings.

China is one huge talent factory, what with its state-backed ability to virtually extract the most pliable young bodies from their homes, send them off to training centers where they will be converted to professional acrobats. Behind their polished faces and impeccable mastery, however, is another story. It is a story of mandatory participation bordering on subservience, of long grueling days spent under the harsh dictates of exacting taskmasters. Whether these children fancy their fates or not, they are forced into the role of apprentice performers, groomed to take their places in troupes that will tour the country or get signed by the likes of a Kenneth Feld or a Paul Binder to perform in stateside rings. Indeed, it is so harsh and painful a life that the famous Chinese multi-talented acrobat Wu Wei, loved by the Brits, resisted encouraging her own daughter to follow in her footsteps.

No doubt, too, many of the young Chinese artists will develop an acquired gratitude for the hand of fate that forcefully lifted them out of poverty and raised them up to be proud wage-earning acrobats admired by peoples far and wide.

Until its demise in the 1990s, the Soviet Union was the single most prolific producer of ring talent. The Soviets were the first to found a circus school. This occurred a few years after the Bolshevik revolution of 1917. Circus arts were taken over by the state and upgraded from side show status to something approaching the refined dignities of a ballet company. The circus classrooms admitted children from both circus and non-circus backgrounds. As explained by a Soviet official to a reporter for *Amusement Business* in 1971, the children of circus families "will, of course, learn the fundamental things from their parents. However, in order to become artists with up to date modern standards, they must attend the academy."

Side-by-side, they all eagerly buckled under, our assumption being that, unlike their Chinese counterparts, they were mostly boys and girls who genuinely wanted to become ring stars. They also took conventional classroom instruction. And if it was an assembly line, it worked very well. Once a student's strongest talents were identified, "the remaining years are spent developing that particular talent into an act," said the official. Moreover, "he does only one act, never two or more, as many western artists do."

Before it careened over a political cliff into oblivion, the fifteen Soviet republics together operated a formidable circus empire. Nothing like it had ever existed. And it did this partly by turning its programs away from real risk, closer to ballet. Boasted the Soviet agent to the *Amusement Business* reporter, Russians viewed the form in a more "serious, critical mood" than thrill-seeker types expecting to be "entertained, as do westerners."

But that was then, and then is not now. Today, what remains of the dauntingly vast Soviet circus world — which at its height employed nearly fifteen thousand people of which roughly three thousand were performers, and had over sixty permanent arenas in operation the year around — is a ghostly shadow of past glories. Until late 2009, when he was removed from the position, president of the new Russian State Circus, gifted wild animal trainer Mstislav Zapashny struggled for a fraction of the state support that had kept the circus such a prosperous enterprise before the breakup of the Soviet Union. Indeed, Communist funding had made his life a dish of caviar and kept him and his colleagues on the payroll whether or not they performed every week, and gave them each a cushy pension after working for only 20 years in or around the rings. Rued Zapashny to *Izvestia Daily*, "The good tradition appears to be fading into the past. For some reason Russia's presidents are leaving the circus to the side." He recalled the Leonid Brezhnev era when he and his colleagues enjoyed the best of times. "Even in the difficult days after the 1998 default, when entertainment seemed far from people's minds, people kept going to the circus! And why? Because humanity has yet to invent a better antidepressant."

How vividly can I still picture a late evening in 1979 following a performance of the New Circus in Moscow, when I was granted an interview with Zapashny. Then, he enjoyed a very good Soviet life, and graciously he acknowledged it, comparing his lucky plight to many of his counterparts in western circus companies, yet careful not to overplay his status. After a most congenial interview, he offered to give me a ride back to my hotel in his luxurious Russian-made automobile. We motored through a frosty night air, sharp and still. How discretely privileged was that long ago visit of mine to the circus under the old Soviet regime. No more.

There are still many outstanding artists coming out of the new Russia, and we in America are still the lucky beneficiaries. In fact, thanks to the fall of the Iron Curtain we are seeing more and more of those acts, for they are now free to work without the restrictions that once kept them imprisoned within their own borders. They are free to accept contacts from foreign producers, so they now star in many of our circuses, alongside the Chinese and the South Americans and, of course, the Europeans. American producers at least have a much wider Russian talent pool from which to draw than ever before.

Inspired by the success of the Soviet model, similarly viable circus schools have sprung up in major cities from Montreal to Paris. A few schools in Africa have turned out some promising talents. And still, back here in the states, so little happens. There are a few serious-minded schools but they are no match, no where near, to the leading foreign training centers. Just take a look at a typical program for an American show, or visit its website, and study the names of the performers. See if you can spot anybody out of an American classroom.

Of course, there are some notable true-blue American exceptions in which we who live here can take pride. The late Baraboo, Wisconsin native Mark David, flew high, effecting a nerve-wracking single trap act routine patterned after the style of the great Detroit born Gerard Soules. Possessing the perfect body to match the form, David spent a few seasons as a Ringling Bros. headliner. He was a thriller when thrillers took real chances, climaxing his air time with a fast "flying heel catch," the trick requiring him to fly furiously forward and cast himself away from the swing, stopping his thrust by his heels catching the bar.

The United States has spawned viable careers for some distinguished animal trainers, to be sure and proud, from the rambunctiously melodramatic Clyde Beatty facing a cage of snarling lions, to the Moore's (Sonny and Bobby) working their hilariously frenetic comedy dog acts. Unforgettable to me is the sight of the diminutive pachyderm, Baby Opal, standing on just one foot atop a pedestal. She was trained by Mack and Peggy MacDonald, whose names must rank alongside the Freddie Logan family, among a number of accomplished U.S. elephant trainers.

There *was* a day, however, over a half century ago, when the United States *did* compete on the world stage in its ability to turn out a steady succession of big top stars. Not a school, a family or a circus was it, but a community in the mid west where many of the best aerial acts wintered in the off-season, a place called Bloomington, Illinois.

The accidental birth in the early 1870s of an informal big top academy took place inside a barn over a blanket of fresh hay spread on the ground below a maze of make-do trapeze rigging. Daily, young boys met up there after school to practice acts on improvised apparatus hung from the rafters. Two brothers named Greene, after whom the barn was named, perfected a gymnastic routine, toured the United States to acclaim, and then traveled abroad performing a Roman ladder number. This all began in a city that is home to the world's oldest and longest-running student big top show, the Gamma Phi Circus, founded in 1929 at Illinois State Normal University. From other barns raised in Bloomington by leading circus flyers needing space to practice during the winter months — among them, The Flying Wards — emerged a stream of well taught young aerialists, signed to appear with our leading American shows. Bloomington soon enjoyed

From the United States of America: Many seasons ago, a thriving circus community in Bloomington, Illinois, led the world in turning out top aerial stars. Seen here, among the flyers performing at the city's annual YMCA circus, are Gracie Genders and, directly in front of her, Bob Fisher of the Flying Fishers. USED WITH PERMISSION FROM ILLINOIS STATE UNIVERSITY'S SPECIAL COLLECTIONS, MILNER LIBRARY.

an international reputation as "…the city that turns out more big time aerial acts than any other place in the world."

Indeed, not a hollow boast. One of the town's best gymnasts, Frank Noble, landed a booking in London. "I didn't know how they came to choose my act, and inquired when I got overseas," he told reporter Robert A. Barracks of the *Decatur* (Illinois) *Herald and Review*, recounting how surprised and flattered he had felt. "They told me that they needed a flying act, and heard of us, and just wrote to Bloomington, knowing that we probably lived there."

Acts were thrown together and practiced all over town. At ice houses. In the Letter Laundry. At the Bloomington YMCA, where a coach named C. D. Curtis, along with flyer Harry Foreman (of the Flying La Mars), installed permanent rigging in 1912-1913. In 1922, Curtis and Bernard Smith began presenting annual Y circuses, stocked by processionals wintering in Bloomington, attended by other pros passing through town and by, of course, the locals. In 1936, the largest spread of trapeze talent — a combination of *six* separate aerial acts totaling 16 flyers — sent four catchers and a dozen leapers into the air!

Probably the Y's most famous graduate was Arthur M. Concello, considered by many to be among the greatest circus performers and executives who ever lived. Discovered by Mr. Curtis, who called the kid "a natural," the kid, known as "a devil around the Y," also fueled debate among locals wondering whether he would end up in a circus — or at the St. Charles Reformatory. Concello would marry Antoinette Comeau, who had been a catcher in the Ward trapeze acts. She was efficiently turned into a full-fledged flyer by her husband-to-be, with whom she would be inspired to master the elusive triple. Art and Antoinette debuted on the Sells-Floto Circus in 1929, and moved over to the Ringling show in 1930. Three seasons later, they were flying over center ring after replacing the Codonas when their legendary star flyer Alfredo suffered a career-ending injury. Concello ended up managing the circus for John Ringling North, at the same time training scores of circus flyers out of the old Ward barn in Bloomington that he and Antoinette had purchased. Concello then booked them onto American shows, including Ringling, and with Australia's Worth Bros. Circus. His most accomplished protégé was Los Angeles-raised native Fay Alexander, who joined the Ringling show in 1949 and, under Concello's guidance and inspiration, caught his first triple three years later. Alexander stunt doubled for Tony Curtis in the film, *Trapeze*. But he did not make the triple a staple in his Ringling act. Concello, who had seen the careers of many similarly ambitious flyers cut short from injuries or death, persuaded Alexander to leave the hazardous trick alone.

At one time in a day long gone, the flyers of Bloomington counted for 90% of all the flying return acts appearing on our shows. This is a remarkable chapter in American circus history, a chapter that thrilled me in my youth when the great Polack Bros. Circus came to Santa Rosa. For in the show those years flew the remarkable Nine Ward-Bell flyers, two of whom, Harold Ward and Eddie Ward, Jr., had grown up in this once-bustling big top city, sons of the Flying Wards. The "triple passing leap" which they performed (three troupes working side by side simultaneously) was a thrilling highlight of the show.

The Y Circus gave its final performance in 1941, only one month after Mr. Curtis had been called to serve in the U.S.O. Today, most of our best trapeze artists hail from outside the States, mostly south of the border. There is something about Mexican blood that seems to inspire countless

Bloomington YMCA coach C. D. Curtis, left, with protégé Art Concello, center. USED WITH PERMISSION FROM ILLINOIS STATE UNIVERSITY'S SPECIAL COLLECTIONS, MILNER LIBRARY.

young men and women to reach for the stars from a swinging trapeze bar. The Wards and the Bells, the Clarkonians and the Alexanders are history. In Recent years, the names Palacio and Espania, Segrera and Gaona have dominated the field. The first quad was flown by Miguel Vazquez.

The producer's challenge is to find such gifted mortals, to sign them to affordable contracts and to maximize their potential impact on the

Antoinette and Arthur Concello, with Eddie Ward, Jr., who caught Antoinette's first triple in 1937. USED WITH PERMISSION FROM ILLINOIS STATE UNIVERSITY'S SPECIAL COLLECTIONS, MILNER LIBRARY.

program. Not as easy as it may sound. The "affordable" part can cause friendly negotiations to take unfriendly detours. If the producer's show itself is a big name operation, he will have an easier time on his side of the desk for he can offer the candidate prestige and payday stability along with likely publicity in major markets. And, most of all, the pride of appearing with one of the "best."

Around the smaller shows, there is the unpleasant need to hire performers who are ready and willing to do more than just one act — worse still, willing, if push comes to shove, to lend a strong shoulder when the tent crews are shy of muscle power. A star one moment, a humble hand yanking canvas out of the mud the next. This dreary extra stuff is known in American circus parlance as "cherry pie." So, let's have some fun paying it a little attention. Here is a letter dated February 7, 1952 from circus owner Clyde Beatty to gymnast George Hulber. Beatty is offering Hubler $75.00 a week for himself and $50.00 for his partner in return for their working a horizontal bar act.

The offer includes Hubler's appearing in a trampoline number the first six weeks of the tour. "While we do not need your trampoline," writes Beatty, "can use you two boys to fill in on Harold Voise's trampoline."

After that, writes the boss, Hubler will be used "in the show on a position to be figured out later."

Those words "to be figured out later" aptly reflect the flexibility expected of a typical circus performer to fill in wherever needed. American producers scouting the globe for next year's attractions do not enjoy quite the same luxury in asking for the world and all the trouping mud that comes with it from a finely trained Chinese hat juggler. And so, the smaller shows are less prone to even try. They would rather default to the "Mexican family plan" which means that the brown-skinned troupes they book will be more than happy to pitch in whenever necessary, be it performing additional acts they have in their repertoire, driving tent stakes or working snow cone machines, or...

Still, the lure of American circus trouping inspires many foreign artists to say "yes" now and face displeasing truths later. In the 1956 movie, *Trapeze*, true to the power he then felt and the respect he was shown abroad, the figure of John Ringling North (played by character actor Minor Watson in the film) looms across the entire story. We see him coming and going at the Bouglione Circus building in Paris, checking up on the progress of an ambitious flyer named Tino who is close to mastering the triple somersault and becoming the first in years to bring it off. During a lively exchange between Tino and North, it is clear that upon landing the triple, Tino will be booked by the American impresario to open the following spring at Madison Square Garden. Paris and London premieres? They can wait.

That was how it was when virtually every star in every circus dreamed of landing a contract to appear with The Greatest Show on Earth. In recent times, other leading outfits like Cirque du Soleil and the Big Apple Circus have taken active roles in searching the globe for talent. American producers are well aware, perhaps to a point of bias, that their audiences respond with keener appreciation to foreign artists. Deserving or not, imported acrobats and aerialists epitomize the excellence of long hard training and a selfless devotion to their art. They bring novelty, and without novelty, without a turnover in the performing personnel, a circus will soon lose its customer base. So the savvy show owner must keep shopping around, must keep his program stocked with new acts and novelties.

Even the smaller shows are sometimes lucky enough to land a very good act; it could be a youngster in a family who is on his or her way up. Carson & Barnes, in its booking deference to Mexico (generally for economic reasons) has now and then carried a young star in the rough;

Fay Alexander, another flyer who mastered the triple under Art Concello's guidance, is seen here on the Ringling lot in Dayton, Ohio, August 1, 1952. At the age of 28, he caught his first triple that year, and later served as the fly-in stunt double for Tony Curtis in the movie, *Trapeze*. Photo by Sverre O. Braathen. USED WITH PERMISSION FROM ILLINOIS STATE UNIVERSITY'S SPECIAL COLLECTIONS, MILNER LIBRARY.

certainly, the riveting young juggler Wally Eastwood was one. There are many mid-level performers who offer the budget-strapped producer both the muscle power to move the show and the star power to sell it. And those who wish to stay in the business are usually more than eager to sign the sort of a contract that George Hubler signed with Clyde Beatty in 1952, which vaguely stipulated that certain duties would be "figured out later."

The Wuqiao Acrobatic Troupe from China, a recent Big Apple Circus feature, execute traditions reaching back over 2000 years to the Han Dynasty. COURTESY OF BERTRAND GUAY/BIG APPLE CIRCUS.

It is hard to imagine such dubious terms being acceptable to one Anthony Gatto, arguably the world's greatest living juggler, who toured with Cirque du Soleil's *Kooza*. But then again, Mr. Gatto has never to my knowledge appeared with an American company. All of his show time has been spent in Las Vegas venues.

And how exotically ironic: Anthony Gatto, you see, did not come out of a foreign circus school, nor did he grow up in a circus family on European soil. No, Mr. Gatto was raised in Brooklyn, New York, and taught by his father, an ex-vaudevillian acrobat. And in 2000, at the age of 26,

Gatto achieved a remarkable first at the Monte Carlo Circus Festival: First juggler ever to win the Gold Clown award, a title he alone still holds.

I told you, did I not, that there are exceptions? Born and trained in the USA, first and only circus appearance so far with a French-Canadian show, Gatto is possibly the greatest exception on earth.

It almost makes you wonder if this juggler's blood does not extend back to a Native American tribe. And if, maybe, there were tribes who, while weaving baskets and worshiping sunsets, tossed oranges and seashells back and forth between each other just for the sport of it. Or maybe to approximate the celestial movements of the stars that so fascinated their quiet souls.

3.
Directing the Impossible

A circus performance is an abstract onslaught of human energy lending itself to any number of structural forms. It begins with a random assemblage of all the acts signed by the producer to appear in his program. From there, those acts are transformed into — a random assemblage of acts, or if there is a director on board, any number of potentially interesting things. The shape the program takes will be determined by the use of lighting, costumes, music and choreography. And even by narrative allusions to some sort of a tie-in tale, as is the fashion these days.

And so a circus is the most difficult of all animals to "direct." Some owners don't even try, content to hand over to their ringmaster or performance director a list of the acts and let the presentation proceed the old European way: One act at a time, each announced. Indeed, so preoccupied for a long period were the Europeans with the act itself, that you will find in Englishman Antony Hippisley Coxe's marvelous, if tradition-trapped, study of performing genres, *A Seat at the Circus*, very little about the staging of the show itself. There is much to be said for the power of such elements as pacing, announcing, costume design and music to transform a random roster of acts into a dynamically pleasing performance. But Mr. Coxe has little patience for presentational showmanship: "Circus acts must also be produced with the utmost simplicity and with purity of style," writes he. "Why today production numbers featuring pop singers or groups should be introduced, I do not know why. It seems to show the theatrical influence of make believe, the invasion of musical comedy and cabaret."

Not so on the other side of the pond, where American circuses at the forefront have thrived on innovation. When he directed for Polack Bros. Circus, Barbette injected imaginative aerial productions into the show, and introduced some of the acts with choreographed flourishes. With one of the more memorable Polack editions came a mini Barbette-directed ballet,

"Carnival in Spangleland," discretely inserted between a family horse riding troupe and the Ward-Bell Flyers at the finale. These surprising images gave Polack Bros. a stature and sparkle. But there was only one Barbette, and it is a pity that he rarely got the chance to demonstrate his full genius.

The problem in the abstract beginning is this: How to arrange the surge of action so that, together the performers can create a certain shape

Eccentric direction from Round Rock, Texas: Barbette wove striking aerial ballets and various theatrical diversions into circus performances. COURTESY OF TEGGE CIRCUS ARCHIVES, BARABOO.

and rhythm that will overcome a stale variety show format and achieve the illusion of unified continuity? A circus is not a symphony concert in which a conductor standing with baton in hand on a podium follows a score composed centuries ago, leading a consortium of musicians up and down a set, rather narrow path.

Nor is a circus a play, a movie or even a ballet, although in some experimental quarters it is growing closer and closer to the latter. A typical roster of performers does not lend itself as a collective to pre-established narrative or structural patterns unless your cast is at the mercy of an avant garde director with a game plan built on a progressive arch, advancing the action, say, from comedy to tragedy, which would theoretically place the clown numbers first and gradually move from ground to aerial acts, the most dangerous feats forming a tense ending. Or, say, should the arc swing from the weakest acts to the strongest (of course, this secret strategy would not be revealed either to the public or to the performers). Ground acrobatics to aerial thrills suggest another from of progression. Comedy capers to daredevils, chuckles to gasps. Progression is itself a dynamic that can work, for it gives us at least a subliminal if not a tangible feeling of development A thrust. A dramatic build. This brings to mind Cirque du Soleil's smartly staged *Kooza,* wherein its leading thrillers begin to surface near the end of the show. Call it effective bigtopian drama.

On paper, the parts of a circus program fairly conform to familiar actions from juggling to tumbling, aerial exploits to comedy. So, how to most effectively connect your diversely talented cast into a collage that is, as they say, more than the sum of its parts? This variety of talent, which some cynics have dubbed post-vaudeville, is not easily merged into a form that can overcome the disparity between the individual artists, especially when animals are factored into the mix. The principle challenge facing the conscientious director is how to create both the illusion of wholeness and yet highlight each act to its greatest advantage.

Before a director can begin to lay out the line up of acts he will likely have to deal with technical considerations, and they may compromise his ideal running order. Let's say that a family has been signed to supply three numbers. Together, its members may work a trapeze act. Apart, one may do a rolla bolla turn; another, a wire walk. And, when needed to fill in for an ailing performer, the family may have a trampoline standing by or a Russian swing at the ready. Obviously, the director must not spot certain acts worked by the same family back-to-back. Costume and prop changes usually prohibit such.

Rigging and props also intrude and can complicate a proposed running order. What do you do while a wild animal cage is being erected or struck? Do you bring in the clowns or send an aerialist over the ring to divert the attention of the audience away from cage removal activities on the ground? Focused lighting can help. It's the same problem for a trapeze net. Something has to happen while it's being raised and struck.

During the planning stages for Ringling's 1955 edition, John Ringling North pushed to have a fountain spotted in the center ring during the finale, "Rainbow Around the World." Personnel director Pat Valdo resisted the idea in a letter to production assistant Ralph Allen: "Anything like dancing waters cannot be set while a thrill act is on."

The thrill act alluded to were the "Nerveless Nocks," who would be performing atop tall swaying spears while roustabouts installed Mr. North's dancing waters. Bubbles were suggested as a substitute.

The fountain did not make it into the show. The bubbles, probably. The show had dropped thousands of them over many of its opulent parades in past seasons.

Costumes can be another source of unanticipated problems. A clever aerial ballet thought up by Richard Barstow, the theme being rags and riches, had the women decked out as Carol Burnet-ish mop ladies in heavy clog-like shoes. Directed to implement a series of amusing dance steps as they entered down the hippodrome track, by the time the mop ladies reached the web ropes up which they would scale to carry out the "aerial" portion of the production, they were too exhausted to give it their all. In deference to grace, the funny shoes were junked.

Broadway choreographer Richard Barstow, photographed here visiting the show in Cleveland, Ohio, on July, 11, 1955, directed and choreographed Ringling performances for 29 years.
PHOTO BY SVERRE O. BRAATHEN. USED WITH PERMISSION FROM ILLINOIS STATE UNIVERSITY'S SPECIAL COLLECTIONS, MILNER LIBRARY.

Once the technical issues have been resolved, once the performers have all been signed, what sort of a director might you wish for — full out innovator or middle of the road taskmaster known for proficiency over poetry? Whatever imprint you may wish to make, if you do not build on your strongest wares, on the best tricks your performers can offer, your efforts will fall short. Performance showmanship is fine and can transform a parade of performers into an inspired spectacle as long as it does not diminish, conceal, minimize, distort or trivialize individual acts.

There are no easy answers for "how to direct." There are some time-proven fundamentals that nobody should overlook: Speed, pep and pace.

Three words any circus director should memorize. Three golden elements of circus action.

Within our early-day troupes, long before advanced staging concepts would elevate the program into a more sophisticated structure, the task of "directing," such as it was, based upon murky accounts, most likely rested upon the man who stood in the center of the ring and cracked a whip

Al Ringling, admired for the ability to merge and pace circus acts into rapidly unfolding programs, hands his ringmaster's whistle to protégée James Agee. Circa 1912. USED WITH PERMISSION FROM ILLINOIS STATE UNIVERSITY'S SPECIAL COLLECTIONS, MILNER LIBRARY.

to pace the horse-riding acts. He was called the ringmaster, or master of the ring. Eventually this figure appeared only as part of a riding troupe, and the term "equestrian director" came to designate the man who stood on the sidelines, gesturing or ringing a bell to signal the end of one act or display and the beginning of the next. None was better known for favoring speed, pep, and pacing than Albert Ringling. Possessed of a theatrical bent, Al was the first to blow a whistle in lieu of ringing a bell, as did his genteel European counterparts, thus dramatizing the equestrian director's presence throughout the performance. While he and his four brothers were establishing a name for themselves, Al was maturing into a no-nonsense director who insisted on a fast-moving performance. Speed, pep and pacing, most definitely. He earned the respected reputation for being able to whip a variable roster of talents into a hurly burly express train of non-stop action. This delighted the crowd, as it still does.

From most accounts, Al's personality was edgy, a bit impatient. He was not one to slow down or meditate. Perhaps he had acquired his strong theatrical pulse while laboring for other shows in his youth. Even the small one ringers, I will daringly speculate, moved with dispatch and dash. After all, inside the tents horses galloped in whirling circles while graceful riders stood daringly erect and hollered high. Circus programs naturally contained energy, strength, action and dexterity.

"Snap is the greatest essential in American circuses," advanced Fred Bradna when interviewed by author Earl Chapin May for his book, *The Circus from Rome to Ringling*. "There must be no waits, no breaks." From whence this propulsive aesthetic? Bradna, while working his way up to the post of equestrian director on the Ringling show, had been well schooled by a few of the men who assisted Al Ringling, and Al Ringling in many ways defined the driving role of equestrian director, more popularly known in recent times, once again, as "ringmaster." Al's brother, John, in an article he penned for *The American Magazine* in 1919, extolled Al's gift: "If I may be pardoned for seeming boastful, I should like to say that, in my opinion, Al was the greatest producing showman the world has ever known. He knew instinctively what the public would like or dislike, and his big success was in his ability to choose good features. In our early days, before we could afford to pay for the high-class attractions, we were, of course, handicapped, especially in the face of bitter and relentless opposition by the richer shows. Al clung to the idea of neatness, clean performances and fast movement. In the circus business he had the idea of speed and 'pep' which George M. Cohan brought into the country."

John Ringling's tribute ended on a high note of candor, and any showman would do well to take heed: "With a dozen rather mediocre acts, by proper staging, by 'doubling,' and keeping the action fast and continuous, he made the show appear better than some of those which cost twice as much to stage. He invented, brightened up, and developed some of the most successful features known to the circus."

From the school of Al Ringling, who blew the whistle for 31 years, to one of its most steadfast adherents, Fred Bradna, pep, speed and pace remained apace. "Nothing is so bad in the circus as a pause," he noted in his excellent book, *The Big Top*. Bradna never once in his thirty-one-year career (exactly equaling Al's longevity) announced a single act. He stood imperially on the sidelines, in the words of Harold Ronk, "a strict disciplinarian who never spoke to the audience. He just made motions to cue the show." At big, long-awaited moments in the program, star artists were introduced by hefty-voiced orators such as sideshow manager Lew Graham. Bradna, who despised the term "ringmaster," referred to Graham as a "ring announcer."

To trim performance running time from several hours, when the circus first opened each spring at Madison Square Garden, down to a tight 120 minutes flat, it took "clockaholic" Fred Bradna either three days total or about a month, depending upon which of his accounts you wish to believe — the one he gave to author Earl Chapin May, or the shorter version he put out, years later, in his autobiography, *The Big Top*.

Masters of momentum, the Ringlings also developed quick and more interesting transitions between displays. Some of the aerialists, for example, would first appear not entering the tent but already above the rings, "in the rigging ready to work before I blow my whistle," in the words of Bradna. "An act may be fined for not being on time. As a matter of fact I can't remember when it was necessary to fine any act for such a cause. Only once in a blue moon do you meet a circus performer who won't do his level best to make the show go over without a hitch. Each gives me all the assistance in his power."

Remember aerialists? Remember animals? A non-stop feast for the eye of horses on the ground, daredevils in the air was what the Ringlings offered their customers through the roaring twenties. The 1929 edition ended with a triple decker thrill: A trio of flying trapeze troupes featuring triple-somersaulting Alfredo Codona over center ring; hurdle jumping horses and hippodrome races, and finally, the coup de grace:

"First appearance in America." That would be Hugo Zazhinni, the "human projectile" shot out of a cannon.

Most American shows during the three-ring era climaxed on high-flying notes. For example, Sells Floto, "the circus beautiful," in 1923 presented two flying return troupes, following which, back down on the sawdust...

"They're off! A thunder of hoofs, a flash of color and the races are on. The tense, rousing, whooping finish of the big show."

Forty years later, the hippodrome races (a quasi Circus Maximus feature) were gone. Forty years later, human projectiles were now called "astronauts."

These timeless staples still work on successive generations. But the delivery format must change with the times. And here is where the clever director can make a difference. He can keep the show looking modern.

When he took control of his family's circus in 1938, John Ringling North hired creative hands from outside the big top, from ballet and theatre. He recruited industrial designer Norman Bel Geddes to refashion the look of the biggest tent. And, as I've already told you, North thought up the elephant ballet, as well as numerous other production ideas and angles. He once even staged a fashion show atop the pachyderms.

"Mr. John North is a most unusual man," wrote his longest-lasting director, Richard Barstow. "I like him because he dares to do…has great enthusiasm and won't settle for anything but perfection. When North gets an idea for a number or effect, he is liable to call you from India or Ashtabula, Ohio any day or night, anytime or place. He once got an idea for a new ménage number and called me from the Biltmore baths and tracked me down to a drug store on Lexington Avenue. It is up to me to decipher these brainstorms and make them work…He expects the impossible and he gets it."

After North and Anderson parted company in 1951, Barstow won the post. He held it for nearly thirty years, lasting into the Irvin Feld era, well beyond North's regime. He considered the circus to be "the biggest challenging spectrum in the world to paint." He developed a form of footwork over sawdust, which he dubbed "jumpy steps." They were easier and safer to execute over the earth's constant surprises on unfriendly lots strewn with rock, weed, and, not infrequently, mud puddles. Out under the big top after the show finished its New York and Boston indoor runs, Barstow rejoined the company for a week or two to restage the circus, from a three-ring and two-stage setting in the Garden down to three rings under the tent.

He had a meticulous attention to detail, and his letters to colleagues reveal intelligent diplomacy. In the heat of direction, however, this Dick Barstow showed a very different face. He could be nasty and sarcastic, bullheaded and derisive. The difficulties in communicating with a multitude of nationalities may have gotten to him on occasion. "What are you going to say? Fifteen minutes to tell everybody to point their toes in seven languages."

Barstow, of course, came up with ideas, as did others on the staff. Some came directly from North, to whom Barstow reported. He called his boss "such a daring man, with such calmness."

By and large, the circus community itself has rarely produced good directors. And so the most enterprising producers, like North, have gone outside for direction from other venues, be they theatre or ballet. Even opera. Barbette, whom North hired to direct his 48-girl aerial ballets, was a rare exception far ahead of his time. Just as strong-willed as was Barstow, when the lines of artistic authority between Barstow as stager and Barbette as aerial director blurred, the circus man nearly drove the theatre man crazy. To Mr. North was sent an urgent letter by Mr. Barstow: "I beg of you to protect me from this mad man named Barbette as I cannot function correctly with him screaming and interfering. I must have it understood and would appreciate it in writing, that I have full charge of all choreography and staging movements, including all GROUND work on the web number." Whatever the outcome, Barbette did not lose North's support. In fact, the very last display seen in the very last under-canvas Ringling Bros. and Barnum & Bailey Circus was partly, if not completely, directed by Barbette. Titled "Hoop Dee Doo," a program note describing it includes this: "Girls in swings held by giant elephants." Pure Barbette.

Onto what the performers wear: Costume design took center ring when Mr. North entered the tent. Up until that moment, by tradition performers wore the costumes they brought with them, and sometimes those threads might have been better left behind. When the Hannefords joined onto Ringling in the 1920s, their preview in a dress rehearsal performance attended by news scribes failed to yield the expected praise. "The Hannefords have a great act, but their costumes are impossible, and they don't know the audience exists," groused John Ringling to Fred Bradna. "Do something about it." Bradna and his wife, Ella, tactfully approached the family of horse riders, referring them to a local costumer and helping them develop a flashier opening. The make over did wonders. The Hannefords arrived.

North commissioned Miles White to design the entire show, and the stunning visual make over, combined with the inclusion of the four production numbers, gave the Ringling programs a more visually captivating look. The splashy parades and festive celebrations, themed after holidays or colorful locations on the map, patriotic events and childhood fantasies, lent variety and shape. The public was quick to respond. After all, the circus is, if nothing else, eye candy, and North gave the world some of the most visually enchanting eye candy it had ever seen.

Preceding the lavish North era, a longer-lasting circus revolution was underway in Russia. Following the Bolshevik rise to absolute political power in 1917, the new Soviet government took serious steps to upgrade the circus scene, then largely dominated by foreign impresarios and artists, into a risk-free form of entertainment. Russian artists had, in fact, been forced to change their names so as to appear foreign, just in order to get work inside their own native land. The measures taken to give the circus a more authentic Russia flavor, and to provide State-mandated security and safety for the performer, would have a profound effect on how circuses are staged and presented today around the world.

I've already suggested that the term "death-defying" may one day be totally replaced by the less threatening one word descriptor: "wow!"

Soviet minister of education Anatoly Lunacharsky was appointed by his good friend Lenin to manage and oversee a more humane transformation of Soviet circuses away from the freak and stunt show mentality. Lunacharsky certainly shook up and shook down the status quo by bringing in outside directors, designers and composers, as would Mr. North twenty years hence. Initially, the Soviet directors addressed the acts themselves. Choreographers reshaped and refined the routines. Original music was composed. These and other highbrow enhancements had the affect, intended or not, of elevating the circus closer to athletic ballet. Secondarily, the Soviets strove to rid their programs of accidental injuries and worse. They accomplished this by implementing the permanent use of a safety contraption called a mechanic. The device amounted to a rope or wire slung over a pulley, one end held by a man on the ground, the other strapped to a heavy belt around the waist of an apprentice during training sessions learning to ride horses or walk wires. Should the apprentice slip and fall, she would be left dangling freely and safely in mid-air, spared misfortune by the mechanic attached to her body, slowly and safely lowering her to the ground.

Now, for the first time in circus history mechanics were worn by everybody who performed risky acts, which included all aerial routines and certain ground acrobatics (off teeterboards, for instance). Everybody. Gone, overnight, was the thrill factor. Even then, the duplicitous Russians continued playing up the idea of "danger" in bogus publicity. Really, their conversion to safety first was a subversive attack on genuine circus. And it would have long-term consequences on circus trends worldwide.

The Soviets also opened a circus school in Moscow, and within roughly ten years it was graduating notable artists, many of whom created their own acts from scratch or added clever twists to old tricks. Established performers were urged if not required to attend classes and hone their repertoire. Animal trainers, it has been recorded, were admonished to adopt the humane training techniques advocated by Pavlov, stressing rewards over the whip.

There can be little debate that the mandatory use of safety belts during the performance effectively removed the single most defining circus feature: danger. Eliminated by the stroke of a bureaucrat's pen were the symbolic realities of artistic daredevilry, which approximated the hazards inherent in the real world. No single episode in its variegated history has done more to emasculate the circus from its Roman roots than what took place over sawdust circles within the young Soviet republic.

And yet, when the Moscow Circus toured the United States in 1963 and again in 1967, it was embraced with raving admiration by both critics and crowds. So stunning to behold were the carefully choreographed acts, each scored by a full orchestra with strings, that few in the audience seemed to bother taking issue with lifelines or the lack of a thrill factor. In fact, most of the performers did not work aerial numbers. And, lest we forget, the mechanic is at times hardly noticeable when the artist wearing it works at a very high altitude in semi-darkness. Some are better than others at concealing their reliance on security.

As I've warned you, as we go deeper into our discussion, you must accept as a given that "circus" has never followed one fixed form. Therefore, this journey may feel disorienting at times.

Next to further expand the power and scope of the director was Cirque du Soleil. It is

From ballet to big top: Eclectic director, Alexei Sonin, appointed head of the Bolshoi St. Petersburg State Circus in 1965, held the post from 43 years. AUTHOR'S COLLECTION.

hard to fathom that so brilliantly inventive a troupe should still be going strong, and even stronger, when most other troupes similarly born of brash, youthful idealism fall by the wayside within mere seasons. Cirque du Soleil is now over 25-years-old. Now, if the Russians gave the individual artist ballet, Cirque applied that esthetic to the entire show. In fact, Cirque is a highly sophisticated extension of the Soviet approach that had thrived up until the collapse and breakaway of the fifteen republics in 1989. Here is the company's first director, Franco Dragone, from his own words as printed in the 1987 circus program magazine sold during the show's appearance at the Los Angeles Arts Festival:

"I don't see why art has to be divided into small compartments, each with its own label. What we do is essentially a circus show in the sense that the emphasis is on the acts themselves. Strictly speaking, there is no scenario. What I try to do is establish realities between the characters and create moments of intensity. Each act is treated as a separate entity."

A separate entity. So you can see that even Mr. Dragone respects the vital autonomy of the act itself, as all ring directors are well advised to do. At the same time, you can see that he is open to fostering little human interactions (possibly suggesting relationships) that may emerge in the shadows. These subtle diversions might be a road to enriching our perception of the cast's humanity. Just as John Ringling North strove to add a more theatrical context to the show in his day, so, too, did some of Cirque du Soleil's pioneering creators.

And now the Chinese are following suit, having obviously been inspired, even challenged by the daunting example of Cirque du Soleil's penetrating influence around the world. A revolution of sorts is now taking place in major Chinese cities, where established acrobatic troupes, long respected around the world for the excellence of their traditional skills, are finally thinking beyond the act into the wider realm of the entire show. Which takes a director. Which could also use a good composer. In Shanghai at ERA Intersection of Time, and in Beijing at the Flying Acrobatics Show, you will discover stunning production values. Laser lights and flying "birds." Body movement and hints of a narrative lurking around the misty edges. A seamless continuum of action. Contemporary original scoring. One show uses a live band. Another, the Chimelong Circus down in Guangzhou, throws open its doors to animal acts, and we are not just talking dogs and horses. Can you spell "tigers"?

The more cerebrally stimulating ERA Intersection of Time is not presented on a proscenium stage, as is the usual custom here, but on a circular, three-quarter round set. Considering its mystical dream-like qualities, we should not be surprised that it was conceived, directed, given dance steps and scored by a triumvirate of well-seasoned Canadians, among them long-time Cirque du Soleil choreographer Debra Brown. Flying Acrobatics Show, arguably a better, certainly a faster and tighter-paced outing, bears exclusive Chinese direction. And its brilliant musical scoring is the work of one of the country's most gifted natives, the multi-talented Guo Feng, a trendsetter in Chinese popular music who contributed to the 2008 Beijing Olympics.

Feng's delicately seductive charts for the Flying Acrobatics Show embrace the modern world from the deeper roots of Chinese restraint; they seem to find their gentle tunefulness in the moods of nature, from a sequence suggesting a tinkling dance of raindrops down a mountainside (the scoring for a remarkably inventive rolla bolla number) to a lonely spare landscape on a windy night, chorally evoked, that invites patient respect for the slowly shifting positions of a trio of young contortionists bound together in sacred concentration. A not insignificant factor that both companies share in common is that they were each *privately funded and produced*, another dramatic change in a country where the vast majority of some 100 acrobatic troupes are supported by government money.

One need only watch ERA one night and Charming Shanghai Acrobatic Show the next to experience the stark differences between contemporary creative staging and a flat traditional format that has grown stale and threadbare. The later show, presented on the stage of a worn down theatre, is a one-act-at-a-time program, with most of the acts announced by a young woman in a white dress who walks out onto the stage holding a microphone in her hand, stops and issues plain-spoken introductions. This makes the evening feel sometimes closer to a high school talent recital than a professionally produced circus.

"At the moment, we are in a very sensitive transitional period in time," says Tian Run Min, a Chinese scholar on the subject and the artistic adviser to the Chinese State Circus in the U.K. "There are many influences with the Chinese acrobats from tradition to a new way. You can't find an authority opinion."

And what has Beijing to say about all this? As Tian Run Min explains, there are only expectations from on high. "The government is officially saying you should present more shows for more people. You should make new acts. You should train the talents. You should win more medals both in the world and here."

This strikes me as ideal. Some believe that to follow Cirque du Soleil is the way. Others, according to Tian Run Min, argue no, "it doesn't make sense, we should make something new and for yourself, and from China and from our traditions."

Out of such creative ferment comes necessary change. To my eyes, they are not slavishly imitative of the Montreal monster. They are slyly adaptive. Think Bill Gates appropriating Steve Jobs. Their fascination with the world stage is all for the better. "I think the world market and also the international circus festivals have inspired the Chinese artists to create something new and to produce the totally new kind of shows like the one you saw last night [Flying Acrobatics]."

I went to China expecting great acts. Not great shows. Having beheld both in equal measure, I returned a believer.

Now, if you want glitz and flash in a high-energy setting, Ringling Bros. and Barnum & Bailey may be your ticket. Direction? A mixed bag,

Preserving and refreshing Big Apple Circus values: the company's new artistic director, Guillaume Dufresnoy, watches almost every performance. COURTESY OF MAIKE SCHULZ/BIG APPLE CIRCUS.

some years favoring Broadway, other years favoring Broadway. And by this I mean the razzmatazz openings complete with stately female dancers strutting stylishly to an original tune repeatedly pushing "we are the greatest show on earth" angle. This form of direction sometimes looks as much like a photo shoot for a Ringling TV promo.

Producer Kenneth Feld has favored, to his credit, a number of directing styles in recent seasons. He has experimented with slight story lines, too, in an apparent effort to please a market perceived to be Cirque du Soleil savvy and therefore presumably in need of a little Cirque fix. Then again, the Felds are digging ambitiously deep to find new modes of presentation now that they have virtually given up on three rings in deference to a more ice show type layout. (You might know that Feld Entertainment also operates all the Disney ice shows.) It does not take a rocket scientist to know that were it not for dwindling traffic through the turnstiles, those three rings would still be up and filled with competing action because the seats around all of them would still be occupied. They are not anymore.

Ringling Bros. became *Ringless* Bros. It is now, as of this moment, kinda, sorta Ringling Bros. with inflatable rings that are blown up to full form during segments in the show requiring their presence (such as during a dog act, those charming dogs would be lost without a ring in which to cavort), and then deflated back to flat tires, leaving the arena as exciting to behold as an abandoned airstrip in the Nevada desert. Except that lately, we are seeing more apparatus on the edges. Call it prop relief. Anything to add a little welcome atmosphere.

And what has this to do with direction? It takes deft staging skill to figure out how to fill up a blank arena floor with a circus that shuns its most enduring symbols of popular appeal, those three imperial circles. This is still evidently an open-ended debate in the Feld family. Facing the winds of inevitable change, you can't blame Mr. Feld, but only respect him, for trying to reinvent a new delivery system for his world famous product. You also have to wonder if he has gone too far, especially when he treats the ring itself like a leftover covered wagon wheel. The traumatic reconfiguration, complete with overhead short-lived video screens, began in 2006. Audiences grumbled their discontent.

Things took a definite turn for the better in 2009 when Mr. Feld put his Gold Unit under canvas at Coney Island and produced a terrific one-ring circus, the likes of which we haven't seen in this country in many seasons. What a difference a tent made. And a live band. And the right acts. And the right direction, all of it thrillingly to the point, and thrillingly free of the extraneous production gimmicks that had grown slightly oppressive over the years. Credit director Philip William McKinley for the taut sleek affair. Opening and closing ensemble segments were picture perfect. Speed, pep and pacing. Yes, all the way. And, adding Fred Bradna's favorite word, plenty of "snap."

The three-ring giant that Kenneth Feld inherited from his father, Irvin, is gone. For now, for sure, we are in the time of the sleek one-ring extravaganza, and if Guy Laliberte and his co-creators need to prepare each new show out of their deeply felt conversations and complex philosophical musings, so be it. Let their fussy French flights of fancy be the spiritual matrix from which the individual acts spring forth, each bearing its own distinctive imprint, each also serving as an integral part of the whole. Let mysticism and ambience have its day too. For, as I will propose up ahead, we go to the circus wishing to be transported to another place, a very special place removed from the grocery store around the block, the big box mall up the highway.

The illusion of an exotic setting need not detract from individual artistry. The three best touring tents shows I've seen from Cirque du Soleil all ended on high circus-rich notes. *We Reinvent the Circus* had the three-person Zhao Family of bike riders whirling around the ring, joined by an additional six more riders from the company. *Varekai* sent two Russian swing gymnasts flying simultaneously in each other's direction, criss-crossing in space one over the other, each landing on the others respective swing! Talk about the wow factor. This wow electrified the house.

Cirque's recent *Kooza*, full of old-fashioned heart-pounding fun, built to a climax on three strong turns down the final stretch: juggling marvel Anthony Gatto; a troupe of wire walkers from Columbia and Spain — Flouber Sanchez and the four Dominguez brothers — working on two wires, one above the other; and a two-man gyro wheel ("wheel of death") display performed with hair-raising daring-do by Jimmy Ibarra Sapata and Carlos Enrique Marin Loaiza. I've never seen this act produce so many spine-tingling gasps.

Three socko acts. Three acts that would move any audience the same way anywhere in the world. A little dangerous? Yes, in fact, more than a little. Skilled? Exceptionally so. And all of the artists cast in that special Cirque mist. Even when you have millions of dollars at your disposal to continue reinventing your circus, no matter how swift you are at staging, how clever with special effects or beguiling soundscapes, without an Anthony Gatto, without a Quiros or a Sapata and Loaiza, you have, sorry to say, not much at all. The "act" is still, and will always be, what the public pays to see. And when the act is as well served as it was in the last half of David Shiner's compelling *Kooza*, direction accomplished.

4.
To Go or Not to Go?

Even more difficult, perhaps, than producing a first rate show is getting you, Mr. and Ms. Public, to patronize it. Fittest among surviving circus owners are those who have mastered the not so fine art of the front-end ballyhoo. Yesterday, that ballyhoo plastered itself in wall-wide posters onto warehouses, barns and low-end hotels. Today, it teases you in high-tech newspaper ad art or seductive TV promos. Yesterday, a press agent's prose; today, a film editor's skill.

Now, what I've referenced above is the higher road, which is where we will start in this front-end discussion, gradually working our way down to the less noble methods, crass and blatantly pandering, concocted by shrewd show owners to lure you out to show grounds. Somehow, someway, if they have their way, they will get you.

Of course, it helps enormously if your circus is a household name, like Ringling Bros. and Barnum & Bailey. Same long ago as now: When two circus men named Dan Costello and William Coup, names you may never have heard, joined burning ambitions to take out a larger tent show, they went right to the heart of the ballyhoo itself, to P. T. Barnum. Brilliant move. Under a five thousand seat tent in Brooklyn on a spring day in 1871, "P. T. Barnum Museum, Menagerie and Circus, International Zoological Gardens, Polytechnic Institute and Hippodrome" was born. Oh, did that name pull them in! Customer demand was so intense, the tent was soon enlarged. In a couple of booming seasons, a second ring was added. Ten years later, Barnum, now operating with James A. Bailey, added yet another! And the rest is history. There you have a brief primer on how Americans came to embrace the three-ring circus.

In his chestnut memoir, *Sawdust and Spangles*, William Coup estimated that he spent up to one half of his entire annual budget on the advance alone. One half. What for? For lithographs and for the bill posters to paste them over city walls, and for newspaper ads. He operated in an era of robust competition. There was a huge circus-going public to fight over. Each show strove to convince prospective patrons that *it* was the greatest, the largest this or the most gigantic that. Billposting crews soldiering for rival circuses literally went to war in the most fought over cities for blank space on fences and barns, buildings and, for all we know, outhouses. They covered each other's lithographss, too, to confuse the public. Show dates were altered

Old time ballyhoo: Sells Sterling pitches a 1937 date at Richland Center, Wisconsin. Photo by Sverre O. Braathan. USED WITH PERMISSION FROM ILLINOIS STATE UNIVERSITY'S SPECIAL COLLECTIONS, MILNER LIBRARY.

to favor the circus committing the touch-over work. Anything to get the town's well-earned farming money first. Remember when most of us milked cows and picked prunes? The trick then was to get your show in just after first harvest, for at that celebratory moment farm workers had well-earned money to spend and the urge to reward themselves on entertainment.

Today, of course, the ticket sales promotion does not pivot on harvest timetables. Gone are the hurly burly men who hustled 24-sheet lithographs, buckets of paste, hammers and tacks. Gone are flamboyant claims of being the largest. Shows that still tout size are touting in vain. The public no longer swoons over such stats. The public has settled into the new one-ring paradigm. And so the circus must market something other than how many elephants or rings it carries. Shows are finding newer hooks: nouveau mystery (Cirque du Soleil); Spectacle and tradition in a new format (Ringling); a circus of stars (Cole Bros.); funky urban grizzle and sizzle (UniverSoul); the show you love and can trust (Big Apple); a charming throwback to the old tent show (Kelly Miller).

Whatever is about to come your way with the word "circus" somewhere in the title (and beware, all kinds of oddball attractions flaunt the word without shame), it must motivate you to spend your money and your time under the assumption that you will be entertained. Let's face it, on the most basic human level we all wish to be sold a bill of goods. Wish to be courted with promises of magic and laughter, thrills, chills, spills. Yes, those well-worn words never seem to go out of fashion. Some words don't. We still respond. Buried deep in our DNA, I suspect, is a desire to be taken into strange worlds of glamour and excitement, spectacle, surprise. Any circus that can successfully address these universal desires is a circus most likely to prevail at the ticket windows.

The circus producer must package and sugar coat his product if he is to snare your attention and motivate you to break free of *Dancing with the Stars*. He must also prepare you for a sense of what to expect so that you will be better conditioned to go with the flow of his program. So, let's assume you are ready and willing to give him a chance on his own terms. The worst thing to happen is for a crowd to have been teased into a tent expecting the very opposite of what it finds. Kelly Miller Circus does not promote itself as a form of Cirque du Soleil; neither does the Big Apple Circus, just as Cirque du Soleil does not claim to be UniverSoul or Ringling. When the lights go down and the artists claim the ring, the audience will compare what is there to everything that came before in the form of advance advertising, poster art, website claims and feature coverage in the media.

Bygone era rivalries between circuses that generated hot press copy are rarely in evidence anymore. As late as 1983, however, in a flamboyant throwback to old-time competitive smear and ridicule, the Ringling show, apparently fearing a loss of ticket sales in Chicago to Circus Vargas, itself slated to play the town a few months ahead of Ringling's appearance, took out this ad:

> *Wait for the Big One!*
> *Accept no Imitations!*
> *Save your money for the very best!*
> *Why settle for paying more for less show and trudging*
> *across a dusty/muddy lot to swelter under a canvas tent*
> *in the hot and humid July-August heat sitting on a hard bench?*

How ironically amusing. Here we had the bizarre spectacle of Ringling Bros. and Barnum & Bailey, whose great legacy was built under the big top it was now smearing. Ringling indoors blasting a large tent show, itself promising the customer "a return to the rich traditions of the circus as it once was in America!"

Press agentry, American style, continues to mimic Wall Street. In recent memory, a blatant illustration of deceitful advertising came out of the same Feld-run Ringling operation. During the 2006 tour of the new Ringless Bros. Circus (and I do mean that literally), a Ringling TV ad included footage of several thrill acts which were no where to be seen in the show itself. In fact, the same promo was evidently used around the country to promote all three of the touring Ringling units. That our nation's largest and once most revered circus would stoop so low to foster such a misconception is but another egregious example of how owners will bend the rules in their favor. They do so at their own risk. Customers tend to remember acute disappointments even if they do not take the time to register complaints with or ask for refunds from the offending shows.

The Big Apple Circus, in its own way, also puts out misleading information by failing to alert ticket buyers visiting its website that its weekday morning shows are reduced by up to fifteen minutes. This means, for instance, that if you happened to attend an 11 A.M..performance of *Play On!* during the 2008-2009 season expecting to see Grandma perform her "Singin' in the Rain" comedy number (I did, and I am still fuming), you would have come up *rainless*. Tantamount to, say, taking in a matinee on Broadway of *South Pacific* and being denied "There Is Nothing Like a Dame" or "Younger than Springtime." Some might dub this Big Apple Circus practice a pre-scheduled "John Robinson" from the old phrase describing a shortened performance under the big top when storm clouds formed, causing management to take preemption action by running the show fast with cuts so as to get the customers out of the tent before heavy winds might topple it onto and around them.

Circus owners have been observed to devise numerous publicity stunts, each conceived to capture your attention and pull you away from Best Buy or your home entertainment center. Circus Vargas once sent an elephant through a car wash in Los Angeles. The stunt landed major television coverage on the evening news; passive TV watchers were turned into active Vargas consumers, their imaginations charmed by the audacity of an automated pachyderm shampoo. Ringling Bros. tried the same thing out at Coney Island in 2009, but without a car wash. Instead, they talked and talked and talked their way up the chain of command from the firehouse to city hall to get a band of firemen to hose down an elephant near Nathan's Hot Dog stand; they also got blasted by hordes of angry citizens enraged that professional fire fighters who might be needed at any moment could be marshaled into serving a circus PR stunt. In this instance, a cheap inconsiderate trick backfired.

Less controversial were the reams upon reams of free press coverage generated by the since-disbanded Ringling Bros Clown College. Founded by the late Irvin Feld, who must rank as one of the most cunning circus press agents of all time, this academy of laugh making recruited and turned young apprentice clowns into paid (if not quite professional) Ringling funny faces. The operation landed extensive feature story coverage in towns along the way from whence the first-of-May jesters had come.

Press men will push the envelope through the grandiose contortion of facts, all of it designed to whet your appetite for a big day at a big circus. Hollywood press agent Eddie Howe, who handled publicity for the highly successful tent tour of James Bros. Circus in 1968, did not return the following season. Nonetheless, he wrote a generously helpful letter to owner Sid Kellner in which he offered advice to his replacement (yours truly). Howe spelled out a shrewd strategy for marketing James Bros. indoors, since Kellner had shucked the tent in favor of playing arenas and auditoriums.

"America's newest and largest tented circus presented here under the auspices of _____ in the comfortable _____ arena, or stadium, etc."

Prescribed "how-to" Howe, "…make them think you are the big famous tent circus temporarily appearing in only a few major cities this year inside of building, etc., due to the lack of suitable and large enough grounds available in this city."

The truth is, the 1969 coast-to-coast ten-week tour of James. Bros Circus, which I fronted, serving as, so read my business card, "national press representative," played in as many small towns as it did large cities. And so, for that and possibly other reasons, I did not go along with Howe's rhetorical recipe. I did try my own ideas, one of them, used ever so briefly, tying circus day to the space race:

Who needs to go to the moon when the circus is right here?

"Briefly," perhaps because it made little sense to anybody but myself.

Another, more sensible line I came up with was also inspired by an imminent moon landing. My brainstorm, not suggested by Mr. Howe or Mr. Kellner, went:

Here Comes the Happiest Show on Any Earth!

It rang nicely, and so I placed it in quite a few ads up the road.

Then came a letter to my boss from a law firm. My bold allusion to a formidable circus title had drawn the ire of that circus's legal department. "We must demand that you immediately cease all use of the phrase 'The Happiest Show on Earth' [a calculated misquote deleting my use of the word "any"] and/or any other phrase deceptively and confusingly similar to our client's world famous service mark, 'The Greatest Show on Earth.'"

Request honored. Mr. Kellner, I supposed, did not wish to tangle with the legal watchdogs over at Ringling central. Suffice it to say, you don't either.

Not all campaigns to sell tickets sell tickets. Especially the case with the smaller shows tagged by dubious or blank reputations. They may spend not a dime on advertising but instead greet you at the check out counter in your local drug store. Yes, there they are, those free children's tickets to the circus. Please contain your excitement.

What a deal! No? You've fallen for the angle before only to be burned under a bad big top? You suffered through a drawn-out intermission while restless Timmy or grumpy Gertrude kept badgering you to buy them a pony ride, an elephant ride, a photo with a clown or a clown face for themselves? You left the circus wishing you had never picked up the free tickets in the first place?

Beware of the freebie. But don't discount it altogether. Many shows hand them out, the number seems to be growing. Free or discount passes are one of the oldest backup plans used by struggling owners to get some people into the tent. Even the most established circuses are offering steep discounts in these economically distressed times. Through its glory days in the mid-1980s, Circus Vargas posted its show dates on Knudsen Milk cartons throughout Southern California. Also posted were cut-out coupons offering family discounts. In 1980, two adults and two children could see the show for just $19.50. And not from end-of-the-tent bleachers. No, from "preferred front side seats," no less. Today, Carson and Barnes includes coupon cut-outs in newspaper ads admitting one adult free when accompanied by one paid adult. Smart move, I'd say.

Unsuspecting, uncritical kids are a market upon which the hard-strapped shows prey because a kid needs a full-paying parent to accompany him if his free pass is to be honored. But children can turn critical and very fast, feeling the onset of boredom and wanting out of the present party and into another. Again, do you want your kid's first or second circus experience to resemble a day at the county fair? No wonder there seem to be less and less grown-up people out there willing to give circuses a chance anymore.

To be sure and fair, let me make one thing very clear: You *can* pick up free tickets to some good tent shows, You *can* grab, if you are lucky, the occasional big bargain discount: Responding to the Great Recession In 2009, Ringling Bros. offered seats to its *Zing Zang Zoom* at Madison Square Garden for as little as *five* dollars, to its *Boom A Ring* under-canvas show at Coney Island for *ten*. And, as for the latter, you got a decent seat. These highly enticing prices, however, all lead to surcharge city, and I am not dissing the thoroughly despicable Ticketmaster. I am dissing those garish concession pits into which you are about to fall, where they will usually get to your pocket book or wallet one way or the other. Five dollars to get in, sure. More than twice that for a program magazine. More than twice that for a snow cone. And we've only just begun. Have I already mentioned the bungee bounce and the elephant rides? Keep this well in mind when you grab that little coupon at the drug store check out. More fun with this subject up the road.

Another way they will get you, and they do a very good job at it, is to sell you en route to your free seats on a ticket upgrade, from general admission into the reserves or "VIP" seating. Inside a tent, your motivation to upgrade will be teased as you are directed down one side of the tent to the far end, rather than allowed to choose a set near the front end where you came in. Why? This trek forces you to notice the superior reserved seats that you will pass on your way to the hard boards. Many customers who got in for nothing end up paying a little extra for a better view of the show in a more comfortable chair. Can you think of any other entertainment that siphons you through its seating options in order to raise additional revenue?

But this old tent show setup can feel customer-friendly, too. I happily recall walking into many a tent and spotting a man perched high on a little portable ticket platform, ready to accept not much money from me to exchange my pass for a reserved seat. And it always gave me a heady feeling of good fortune; I had elevated my status inside the big top. How easy it was! How lucky I felt! Today, now that our tent shows have all scaled back to one ring, virtually all of the seats offer reasonably good sight lines to the action.

These tactics are, any way, on the up-and-up. Stick to the free seats you came in with and you'll still be fine. Many shows now offer everyone a chair. The $10.00 Boom-A-Ring ticket at Coney did. What a deal.

So, let's say you are short on cash. You resisted a seating upgrade. You're happy enough with your seats, looking forward to being entertained. The feeling might not last very long if you or your kid can't resist the call of the "candy butchers," those fast moving fellows who unload tasty treats into the captive hands of sugar and salt feigns. For a fat charge. Remember, circuses tend to overprice their concessions as if the world were in the grips of a cotton candy famine. They need to make money somehow in order to compensate for all the free passes they give away.

Veteran concession man and blogger Dick Dykes defends the value of candy apples and hot dogs: "I have had many show owners tell me that they have days that if it were not for the concessions the show wouldn't have moved."

Ringling Bros. Circus is the worst offender because of its outrageously high prices, a point made by Dykes: "The trouble with the Ringling show, they want it all! And when it gets right down to it they are keeping a lot of people from attending any circus after they get done with them! I'm sorry but that's the way I see it."

But Ringling is not the only circus to have this negative affect on the public, as I will show you in the next chapter. Many shows, each in their own way, can leave the "customer" worn out on its incessant concession pitches from every angle and direction.

At the very small bare bones Circus Osario, which I caught in 2008, a woman and her son sitting on the plank in front of mine went back and forth about the boy's desire for a bag of popcorn ($3). His mother pointed out to him how much it had cost for her to get in (around $23.00). Obviously, she was reluctant to spend anymore. They sat there and watched the show. The subject came up again. "When we go home," promised the mother, "I'll make you some popcorn, okay?"

After intermission, they did not return to their seats. I assumed they had gone home early so that the boy could have some popcorn or because they were both equally unimpressed with a very weak program.

There is, let's be clear about this, a thick wide line separating a Ringling circus, which generally puts out a high-quality program, from the bottom feeder big tops like Circus Osario, built around and framed on the backs of a Mexican family or two.

Even lower down the ballyhoo chain, below the Mexican Diaspora, are the aggressive "boiler room" promoters who form shady alliances with police and fire departments, with chambers of commerce or the Elks or the Lions. And they go to work on local merchants: "I'm calling on behalf of the Policemen's Protective League. We are putting on a circus to raise money for the crippled children. May we sell you a book of tickets to distribute to children in need?"

Now, if you are the businessperson at the other end of the mock-compassionate phone call, do you dare say "no" to your local police department AND to the crippled children upon which it claims to be showering dollars and good deeds? The only issue worth noting here is where all the money goes. And, yes, if not today, certainly in recent times past most of it slipped quietly into the deep pockets of the boiler room king and his charity chasers. These deceptive rip offs, which I refuse to condone in these pages, thrived throughout the seedy 1970s. Largely since outlawed by local and state governments, the shows that once upon a season dialed for charity dollars are now smiling at all the adults buying adult tickets so that their sons and daughters can get in free on all the freebies handed out in advance.

During the American three-ring heyday, circuses were pushed by a public conditioned to judge a show on its size. The modern-era embracement of the older European style helped to deconstruct this uniquely American fetish largely engendered by Mr. Barnum and his colleagues. Now, in lieu of magnitude and spectacle, atmosphere and artistry are preferred. Consequently, ticket buyers no longer count the number of elephants. And this is why, I suspect, that in and around the Ringling show there has been so much producing schizophrenia concerning how many rings, if any, to use, and whether to use them only at intervals throughout the performance when there is a clear purpose.

The intensified emphasis on the artist seems to have hastened a trend favoring fewer acts, a trend no doubt welcomed by the producers for it means less performers to employ. A Ringling program in the last under-canvas days might comprise forty or fifty acts, although many performers appeared in more than one of them. Today's typical single ring show may incorporate as few as twelve acts, and even without garish spectacle, the overall affect of a masterfully directed performance can register a strong impression. The challenge more than ever is how to heighten the impact of the individual artist. Who can quibble with this esthetic?

Today's marketing techniques have also evolved. Again leading the way, Cirque du Soleil refined the art of newspaper ad design and placement. They place full-page teaser ads months preceding a date. "Michel-Thomas designed all the images and illustrations for the shows from 1985-1994," wrote Cirque's first marketing director, Jean David, on his blog. "Some, like *Saltimbanco, Alegria,* and *Mystere* visuals are still being used. Ideally, the marketing and artistic teams agreed on the choice of a show's base line and visual. We held lengthy discussions, trying to identify the aim and intent of every show. These discussions would end just in time for us to launch the advertising campaign…Each group had its legitimate needs, and when the discussions came to an impasse, we let [owner] Guy Laliberte decide."

How markedly different are the stylishly spare Cirque ads from the gaudy, prose-intense ones put out by American circuses even in recent years. The Cirque style stimulates the imagination but with a single image and logo, and with the show's name in smaller type. Subtle enough to identify the brand. This deft marketing of each new show would in time be followed by Ringling Bros. and Big Apple. Those two outfits, among a growing number of others, assign a new title to each new opus. In 2009, Ringling came out with *Zing Zang Zoom*, Big Apple with *Play On!*

Television still offers probably the most effective medium because circus imagery can be so visually captivating. Ringling's TV promos are brilliantly fashioned to give fleeting snippets of its best acts.

The value of a newspaper ad, in comparison, is that it gives the reader a permanent source of information, and the longer the paper hangs out on the coffee table, the likelier are the chances that it might be reread and reconsidered. One of the best damn circus ads ever was placed by the Moscow Circus for its engagement at the Radio City Musical Hall in 1988. Taken out in *The New York Times*, the full page pitch featured a bear standing nonchalantly atop the iconic Radio City neon sign. Read the text:

> "Moscow at the Music Hall. The circus that delights over one hundred million people around the world every year is coming to the Radio City Music Hall."

That impressive "one hundred million" figure makes me wonder if old-time press flack Eddie Howe handled the calculations.

So then, back to this chapter's main question: Should you go? After everything is said and considered, after you might have done a little website checking for reviews or consumer feedback, and assuming Yelp! has not trashed it; unless you are holding free passes to a show you have never heard of which is playing in some obscure location in a dicey part of town; unless it's a charity event setting up in the old municipal auditorium and you have yet to spot a single thing about it in the newspaper or on television; if unless does not apply, then you might wish to take a chance. Did you ever take a chance on a Broadway show, investing big bucks only to get burned? At least your investment here will be closer to donuts than diamonds. Fact is, every circus changes from one season to the next. Even the best of them have off years.

As for your possibly checking out "reviews," remember that reliable professional feedback is hard to come by because circuses rarely get reviewed except in the major cities. And even there, a newspaper may send out the most unlikely candidate to file a report. Could be a society editor (are there any of those left?) Or a sports columnist. A movie or ballet critic would be better. Any of these free lancers may have the journalistic chops to deliver a fair notice. As for Yelp! and other on-line consumer rating sites, keep in mind that hidden agendas can motivate some of the comments passing as legitimate feedback. Many of the so-called "consumers" who post reviews may actually be shills working for the show you are considering, or against it if they are surreptitiously shilling for a rival circus. They could be animal rights activists seizing upon every opportunity to pillar a show that dares parade pachyderms in plumes, dogs in clogs, no matter how good it might otherwise be. Conversely, those same activists may issue glowing marks to most any all-human circus.

Another good form of advance checking is to study a listing of the acts if you can locate one on the show's website. Most circuses now offer these, though not all are up to date. Look for features that appeal to you. If there is a YouTube or video sampler, by all means watch it. Do you like what you see? Are the performers skilled and engaging? Look for breadth and balance in the footage, from aerialist to acrobat. Do you spot too many secondary items like hula hoops or, say, roller skating? My best advice is this: Go for variety. A circus whose photos promise variety is more apt not to let you down.

It's an enterprise in discovery, and one experience will never match another, which is what makes chasing circuses both vexing, now and then rewarding, and on rare occasions flat out glorious. Expect something somewhere in the middle. If you are going with your kids on free passes, lower your expectations.

There is choice excitement in finding yourself at a very good show from fanfare to finale. This, trust me, can happen under a tent large *or* small. When Ringling Bros. deconstructed down to half a ring in 2006, hordes of ticket buyers took on management for inferior showmanship. Many were outraged. How could "the greatest show on earth" stoop so low? Well, the co-producing Felds, Kenneth and his daughter Nichole, had embarked on a creative journey into a new world of their own inevitable reinvention. Mr. Feld listened to customer feedback. And he made changes accordingly. Before the year was out, in came a white tiger act. Ringling audiences still wanted exotic animals. Other changes welcomed by the fans have been made, and more are likely on the way. The Feld future, indeed, the future of all shows, remains an open ended experiment in reformatting.

Which is why you, too, should remain open. The circus that left you cold one summer may, the next, rouse your spirits. And the price of a snow cone may have by then melted down to something half way human, like, say, not a penny higher than the cheapest seat. Just hope that the "cheapest" seat does not go up much.

Before circus animals became an issue, Americans flocked to the early morning set up of Ringling Bros. and Barnum & Bailey. Circa 1954. PHOTO BY TED SATO/AUTHOR'S COLLECTION.

5.
Midways on the Way

The heart beats faster. In the distance, you spot a circus tent around which pennants are galloping gaily in the wind. How I miss the old canvas tops that swayed and flapped from side to side like wind-tossed willow trees. You could almost feel them breathing in and out, expanding and contracting in size as if they had a life of their own.

No wonder the gradual exodus in recent times out of the indoor arena, back to canvas. Some shows now emblazon their names in electric signage across the tops of their tents, flashing out neon invitations to passing motorists. The circus is here! The more elaborately designed are they, the greater our motivation to park the car, get out of it and check on show times and ticket prices.

At the forefront of a big top transformation, Cirque du Soleil creates the aura of a cinematic fantasy. Other shows have followed suit, usually with less opulence to flaunt. Just as the world moves on, so too must the circus. The costly vinyl arenas from Italy represent a step up in esthetics. By keeping the natural light outside from seeping through (a feat first achieved by John Ringling North in 1939 when his Norman Bel Geddes-designed big top was made of blue), sophisticated theatre lighting is now a reality under the big top.

The more visible the location, the better the chances for attracting crowds. That is, if the location is not next to a city dump, a liquor store, strip mall or smack dab in the middle of a gangland shooting range infested with druggies, hookers, crack addicts, *et al*. Visible in the affirmative would be something like a fairgrounds or decent open space close to a freeway, but not to an incarceration facility. Unfriendly rental fees are a deciding factor that have driven some show owners to settle for cheaper lots precariously vulnerable to heavy rain storms. This can make circus day for you a muddy ordeal compared to visiting your local Shrine circus at the old municipal auditorium, that is, if the place is still in operation and not in the middle of a Section 8 neighborhood during a drive-by shooting festival.

Shows that play shopping malls effectively circumvent getting mired in Mother Nature. Asphalt is a more reliable if less poetic surface to perform on. Dry. Level. Firm. There should also be plenty of parking space, another big advantage to the customer.

A crowd waits for Mills Bros. Circus to opens its doors in 1958. PHOTO BY SVERRE O. BRAATHEN. USED WITH PERMISSION FROM ILLINOIS STATE UNIVERSITY'S SPECIAL COLLECTIONS, MILNER LIBRARY.

Now, if you favor an idyllic circus setting and don't mind getting a little terra cotta on your designer jeans, nothing beats a green grassy field, even if it's more brown than green. In my seasoned view, this more natural setting compliments the organic vitality of the circus experience, especially if the show includes animal acts. Who wouldn't rather see a circus parade over grass or dirt than across the white lines of a mall parking lot?

First impressions can't be denied. I'm talking even the condition of the trucks that haul the show, the tents and the concession booths. How freshly painted is everything? How bright and appealing, or seedy and run down looking? Take a quick once-over look and decide for yourself, how impressed or unimpressed do you feel at first glance? Give your gut impression a grade. Not too promising? You already bought tickets. Okay, then move ahead. You've not bought tickets? Okay, then step back and rethink. Check out the cost of adult tickets. They almost certainly are not free. If there are children with you, the deal may already have been sealed. After all, would you dare turn your back on your own child? Impossible, yes. Proceed, of course.

Let's play devil's advocate for a moment. Say you have just arrived with but one child. You spot a not very large tent. Yes, *that's* the "big top." It doesn't have to be big, only the biggest tent on the lot. You might have been lured into a Mexican family circus (the name will tell you). Most of these modest, barely surviving outfits manage somehow to feed and shelter themselves on the hand-out of free passes. The programs they offer usually range from very, very weak to maybe almost pretty good. You may spot a Mexican tent at the fairgrounds, or at some shady location further adding to the likelihood that they are only a few bum turnouts away from selling their trucks for tacos and heading back south of the border.

Ideally, a circus tent is at its most appealing over a grassy lot. Good luck in ever finding one. Realistically, you are more apt to find yourself traipsing across rough terrain, up a slippery slope or down through a weed patch next to a crocodile pool. Good circus lots are harder and harder to come by. The farsighted Otto Ringling, known affectionately as "King Otto" by troupers, once tried talking his four brothers into an audacious long-term plan to snap up prime real estate in the major cities regularly visited by the show. Otto projected that in future years, as urban renewal claimed open fields and vacant lots, the show would end up at a disadvantage, unable to secure space close to the city center well served by public transportation. Otto's brothers nixed the visionary proposal, and within fifty years, the huge touring Ringling Bros. and Barnum & Bailey Combined Shows wrestled through an increasing number of markets to secure exhibition space on grounds close to the cites and large enough to handle fifteen acres of canvas. The geographical symbolism of Ringling's last stand under canvas in Pittsburgh, Pennsylvania on July 16, 1956, was hardly atypical. The circus appeared under the big top on the Heidelberg Raceway parking lot, *15 miles* southwest of the city.

Parking became another daunting problem fifty years ago. Even if a circus could secure sufficient acreage to house all of its tents, it still might be unable to host a mass convergence of gas-guzzling patrons onto the show grounds. This problem led to circus owners making deals with shopping malls. The arrangement proved good for both. The circus had a flat solid surface to show on, although driving stakes into asphalt is more labor intensive and the holes left when the stakes are removed have to be filled in before the show leaves town. The mall benefited by the increased traffic drawn to the circus. Other similar locations with built-in parking lots, like fairgrounds and stadiums, have worked well for circus owners. And they work well for you, the customer.

And then there are those lots from the other side of civilization. Could

Under the new — and last — Ringling marquee, in Brantford, Ontario, July 7, 1953. PHOTO BY SVERRE O. BRAATHEN. USED WITH PERMISSION FROM ILLINOIS STATE UNIVERSITY'S SPECIAL COLLECTIONS, MILNER LIBRARY.

be the condition of the ground. When I traveled one summer with Wallace Bros Circus, we once set up on the side of a hill; was *that* a challenge erecting the seats and getting the customers to feel comfortable sitting in them. Another time we pitched the tents over what looked an awful lot like an abandoned cemetery. Advance site-booking agents, pressed to nail down dates at the lowest terms, have been known to settle for dubious open spaces, which they may not have taken the time to personally vet. More than a hundred times have circuses at the last minute ditched one lot for a "better" one. Of course, when the weather prohibits, shows may have to dump one-day dates altogether. Usually, however, they will persevere by hook or by crook to at least pull off one performance. Anything to add a few more pennies to the kitty.

At the Oakland Coliseum near a depressing freeway named Nimitz, there lurks one of the ugliest "lots" known to the circus world. A clumpy patch of dirt and weed reachable by utility roads serving freeway on and off-ramps. This no-man's-land has hosted, incredibly, a number of regular touring tenters, including the Carson & Barnes and UniverSoul shows. Circus Vargas tried it one time, but has yet to return. It is a dreadful place, dreadfully located in a crime-infested corridor of Oakland. Amazing to think that any circus can draw a crowd there. Once, wanting to take in a performance of Circo Caballero, I called an 800 number and was connected to a fellow in Southern California. I asked about early show times. He mentioned a matinee but warned me that I might be better off waiting for the night show. "If not enough people show up, they probably won't do the first show."

Another time, risking high urban stress, I took BART out to the Coliseum station and walked about half a mile from there in an effort to take in a performance of the UniverSoul Circus. The tent was reachable across a pedestrian obstacle course of rock and weed and slippery mud. Here was a spot I could easily imagine the Native Americans even shunning in their time. Nor did the presence of hip hopper types quell my apprehensions. When I got to the ticket windows I was told the performance was sold out. And all of my panic for naught! So I returned another time or another year but on this occasion with a ticket in hand that I had purchased online in advance. The circus, to my relief, was sanely patronized, mostly by young mothers and their kids. No problem at all. Nonetheless, I will not be going back to that living wasteland. Even UniverSoul has not played there in a few years.

Location. Location. Location. When UniverSoul's first ringmaster Calvin "Casual Cal" DuPre quit the show, one of his departing regrets concerned management's preoccupation with an African-American audience base. He felt that owner Cedric Walker should be reaching out to more culturally diverse markets. This is a proud black owned circus that has carved out a durable niche for itself within predominantly black communities. Why it will not pitch its tents in decent San Francisco Bay Area location remains a mystery, unless the show's profit margin is too narrow for it to afford higher rental rates. Jack London Square in Oakland would be ideal.

Of course, not to play favorites, our nation's largest and most profitable circus, Ringling-Barnum, also appears in the same creepy Oakland district not far from that hostile location just described. But Ringling plays in the Oracle Arena, which provides ample parking space, security, and a direct walkway to the adjoining BART train station.

Okay, enough urban paranoia already. You have reached the midway, be it on a green meadow in a pretty little town or in front of a metropolitan sports arena. You are now on their turf. Look it over, and look all around, as I've recommended, and give it a grade. Unless it looks really creepy (punks in baggy trousers engaged in target practice), or you fear being ripped off (strange man with long fingers keeps eyeing the bulge in your pockets), then proceed further. You can still turn around at any moment.

The "midway," in case you are asking what that is, consists of everything you will pass through *until* you step into the main tent. Your ticket may, in fact, be taken upon entering the midway, a security measure implemented in modern times to thwart the free passage of animal rights zealots, or it may be taken when you enter either the big top or a small tent just ahead of it called the marquee. And here, I must warn you: Don't judge a circus by the midway. True, some are accurate preludes to substandard amusement. Others may mask a fine program on the inside. Keep in mind that these carnival add-ons are there to raise additional revenue from circus souvenirs, rides and "pit shows" (snakes and animal oddities). So, yes, a midway may ill-reflect on the circus performance you are about to witness. You simply should not make an educated guess based purely on all the stuff out there in front of the tent. Now, if it suddenly dawns on you that you have seen this particular circus before, the memory of that experience may serve as a general indication of what likely lies ahead.

Circus Chimera was born out of a plan to give the public an affordable Cirque du Soleil type of program. It's big top was fronted, however, by an old fashioned pit show midway that harkened back to the 1950s and before. It did not belong to a circus desiring to appropriate the Cirque look and feel. And so it sullied customer expectations. And yet, in other ways, its old-fashioned midway epitomized a struggling operation unable to fully define itself to the public. The Chimera experiment was too schizophrenic too succeed, and a well-intentioned enterprise which never actually turned a profit was out of business after nine straining seasons.

These carnivalesque thoroughfares en route to the main show, with which I have few qualms, after all are clearly not a part of the performance itself. And if they are, I do have qualms. But this topic must await my assaulting it head-on once we get inside the tent. At its best, the midway offers pleasures to children whose parents can afford the cost of a pony, camel, or elephant ride. At its worst, a scruffy midway tags the show as second or third rate whether it is or is not. The public does not forget. Every item on the lot influences your perception. Chimera's failing, I believe, was its split-personality layout — old carny out front, ersatz nouveau circus inside. The crowd that Chimera aimed to satisfy did not really exist in sufficient numbers. People who tend to prefer a circus without animal acts have too much money to settle for the lower-end Chimera product. The few who did venture onto the lot took smug satisfaction in being able to draw comparisons between the evil animal circus (Ringling,

Al. G. Barnes, 1934: Gone are the sideshows that promised strange exotic features. PHOTO BY SVERRE O. BRAATHEN. USED WITH PERMISSION FROM ILLINOIS STATE UNIVERSITY'S SPECIAL COLLECTIONS, MILNER LIBRARY.

of course) and the good troupe (Chimera).

Now, to be all-inclusive, let's switch settings. You are about to enter in a building and the name of the show is Ringling. You will come upon atmosphere, all right, most of it supplied by a festive string of food, concession and souvenir stands. Say what you will, these colorful displays compensate somewhat for the lack of tents and pennants. They also serve as a signal to the savvy consumer: beware; you are entering a high tech retail zone. Hold onto your wallet. The Felds have made a high art of maximizing concession sales. If you are willing to play their game, or if your kids are swift at working you over for fun money on such occasions, you may contribute mightily to the Ringling coffers. But we mustn't take to task Ringling alone. All of the shows get what they can at the popcorn and cotton candy counters.

You have reached the ticket windows. A typical ticket seller will treat you with gingerly respect and patience. No show I can think of does a better job at customer service than Circus Vargas. The moment you hit their premises, you are greeted by a staff member with clipboard who will gladly help you make your seat location selection. These people work the gathering crowd to help speed up the flow of traffic from ticket window

Typical of today's shrunken midways, Carson & Barnes Circus sells opportunities to ride upon and interact with its animals. AUTHOR'S COLLECTION.

to entrance. The Vargas staff is Class A all the way. In fact, you may spot the person who sold you your ticket in the actual performance riding a unicycle or dangling lyrically from a rope. On the smaller shows by tradition as heretofore mentioned, performers often handle other jobs for a little extra money.

Where to sit? One of the advantages inherent in the one-ring circus is that since the tents have gotten smaller, virtually all of the seats are close enough to the action. If you are on a tight budget, the cheapest seat in the tent should work just fine. Most of our shows now carry advanced understructures that support individual contoured plastic chairs similar to those in baseball stadiums. Another advantage of going "cheap," is that, the farther away you place yourself from the ring, the greater the chances that you will have ample space in which to stretch out because you can usually find sections of vacant seats in the upper reaches. When I took in a performance of UniverSoul Circus, that is where I ended up after first being seated only a couple of rows from the ring. Great seat? No. Above me hooked to a tent pole were music amplifiers that sounded like jackhammers against my ear drums, no thank you, Hip Hop Circus for the hearing impaired. I fled to a cheaper seat, possibly the cheapest, as high in the tent as I could go, as far away as I could get from High Decibel Damnation.

Ideally, I recommend purchasing your seats a few rows back of the ring unless you enjoy studying theatrical makeup or you are attending a circus called UniverSoul. Sit back a few rows and enjoy the illusion.

Some circuses use seat wagons. They provide solid support, if not cushy comfort. You could end up on a plant rather than in a chair. Beware Carson & Barnes: the backrest to a reserved seat I upgraded to leaned too far back, making me feel instantly uncomfortable. Back problem city I was not about to visit. Since there were so few people in attendance, I easily relocated myself to another plank and back rest. Okay.

Most shows nowadays offer "VIP" seating. Be careful when ordering to *insist* on the *front* row. Why? At most of the smaller outfits, the VIP chairs are placed flat on the ground as opposed to raked theatre seating throughout the rest of the tent. You could end up feeling stranded behind a tall somebody and having to crane your neck this way or that around or over that somebody's head. VIP, in my book, also stands for "Very Inconvenienced Patron."

Putting tent show atmospherics aside, indoor circus fans can point to a number of distinct pluses, not the least being that your trip to the show is guaranteed to be raindrop and puddle free. Indoor arenas usually control the temperature. Compare this to a torrid summer day under a tent, or to a frigid spring or fall day under a tent. A few of the high-end outfits, among them, the Big Apple Circus, carry heating and air conditioning systems to their marketing advantage.

John Ringling North tried cooling down the big top in 1939. His ambitious plans overreached the technology then in existence. Before him, his five uncles bucked a profit-making tradition by ordering canvas crews to *lower* the sidewalls during heat waves and let the breezes in, a very humane gesture designed to give customers as much relief as possible. Soda pop sales dropped, but respect for those customer-loving Ringlings soared. How very different from my times under a torrid Circus Chimera tent, wondering if management could not have done more to cool it down.

Your interactions with the staff at the ticket windows and concession booths form your first impressions of the kind of circus company you are about to keep. The warm hospitalities you ordinarily come across on the smaller shows are the mark of a grateful work force. These people struggle day in and day out to bring you circus day. They rarely make a lot of money. They need your patronage. And so they tend to treat every last customer with special attention. They are, indeed, as happy to see you as you are, I hope, to see them.

Inside, you may come upon a pre-show concession party of sorts in progress. And it may look like the midway followed you right in. No, it will never completely go away, so you had better get used to it. More photo ops. More animals for the kiddies to ride. And all of it rendering obsolete the idea of any circus ever again starting exactly on time. Sell. Sell. Sell.

Considering all the shows whose rings are cluttered up in this philistine manner, what a pure unmolested joy it is to be seated inside the gorgeous Big Apple Circus tent and gaze upon a still and vacant ring. Bravo, Big Apple!

At the Ringling circus, an "all access pre show" event is staged down on the arena floor. Kids and parents mingle with select performers; autographs are given, which, of course, helps sell more coloring books and program magazines. Young aerial dreamers are lifted onto trapeze bars to sample a rare feeling. Boys cavort with clowns. Most amusing of all is to watch a Ringling elephant stroke a brush across a sheet of canvas placed on an easel, "painting" a picture in progress. This alone is worth a walk down there. I have always been leery of these intimate interactions between audience and artist, for they intrude upon the mystique of the circus, reducing it to the level of a street fair. On the other hand, the Ringling pre-show parties are all free, no money-making concessions going on, which sets them apart. And then there's the delightful pachyderm Picasso. How I wish he'd been wearing a beret.

You have been ushered to your seat and are waiting for the show to begin. The moment comes and it does not begin. Be prepared to wait longer. And maybe yet a little longer. Maybe by fifteen or twenty minutes, depending upon how many things are being sold and how many people are still waiting in line to buy those things. The Sarasota-based Moscow Circus of Stars took up nearly a *half hour* selling stuff. At a Shrine Circus in Sacramento in 2005, the pre-show party included 20 female acrobatic students from a local private school, given plenty of time to demonstrate their repetitive skills. I wondered what in the world they were doing there. Maybe they were a generous sponsor exacting a payoff in the form of a pre-show promo. Also included were local Shrine clowns literally falling on their faces, all of it needlessly time consuming and a direct affront to professional circus entertainment.

When I was a kid growing up in Santa Rosa, California and the Shriners brought Polack Bros. Circus to town for a couple of days each spring, there were no animal rides for sale. No photo ops or slides. No Shrine "clowns" mucking up the ambiance. Into the Grace Pavilion at the fairgrounds, just before the circus began, marched the men in red hats, briefly and to the point. We applauded them gratefully. The crowds were large and animated. The show was top-drawer from front to finish. The clowns who made us really laugh were not local wannabes. They were pros, period.

I doubt the performance started more than five minutes late. And even without a carnival of concessions that today is said to compensate for the mass free ticket giveaways, the Shriners handed out plenty of free tickets to kids. I can still remember, with a lasting thrill, the sight of a tall man outside the Grace Pavilion looming over me one afternoon, not long after I'd gotten out of school and had run down to the fairgrounds. For weeks I had been glued to newspaper ads illustrating images of people performing stupendous tricks. Polack Bros. Circus was coming to town! And now, at last, I was so close to my magical destination, and the tall man in the red Shriner hat was holding between his fingers a block of passes to the circus and asking *me* if I'd like one. Boy, would I ever! Thank you, sir!

Back then before inflatable slides and elephant rides, before you could get a clowny look painted onto your face or have your photo taken with a big snake wrapped around your shoulders, when the "circus" came to town, "*circus*" was what we went to see.

6.
A Special Place

Now that you're inside the tent, your next circus day assignment is to play big top architecture critique. First, a brief primer. Tops, as we call them, come in all sizes, shapes and colors. No longer plain white canvas. Now usually a thick plastic. The best of them transport you away from the everyday world into another place. A place you have never seen before. That last idea came to me from my friend Boyi Yuan, who was raised on a farm in Southern China and only once saw a circus under a tent, and that was after his family immigrated to the States. That one experience left him with a distinct appreciation for the magical difference between a typical indoor venue and a tent. Said he, "I want to go to a place where I have never been before, not a place where I can see movies or musical shows. The circus should be in a special place. Light coming through the top of the tent."

So now that you're inside the tent, take a look all around. You might make a mental listing of things you like as well as things that put you off. To be specific, how much of that other stuff against which I have been railing do you also see? First impressions, you've heard, can be lasting, and so I only wish you many excellent first impressions upon entering our big tops.

At every circus, the first thing to do is to look up: how much rigging do you spot? Perhaps unfairly, I tend to pre-judge a show by the evidence of cables, wires, pulleys, swings, trapeze bars, and all the other hung apparatus that will be employed during the program by daredevil specialists. The more the better as far as I am concerned. A dense maze of rigging promises an abundance of aerial gymnastics, which can only heighten our expectations.

When a young Ken Dodd, who would grow up to become producing clown for Clyde Beatty-Cole Bros Circus, stepped into Ringling's huge canvas amphitheatre in 1948, he was spellbound by a mind-boggling maze of overhead rigging — revolving ladders, loop-to-loops, single traps and cloud swings, irons jaws and webs. Every possible space taken. That season the show was presenting the "Monte Carlo Aerial Ballet," a mesmerizing production designed by Barbette in which 48 "North Starlets" performed simultaneously. It left Dodd with a dazzling impression of circus spectacle.

I was nearly as dazzled during my boyhood years in the 1950s when Polack Bros.. Circus assembled itself aerialistically inside the Grace

Americans return to one-ring intimacy under the Kelly Miller Circus big top in Brewster, New York, 2010. AUTHOR PHOTO.

Pavilion at the Santa Rosa fairgrounds, only a few exciting blocks from where I lived. The fascinating set-up phases drove me to skip school without a shred of guilt. What would they unpack out of the big wood crates and canvas bags, the trunks and off the back ends of the trucks? Everything charged my imagination; how would each of the contraptions be used in the show? Indeed, one of the most interesting things about watching a circus is to contemplate how all of the props spread around the edges of the performance area will be put into action when the performers whose props they are bring them to life. These magical shapes in the shadows serve as a kind of tease, helping to sustain our engagement as the program unfolds.

Okay, that is all in the plus territory, and we hope that's where your immediate observations stay. However, the realities of big top survival will dictate that you are just as likely to come upon a whole different array of objects that have nothing to do with the program you are about to see. I must regretfully return to the issue of carnival amusements. Yes, I am talking all manner of concessions and rides that clutter up the ring(s). If this you encounter, your circus rendezvous may have already been tainted. Take heart, however, this does not necessarily mean that the show itself will fail you. Now, assuming you have children in toe who got in free and

When animals and aerialists ruled the program: Ringling is set up and rigged for Madison Square Garden. Circa 1924. PHOTO BY CHARLES CLARKE. USED WITH PERMISSION FROM ILLINOIS STATE UNIVERSITY'S SPECIAL COLLECTIONS, MILNER LIBRARY.

there are pony and elephant rides for sale on the premises, you'll probably overlook these crass slights to circus art, but you may begin to understand a deal you have made with a circus devil: In free, but once inside, no longer free. Good luck placating tiny Tim or nagging Nancy as all around you cotton candy and snow cone vendors are working their spiels.

The "special place" that it should be is not always the place you have reached. Have patience and concentrate away from the money changers in the tent, away, too, from any other setbacks to that idyllic circus day of your dreams. I learned this at a very early age when King Bros. Circus came to Santa Rosa one hot, late summer day. My mom, sister and I stood out on the midway for what felt like an eternity. Unbeknownst to us, the seat truck had broken down en route from the last town played and management was scurrying about to find substitute chairs. While we waited in the sun, I glanced up every now and then at the tall side show banner lines, and, boy, did they seem to stretch clear up to heaven. I exulted in this strange and wonderful place, my first trip to the circus under a tent. The white rippling canvas bedazzled my young eyes. When finally we were admitted inside, we found seats for ourselves among a makeshift array of chairs from a local church or school that had been hastily assembled over a grassy field. But when the show started, it was magic, pure magic.

Why had that circus left such an impression on me? I suppose because of my being placed inside a tent especially made for the circus, rather than in a building that housed other times of the year numerous non-circus events. Floyd King, the man who brought King Bros. Circus to Santa Rosa, had also worked as a press agent for other shows, and the flowery prose he produced yet hit the mark: "Strange and glamorous is life under the big tops," he penned, as smooth as a candy butcher spinning cotton candy. "Our astonished eye will gaze upon the gorgeous pageant and the parade and, returning to the grounds, will peer freely and familiarly about the place of strange sounds and entrancing sights."

Indeed, we wish to be removed from the humdrum world that marks our daily steps and obligations. This is not nearly as possible inside a 10,000 seat auditorium, even inside a 5,000 auditorium, for those venues remind us of all the other activities from ice hockey and rock concerts to Christian revivals and Gem Fairs that also take place inside them. When the lights go down, yes, a semblance of circus magic may be glimpsed and felt through the riggings and props, but only a semblance. We are still seated in a place not of the circus.

Inside a tent, especially one that has been pitched over a natural field, we find ourselves in a distinctly different environment. Under a tent, the animals look more at home. The sway of the canvas and the smells of the earth compliment the primal sounds and movements of lions and tigers, elephants and monkeys, horses and dogs. For this authenticity of place, many of us are willing to endure the occasional inconvenience of raindrops and mud puddles that can be an unexpected part of the package.

During the American three-ring heyday, when dozens of circuses criss-crossed the nation on rails of steel, scholarly press agent F. Beverly Kelly dubbed the fascinating ritual "the city that moves by night." Americans wanted spectacle and action in three rings, nothing less. The smaller trucks shows gave them the imperative norm, too. "Downie Bros. Big 3 Ring

Wild Animal Circus, Museum, Menagerie and Real Wild West. The Largest Motor Circus in the World"

The more the better, as witness this rhetorical program magazine buildup to the opening parade, "The Birth of a Rainbow," presented in 1920 by Sells-Floto:

> *"There is a grand stirring, as the children of all ages, the joyous joyful of heart and the seekers of happiness, of fortune, of love, begin again the chase. Round and round they go, for there is no journey's end. It is just ahead. The goal, the glowing, the golden joyful goal. Riches, Rapture — They are there, just ahead — There! For at the end of the rainbow there's a pot of gold."*

Over pure green grass (rare) or dirt and dung (less rare), the parade unfolded to the oos and ahhs of the crowd. Put that same parade inside a building over cement, or outdoors on an open nondescript field like a ballpark, and something is lost.

During arguably the two bleakest periods in Ringling circus history (notwithstanding the horrific aftermath of the 1944 Hartford fire), the show performed in settings so far removed from what the public had grown to expect as to look stranded in time. First episode: After it left the big top in 1956, for the next several seasons Ringling engagements were played, not just in arenas, but in front of racetrack grandstands or at ballparks. Never would its "performance" look so lost and so formless, so insignificantly out of place. Some called it "beer can circus," alluding to tossed cans strewn about baseball diamonds.

Second episode: Forty nine years later, in another drastic redefinition of its program format, the show that had defined three-ring extravagance shucked aside all three rings. Suddenly it seemed disoriented, disjointed. In an eerie way it looked much like it had looked in 1957, foundering in the absence of a clear context. In both instances the show had eliminated significant set pieces: In 1957, the tent; in 2006, the ring. So let us now address the subject of circus sets and their critical importance to the artistic impact of the show.

In recent times, circuses have gravitated back to their own special enclosures.

When Cirque du Soleil bolted onto the international scene in 1987, one of its most brilliant moves was to restore the unique atmosphere of a tent circus in ways unmatchable inside a building, to turn the tent itself into a temple of intense mystery. A Cirque layout includes the performance top plus a few smaller tops, all of them uniformly designed to compliment each other so that we come upon a portable village that may call to mind the land of Scheherazade. We are taken in at first sight. Other shows have followed suit in one way or another, upgrading their physical layouts to approximate a Cirque look, all of which, in contrast, only makes the indoor venue look less inviting, less relevant.

Pity today's tentless circuses! They are drowning in thousands of seats they no longer can fill up, stuck as they helplessly are in the middle of vast performing spaces that cry out for the three rings no longer fancied by the public. What are these companies to do? How to foster an air of intimacy over cavernous concrete floors? How to connect with small crowds sprinkled over thousands of seats? Most of the Shrine Circus producers carry tents, ready to play either indoors or under canvas. Not always the smoothest transition. For instance, the 2005 Shrine Circus in Sacramento was presented in a medium sized tent. The producer, Jordan International, managed to squeeze three small rings together by overlapping them at the edges. This gave the setting a claustrophobic look and feel. Apparently, lacking sufficient space to hang the rigging for a flying trapeze act, the rigging was erected outside in front of the tent. On the day I attended, however, the flyers did not fly before or after the regular performance, the reason being, I surmised, that a light drizzle might have endangered their mid-air maneuvers.

Particularly off-putting was the flimsy, bare bones seating structure inside the tent. Raindrops escaping through made the steps more precarious to climb. I stayed put down on the front row, my feet flat on the ground. That flimsy set-up did not instill a sense of security or stability. In a Twilight Zone kind of way, it symbolized the plight of the American circus semi-stranded between its old-time big top ways and a future yet to be fully embraced and validated by both producers and public alike.

When John Ringling North struck the tents in 1956, opting to entertain in large arenas (within a few years, he was out of the ballparks and the race tracks), three rings were the norm, but the cost of running a colossal railroad show had grown prohibitive. It seemed clear that North did not wish to scale back the size of the show itself to fit a drastically smaller tent, thus placing himself on the same level as smaller shows. The only way he could then maintain the circus he wished to continue producing was to tour sans canvas. Overnight, North cut his costs by more than fifty percent. It made perfect if sad sense at the time, and it worked well for many years. Often enough, they filled up at least half of the seats in the average arena, and it's an old tent show axiom that if, on average, you can draw half houses, you will do okay. Mr. North did more than okay switching to hard tops.

Fifty years later, the story has changed. Traditional circus entertainment itself is no longer so irresistible a magnet for Americans. Blame either the Feld family, who took over operation of Ringling Bros. and Barnum & Bailey in 1967, or simply inevitable shifts in American culture.

The immensity of it all, and from a bare seat plank when that's all you could afford. Ringling Bros. and Barnum & Bailey. Circa 1924. PHOTO BY CHARLES CLARKE. USED WITH PERMISSION FROM ILLINOIS STATE UNIVERSITY'S SPECIAL COLLECTIONS, MILNER LIBRARY.

When Kenneth Feld assumed control of the show following the death of his father, Irvin, in 1984, he would soon confront a pair of daunting challenges born of Cirque du Soleil: (1) Cirque du Soleil's one-ring paradigm; and (2), declining patronage at his own shows likely influenced partly by the impact of Cirque du Soleil's animal-free profile.

Given these two formidable realities, do you keep your world-famous trio of rings when you are playing to fewer customers and when, all around you, other shows are reverting back to single-ring formats?

So here was producer Feld facing an opposite set of public expectations incongruous with those that his circus once had to satisfy. The customer *seemed* to have fallen out of love with a surfeit of simultaneous action in multiple circles. How to address the situation? Shrewdly, the Feld of Felds solved the two problems by eliminating use of about a third of the seats at one end of the house and erecting a European-style performer's entrance to help obscure the blocked-off seating. This may have justified the downsizing, in the customer's eyes, as an artistic rather than a commercial alteration.

To Feld's credit, the truncated layout does lend a slightly more intimate feel to what can otherwise seem a sterile setting, especially when you compare the size of these arenas to the much smaller size of a typical one-ring tent circus of today. However, the smaller the performance area becomes, the more unflattering the contrast between it and the preponderance of concession kiosks that emblazon the walkways like a Vegas trade show. You may then ask, is that why I am really here?

We have talked ourselves almost into an aversion to the elements of size and scope once linked to the famous slogan "the greatest show on earth." Too much. Too yesterday. Too retro. The three-ring holdouts that linger on inside hard tops are looking more and more like gilded dinosaurs. I can hear sponsors telling producers who pitch to them, "We don't want the three ring thing anymore. We want a higher quality show. Better lighting. Some special effects. Maybe a character or two, you know, a little story woven into the program? More up to date like Cirque du Soleil." The Shriners in some ways are more in touch with the audiences than are the producers who supply the acts. Some of the temples, for example, talk down the old opening parade in favor of the faster moving charivari, the sudden high-energy rush of performers into the ring executing some of the action to follow, all of it colorfully embellished with bravura posturing.

Are the Felds letting go of too many traditions and set pieces? When you end up without even one ring, you risk obliterating what is called "product identify." And this they risked, indeed, in their 2006 breakout edition, the ringless version I've told you about. Well, there was half a ring at that, so all was not lost. Every form needs its enduring set piece. The concert hall has its podium, the stage its proscenium, a baseball game its diamond. And so too the circus, perennially centered in the ring. And those who retire it from view risk self-annihilation. The Ringling show has since returned to ringhood, but only during select moments in the program when rubber tubes are inflated and joined to foster the image of rings. Cole Bros. Circus of Stars was, in fact, the first to retire the rings completely when it reconfigured its performance area into a rather amorphous rectangular shape.

A bigger ongoing challenge facing the Felds may be the venue itself. Will they be able to reinvent an indoor circus format of their own attractive enough to draw lush crowds well into the future, or might they inevitably have to bow to change, reverse the course taken by North over fifty years ago, and go *back* to the big top?

Kenneth Feld dabbled in a high-tech tent show just as the last mil-

China in a ring: At the Shanghai Circus World's circular theatre, in 2010, traditional stage-bound troupes are adapting to the universal set piece for circus. PHOTO BY BOYI YUAN.

lennium was drawing to a close. In this promising new career chapter, he had obviously set out to capture a substantial slice of Cirque's market. He called his derivative brainstorm *Barnum's Kaleidoscape*, and it lasted not quite two years, reaping excellent notices and pulling in respectable crowds. But it still lost money, and its populist producer was the wrong person to hang in with a good idea for the long haul. In fact, the long haul of too many trucks needed to move the costly *Kaleidoscape* between engagements is thought by many to be the real reason why this impressive new venture went no where.

Exactly ten years later, the shrewdly adaptable Mr. Feld was again testing a tent, and over it he placed name Ringling Bros. and Barnum & Bailey. For the first time in over fifty seasons, the greatest show on earth was back under canvas. Not the biggest spread. Those 10,000 seaters are dreamscapes of a bygone era. This new tent, made in Italy, as virtually all of them are these days, seated about 2,400. It was raised over Coney Island in the summer of 2009, raised to stand proud for three long months. A kind of test run, the optimistic projections favoring an annual Ringling summer visit. New York Mayor Michael Bloomberg, who fought hard to get the circus under canvas at Coney, envisioned it becoming a major component in his plan to revive the ghostly old amusement park that had turned seedy and dangerous, infested with gangs and their like.

I've told you of the outstanding performance that blossomed inside that tent. Of only a few New York critics who came out to review, most filed glowing endorsements, finding it superior to Ringling's larger arena productions of late. And for a moment of high promise, it seemed as if this more artfully disciplined and scaled down version of the Ringling show might help restore some of its lost luster. But business during a nearly three-month run, arguably far too extended a stay, was only fair.

Ringling went back to Coney in 2010 for another summer-long splash with a very good show tilted *Illuscination*, though not up to the excellent standards set by the superior *Boom-A-Ring*. Opening night, unlike the previous year, was far from a sellout. Business, overall, seems to have been unspectacular. And the annual Ringling visit imagined by Mayor Bloomberg came to a premature end. Likely the canvas was retired because, by then, a new arena was under construction near the Atlantic Yards in Brooklyn, and Mr. Feld had already inked a contract for his circus to appear there.

And, so, another brief interlude under canvas for the Big Show is now a memory. An interlude of fleeting one-ring excellence. How bittersweet to recall that in a tent much smaller than the elephantine arenas it has been dating for decades, The Greatest Show on Earth looked better to my eyes than it has in ages. Heck, it almost looked like The Greatest Show on Earth.

7.
On With the Show!

A windstorm of trumpets. A thunderbolt of drum rolls and clashing cymbals. Darkness then spotlights. The blast of a ringmaster's shrill whistle signaling *start*! A rush of shimmering bodies straight into the ring with bolting twisting force. Somersaults and back flips. Clubs in motion. Twisting, twirling wizards yelping across the sawdust — we're here!

If it's a good "here," it has **drive,** rhythm, force and form, its own. It has fast forward. It exudes a certain something that is hard to describe, a certain something whose various parts create a buoyant stream of ever-changing action. From sensory overload to sweet simplicity, a circus program either takes shape and pulls us in or just wanders in and out of our flagging attention. Like any other form of entertainment, rare is the big top show that will generate a standing ovation. Coming close to that is something to which every serious producer should aspire.

In my boyhood, when my expectations were naive and fundamental, when, indeed, a very average circus might excite and enthrall my young eyes, seeing King Bros. Circus on parade under a big white tent worked wonders. I had so little to compare it against; only one previous trip to the indoor Shrine circus in San Francisco when I was too young to remember much other than the sight of a big flying trapeze net, a few elephants lumbering about and a funny clown gag where they lit off a huge cannon that made the tinniest noise, and then a small fire cracker that produced a colossal blast. King Bros. on parade may have been simple, even a little crude, hokey and sparse, yet it accomplished something fundamentally important: it got the show off to a stirring start.

During its sleek early indoor years through the 1960s when Richard Barstow cracked an exacting director's whip, Ringling's three rings all lit up just as darkness enveloped the arena. Rolling drums and blaring brass charged the air. Harold Ronk blew a commanding whistle, waving his arms high with a flourish, and we waited to hear him thunder as only he could:

> "Children of alllllllll ages! John Ringling North welcomes you to Ringling Bros. and Barnum & Bailey Circus, the greatest show on earth!"

Today's troupes favor opening in Charivari fashion. COURTESY OF BERTRAND GUAY/BIG APPLE CIRCUS.

Powerful, compelling, to the point. As fast and defined as a rush of tumblers down the track and up off a rickety springboard's tip into leaping gusto.

A well-paced parade that bears a distinctive spark rarely disappoints. Who does not, after all, love a parade, especially a parade under the big top? We await that first burst of action, wait to be teased and thrilled, amused and astonished. Who are those smiling acrobats vying for our adoration? We may try assigning each of them a specialty: He could be a juggler; she, a wire dancer; those dark skinned beauties in capes, a family of flyers.

Be it simple, be it spectacular, the opening segments need to seize our attention immediately. Without intellectual pretense. This is not a genetics-in-space workshop for jaded computer hackers. This is a circus, all right? In older bolder days, usually the show threw up high-voltage action in the form of a parade or big cage act. In 1949 when he directed Cole Bros. Circus, Barbette is said to have opened the show on pachyderm power; he had the entire herd circling the track and roaring up into a long mount. Can anybody deny the spellbinding impact of *that* for a start?

Most of the opening parades traded, with little scholarly input, on exotic far-off atmosphere or ersatz fantasy legend. For his inaugural season as Ringling producer in 1938, Mr. North engaged Hollywood costume designer Charles Le Maire to glorify the initial splash, which they called "Nepal," and which starred "bring 'em back alive" hunter Frank Buck. The take-note pageant flowed into a trio of wild animal acts, with two groups of the Pallenberg Wonder Bears cavorting in the end rings while Buck worked black leopards in the center spot. Program magazine syntax described it, "Midnight-Hued, Sinuous, Slinking, Snarling Haters of Man Forced to Respect the Law of the Ringling Bros. and Barnum & Bailey School of Advanced Wild Animal Subjugation."

Next came Dolly Jacobs supervising the display of a lion and horse appearing as compatible partners. "Natural enemies since time began perform together in perfect harmony," promised program notes.

The entire opening segment wowed the crowd. Critics issued glowing adjectives. The circus world discovered something excitingly different. Mission accomplished

Thirty years later, North's production team, now headed by Barstow, uncorked one of the best opening romps ever, and it was about as atypically simple and was "Nepal" traditionally opulent. Out marched a line of high-stepping showgirls clad as ringmistresses in red coats and silk hats. Harold Ronk sang an infectious original ditty composed by the director himself:

Take a ride on a bubble
whether eighty years old or eight!
Children of all ages,
It's circus time!

The song transitioned into Rodgers and Hart's "The Most Beautiful Girl in the World," then back to the original theme.

Briskly confident. A spirited walk around merged smartly into a parade of animal stars following the showgirls and into the rings: elephants, llamas, zebras and camels in the outer circles; a pony drill in the center. Their cantering pep sustained the bright cadence established by the sexy hoofers. And therein lay a fine example of a different kind of circus opening. It takes the hand of a canny director thinking against the stream to think up something so original. Richard Barstow had what it takes.

That same memorable season of 1968, Dobritch International Circus, which drew large crowds to the Los Angeles Sports Arena during a spring gig, got underway with a series of quick, startling developments: Lights fell to pitch darkness. One long spotlight found a man falling in a horizontal position down, down, down — onto a tiny pad. A cannon went off. A woman leapt recklessly towards a trapeze bar…and missed! Down she plunged, at the last moment spared the unthinkable by ropes encircling her ankles. The house gasped in shock, then relief. Great old circus maneuver. Shafts of light raced across the darkened arena to meet a parade in progress. House lights returned. The arena was ablaze with color and animation. "Dobritch International Circus!" cried ringmaster Paul V. Kaye.

A circus, may I impatiently propose, should avoid gratuitous local celebrity introductions and all manner of back-slapping sponsor endorsements (this is *not* the place), but get to the point at once: start the show and the *show* only. From the get-go, a great circus program speaks in broad strokes, not in tired ceremonial gestures such as having one announcer come out to thank this or that sponsor before then introducing another person who might be the actual ringmaster. Such anti-climactic hot air dissipates the impact of a proper big top blast off.

Some of the more effective openers have been produced by the Feld family, operators of Ringling-Barnum since 1968. They've made an art form of setting the circus into confident motion with glitzy show-off production numbers set to appealing original songs. Sometimes it all works. Other times, as I think I've said, it can look and feel more like a commercial for the circus, as when song lyrics inform us over and over again that we are at the greatest of all shows, until we feel hammered over the head. All of which can make it feel as if the ballyhoo followed you all the way into the tent and you are still being hawked a show that you have already paid to see. Enough, already! The Felds have never shied away from overkill.

Okay, this Feld-run version of Ringling, you could argue and I would listen, needs these flamboyant in-our-face arrivals to compensate for the lack of tent show ambience inside the impersonal arenas it plays. Indeed, Ringling must find new ways with fewer rings to sustain the illusion of size and stature, to uphold its "greatest" slogan.

Down to one lonely circle in a much smaller and more confining tent, and the old opening spec has been squeezed out of existence. Where do you parade your people when your back door abuts up against the ring, eliminating a complete passageway around it? Let me put it another way.

How do you put on a parade when there is nowhere to parade? When circuses came with three rings and a hippodrome track encompassing the three rings, how could they not parade at some point in the program? No longer. Of course, the cast can march into the ring and around it, which does not make for much of a march. And so our U.S. shows have reverted back to the European style charivari, which fosters an ensemble burst

Another view of the 1924 Grand Entry at Ringling Bros., apparently following days of rain and mud on the road! PHOTO BY CHARLES CLARKE. USED WITH PERMISSION FROM ILLINOIS STATE UNIVERSITY'S SPECIAL COLLECTIONS, MILNER LIBRARY.

allowing for each of the performers to demonstrate a few of their respective specialties. Together, they can create a colorful collage of fast-paced action.

You will see this today at the Big Apple Circus, which favors the collective attack. Charivari can reveal the flair of a good director, as witness their differing qualities. They invite the cast to combine their respective talents into a fast moving sampler. When handled with deft imagination, they cast a delightful first impression. Pickle Family Circus founder and artistic director Larry Pisoni possessed a natural bent for first-burst choreography. Too bad that he did not try for or succeed at a second career, post PFC, as a director of mainstream shows.

In 2008, Circus Vargas staged one of the most captivating openings I have ever seen. It began with a trickle of performers slipping mysteriously through the back door into the ring. The choreography was beguilingly basic. An original theme song, sung with force by ringmaster Ted McCray, hit the mark ten times over. Gradually, the ring blossomed with more artists until they exploded into charivari-like patterns. Here was the start of something great, if only what followed had been great, or anywhere near. Powerhouse openings that do not deliver on what they promise can turn one into a critic fast. On the other hand, the best openers leave a residual luster that may color everything that follows in a more flattering light.

Cirque du Soleil rewrote the script on how to pilot light the program. Turning away from Broadway bombast or animal power, Cirque's directors opted for the ultra surreal. Strange alien characters may emerge through a maze of murky foreign settings and soundscapes. Fantasy figures convene amidst abstract motifs calling to mind fairy tale mythologies. In a sense, what we sometimes get is a modern version of the "Nepal" spec. Cirque employs advanced special effects to create a multi-layered experience, submerging us in sensory overload, and is this not a form of old three-ring circus pageantry? While we are watching Cirque du Soleil, it can also feel like being inside a Hollywood sound stage when a bizarre fantasy is being shot. That is not unlike the reaction some people had to a circus produced by Mr. North when he first hit the scene with a deference to lavishly costumed productions interspersed throughout the program.

Cirque's more fantastic sets and ensembles (unlike the readily familiar locales and historical figures of North's productions) have had a way of redefining the art of the performance itself, so that the individual tricks of the artist seem fresh to the eye. The risk here, an issue to be addressed head-on later in these pages, is that these softer, more cerebral touches can emasculate the act itself.

Okay, the show is on. In some way or another. You may feel excited. You may feel only halfway excited. You may even be already glancing at your cell phone, wondering why you bought into this instead of staying home to watch *Dr. Phil* or *Wheel of Fortune*. Pray tell that is not the case. Now you have reached the point of voluntary evaluation. How to sharpen your critical pen? What should you be looking for as the program unfolds? There are a number of fairly obvious factors, if they are at work, that should be constantly in evidence. Let us begin with music, for music, as I've noted, has more potential power than any other single production element to bind the acts together and unify the performance. A good circus score should be both relevant to the action, act by act by act, and at the same time appeal to contemporary ears. What sounded zippy and spot-on fifty years ago may please circus buffs of a certain vintage. It will not move a mainstream crowd.

The importance of *what the customers hears* is too often slighted by producers operating on the fly. A good live band can make a circus twice as exciting than otherwise it would be. In days gone by, circus crowds on the larger shows were served a wide-ranging concert drawn from pop to classic; The old Ringling bandstand, led by Merle Evans, held 25 to 30 musicians. A copy of its 1932 program magazine which I own was obviously purchased by a patron who valued many of the tunes played during the show, for said patron penciled in the titles of a number of them over the names of the acts for which they were played: "Wash Board Blues," "Can't We Talk it Over?" and "My Common Ordinary Gal" while prancing high school horses filled the rings and the hippodrome track; "Indian Love Call" during a diverse seven-act display of acrobatic maneuvers featuring in the central circle Bombayo, The Man From India; "Keep on Smiling" while comedians cavorted in family horse riding acts; and "The Skaters Waltz" as the greatest flyer on earth, Alfredo Codona over center ring, swooped majestically through the air. And so on. It seems reasonable to assume that circus customers went to the big tops banking as much on the music as they did on a good show.

Today, certainly this holds true for many avid Cirque fans, albeit for musical scoring no longer drawn from popular hits but created from scratch. On the web site, *The Cirque Tribune*, which is devoted to the sharing of information and the hosting of discussion groups among Cirque aficionados, one need only consider the attention given to Cirque scores to know how highly valued they are by the people who buy the expensive tickets. For examples, in December, 2008, Evil Jeremy contributed this to a thread about *Coreto*: "Cirque du Soleil is nothing without music, and Cirque has always been the king of show soundtracks." Another website member, MSam. offered this about another show: "*Dralion's* score is fantastic, and I felt so lucky to hear it live." Which brings to mind a posting, not at hand, about yet another Cirque program, the contributor in so many words stating, "I'm not sure the show will be that good, but I go mostly to hear the music."

We live in trickier times. The cost of a live musical score has become prohibitive for the smaller and mid-sized shows. Even the fairly formidable UniverSoul Circus no longer carries a band. And modern trends have favored the downplaying of pop tunes in favor of original scoring; fees to ASCAP may have played a part.

Enter the CD. As far back as the early 1930s, one circus, Sparks Bros., played 78 phonograph records, a not very successful trial run using primitive sound recording technology. Sparks did not return to the road ever again.

Since then, of courses, the impressive advances have made the playing of recordings superior to a very small band, especially one not graced with graceful windjammers. There is, I will grudgingly grant, something to be said for the CD, that is, if you can't afford to go live. Electronic recordings bring the sound of a major band or orchestra into the smallest tent. But with a pre-recorded score made up from a bunch of miscellaneous CDs comes another setback. What you hear may sound disjointed and random, as if someone were switching from one radio station to another up and down the dial. This happens when the respective acts on the show bring their own music with them. The result is a hodgepodge sound track which does nothing to help unify the program. What you are subjected to may sound as slightly distant and detached as that radio station. Something is missing. And that something is the hand of one musical director arranging the score from start to finish. Which is not to say that any old band will do. They, too, can produce an unwelcome clash of musical genres.

Some shows take a higher road by producing an original score that is taped for replay. The downside to this practice is that, on some of the smaller troupes, the tape may be reused during subsequent years with diminishing impact. As acts come and go, as seasons come and go, last year's "score," no doubt recycled to save money, will not fit everything on this year's program. There is no substitute, really, for a musical director working daily with a group of competent musicians to accompany the acts at hand. During its halcyon years in the mid 1980s, Circus Vargas proved that you do not need more than five or six players on the bandstand to produce excellent scoring, not when they are the right five or six piloted by the right director and you've got the right sound system.

Next item: Are the acts introduced? There might be a ringmaster. There might not be. Tanbark orators are hard to come by. The one and only Harold Ronk, who defined an idyllic view of a "classic" ringmaster that probably never existed, would today likely be out of his element in a single ring. Whoever is given the job of introducing the performers should specialize in brief articulate intros, such that they do no get in the way of the show. Stay clear of florid adjectives, a thing of the past.

The best of announcers serve as cool, slightly aloof figures of authority who avoid hoarding the spotlights. Too intrusive and they come across as blowhards. There are plenty of overbearing blowhards in love with their own voices, confusing sheer volume for talent, who perpetuate an overblown cliché associated with the "golden age" of the gigantic three-ring circus. Those circuses, in fact, rarely if ever heralded each and every performer. With Ringling in 1946, while Fred Bradna as usual remained silent, an announcer named Arthur Springer was hired, and his ability to "announce" required that John Ringling North lift a ban, then in effect, against all announcements. This resulted in Mr. Springer (dubbed "Sphinx Springer), uttering a grand total of *six words* throughout the entire performance: Con Colleano!... The Wallendas!... Justino Loyal!

Even during Harold Ronk's celebrated reign in red, following a Ringling tradition he did not always presage every act in the program.

Onto costumes: How original and tastefully executed do they appear? Do they bear the imprint of a single creative mind? Are the colors coordinated, or do you detect a mishmash of styles? An increasing number of shows are now handing over design work for the entire program to one person, thus giving their programs a more visually sustained look. The results can sometimes be stunning; I am thinking, in particular, of the Big Apple Circus's 2004-05 masterfully wrought *Picturesque*. Costume designer Mirena Rada paid sensitive tribute to the styles of a number of famous artists, among them Chagall, Degas, and Toulouse-Lautrec. Her captivating creations lent a rare unifying air to the circus that memorable season.

Now, to the three most critical elements, often overlooked by second rate directors: Variety, Transitions and Pacing.

Variety: The wider the spread of circus action, the greater the chance that you will feel continually engaged. From pole vaulters to jump-roping dogs, elephants to clowns to fearlessly nimble wire walkers, you should feel a range of emotions from delight and glee to trepidation and suspense, triumph and elation. Conversely, a program riddled with redundancy may push you to an early exit. I've seen virtual duplicate acts even at the Big Apple Circus, a programming misstep that compromises the show, especially if the weaker of the two performs in the latter slot.

Transitions: Here, I am talking about those moments between acts. When one group takes their bows, how quickly is your attention directed to the next? Or do you find yourself sitting on your hands while prop hands struggle to reset the ring, or, worse, through a puzzling pause when nothing seems to be happening at all? I've already alluded, not with glee, to the old European format wherein the ringmaster would walk out after one group finished to announce the next. Very predictable. Some of our better-directed American shows found ways to vary entrances and exits.

For examples, just after a teeterboard troupe marched off to applause, the spotlights would channel our vision to an aerial troupe overhead and already in motion. This is an example of smart pacing.

The placement of acts should create contrasting moods. Richard Barstow was once observed to exclaim, "Okay, we've been on the ground now for half an hour. Let's get up into the air!" A slow contortion number should never be followed by another slow turn. Nor should the slower acts be spotted near the end of the show when audiences are growing tired and need faster fare. The 26-display Ringling-Barnum 1955 opus ran around two and a half hours without intermission, and its excessive length caused a number of patrons to leave the tent before the show had finished. When I saw the circus that same year in California, I recall a few dozen walkouts in a near-full tent of around eight thousand people.

During one road performance for which a tape recording exits, twice during the second half of the performance the ringmaster encouraged an apparently restless audience to stay seated, promising them a lot more action still to come. "The show is definitely not over!" But the show was too long. Or maybe ill-organized. Troupers would question the placement of hand balancer Alfred Burton, Jr. near the tail end of the program, arguing that so slow and time-consuming a turn would have been more effectively spotted in the first half.

Pacing: Does the program move straight ahead with a sure sense of polish and momentum? Are the acts linked tightly together, back to back, by clean crisp transitions? Does everything seem intricately a part of the same well-connected program? Or are there dead spots and lulls? Time to re-quote Fred Bradna's advocacy of what he called "snap." And of his insistence on there being absolutely "No waits. No breaks." In his day, two hours flat. No excuses.

However well directed the performance may be, still it is the acts themselves that will make or break the show. You can have the best-paced program in the world. If you don't have the talent, your pacing and transitions are all for naught. So, how do you judge each individual performance?

First Impact: Does the artist own the ring *immediately*? Does she acknowledge your presence? Does she exhibit self-assurance and a desire to entertain you? Does she, indeed, convey pleasure in your patronage?

Fast Start: How quickly does a star go into his routine? Wirewalker Harold Alzana grabbed instant notice by running across the ring and jumping onto an inclined wire, up which he restlessly scampered to reach his rigging aloft. Talk about drama. Then there was juggler par excellence Francis Brunn, who tore into his program like a half-mad genius as if his very life depended on his success in seizing hold of our attention and possessing it every moment he was on.

Immediate Persona: A crazy-looking fellow commuting on a bike, holding the wheel with one hand, a suitcase in the other, might be on his way

Comedy contortion from the Long Twins at the Big Apple Circus.
COURTESY OF BERTRAND GUAY/BIG APPLE CIRCUS.

to a job interview or, who knows, to a circus hoping to land work so that he can then afford to book a hotel for the night, and you can't take your laughing eyes off this character: Justin Case.

Lady on horseback riding madly down the hippodrome track is unexpectedly whisked off her steed and high into the air by catching hold of a free hanging ring: Sylvia Zerbini.

Technical Skills: These are what we ultimately judge the artist by. Mr. Case, from above, ends his hilarious turn by sitting on and peddling an incredibly tiny bicycle through a flaming hoop. How difficult are the skills they perform? How inventive? How smoothly executed? One flub should not be judged too harshly. A second causes concern and doubt. A third, sorry to say, renders the routine a failure. Yes, you could still find sufficient entertainment, but you will be left with a dithering impression of incompetent preparation. We pay to see top artists accomplish remarkable things. Stress *accomplish*.

Precision end points: Nothing better proves the competence of an act than emphatically precise landings, be they on hands or feet or, for that matter, on any part of the body. Be they executed on the shoulders of a partner, the back of a horse, an aerial platform, the sawdust itself. The

Queen of the center ring, aerialist Lillian Leitzel poses here with equestrian director James Agee, who would "rescue" her following occasional staged fanning spells at the conclusion of her act. USED WITH PERMISSION FROM ILLINOIS STATE UNIVERSITY'S SPECIAL COLLECTIONS, MILNER LIBRARY.

landings should be rousingly upright at the split second end of the trick or caper if the artist is to completely win over the crowd. Of course, given the precarious nature of circus acts in general, there are those moments, such as while standing atop a cantering horse, when the performer must valiantly struggle, or so he may make it appear, just to maintain his balance, and of this struggle he may stir additional excitement if he can turn a flailing mass of arms and legs into a statuesque pose, stout, solid, imperially erect. That, too, is circus!

Consummations: Upon the successful completion of each item in her routine, does the artist share with us a sense of accomplishment?

Originality: Very difficult to judge unless you have seen a good sampling of the acts in any given category. What may strike a child as novel may be a trick the rest of us have endured a hundred times. So, if you are new to the circus, I envy you, for much of what you see will probably please you. The more shows you take in, however, the better a judge you will become at assessing talent.

Build and Climax: The most accomplished acts start off with their easiest items and demonstrate increasingly more challenging tricks, saving the hardest and most spectacular for the last. It is a pleasure to observe an escalation of difficulty that leads to a surprise payoff — the big finish. The best acts reach a climax that seals the deal. You will feel totally convinced, totally sold. *Yes!*

Comedy: Some performers incorporate comedic touches that add considerably to the mix. The bareback riding Zoppes had Cucciola, a little guy who, hooked to a practice mechanic, tried being a rider and ended up flying over rather than on the horse most of the time, the wig he wore sailing through the air on its own. After being thrown off the horse, Cucciola would stumble across the ring curb and into a passing popcorn vender whose stack of boxes he sent flying. Very funny to watch. Every time. Now, who was the star of this act? You guess.

Tarzan Zerbini in the big cage was as much a comedian as he was a master of wild animal training. He would place his head into the mouth of a tiger, and then, in revulsion eject himself. The reason, Mr. Zerbini? "Bad breath!"

Young Adrian Poema, Jr., on Kelly Miller Circus, lights up the ring like a seasoned star. Indeed, he gives his family's risley act wonderful levity and charm, he is such a natural ham at working the crowd. You can't take your eyes off his giddy look-at-me enthusiasm. Perhaps goading him on is the spirit of the celebrated comic horse rider Poodles Hanneford, whose English family line extends down through Nellie Hanneford, Adrian's mother.

Europe once produced, I would ruefully guess, more excellent ground acts, such as the horizontal bar routine, that were as amusing as they were accomplished. We could use more Justin Cases.

Showmanship: What is this elusive element that only a few possess? It is that rare ability to connect more intimately with an audience. In total, it encompasses everything that I have mentioned plus whatever additional tricks the artist may bring to the ring A sense of high drama certainly helps. The tempestuous aerial thriller Lillian Leitzel was vividly remembered for casting a hypnotic spell. So intense was her devotion to moving a crowd that, on select occasions when the tent was packed or celebrities were in attendance and she felt the urge coming on, Leitzel would fake a fainting spell at the end of her routine. To her side rushed equestrian director Johnny Agee, retrieving our fallen bird from the sawdust and placing her into the big protective arms of her giant assistant, Willie Mosher, who carried her dramatically out of the tent. Fred Bradna called her "the greatest star." John Ringling North in his own words issued the same judgment.

In less manipulative fashion, other ring stars have captured the crowd with near-equal force. Poodles Hanneford had what it takes. So did, in spades, juggler Francis Brunn, single trapeze star La Norma, flyer Tito Gaona. And yet there is another breed of performer, like the more accomplished Miguel Vazquez, like the ethereally absorbed Pinito Del Oro, and like even the understated Gunther Gebel Williams, who may succeed brilliantly despite maybe *not* having it. Their star power was born of their exceptional exploits displayed with atypical restraint, perhaps purposely so to honor their craft. Too much showmanship, after all, can be worse than too little. Have you heard the word "milk"? Not everybody can convincingly stage a fainting episode.

Now, I've given you the major points to think about as you watch the show. Your awareness of these elements, I hope, will deepen your appreciation of circus. And it should help you realize why you prefer certain performers over others. As an exercise, at your next circus focus on a few of the acts, and while they are performing keep uppermost in your mind these main judging considerations. Keep a mental checklist and see how well each of them do.

The successful integration of performers and production into a solid rhythmic force can produce an exhilarating outcome. One that takes you on an emotional roller coaster, from fear to elation, dread to delight, rare is the emotion we do not feel at a complete circus.

During the next few acts, let's stay on this high, okay? And let's discuss some other features of the show in closer scrutiny. There will be ample time when the program comes crashing down, and it will, to examine how and why this ideal performance that I am advocating can sometimes seem as elusive to come by as affordable passage to the moon.

And why it can be as rare to find, no matter how much you are willing to pay for a ticket, as it is difficult to create. Going after it, I must warn you, may turn you into a hopeless fan, something like a junkie in search of another fix. Only for "fix," substitute "circus performance to remember."

Star power at Kelly Miller Circus: Adrian Poema, Jr., brings charm and comedy to his family's risley display. COURTESY OF KELLY MILLER CIRCUS.

8.
Clowns Are Us

So full of themselves, those blowhards and wise guys. Misfits on a mission: "I'm a circus star, too!" Pretentiously they perform. Invariably they flop, smack dab on their fannies. They can't get enough of us. Can't stop trying to steal the show.

The great come-in clown Otto Griebling, who began circus life as an acrobat, matured mightily in older age to clown alley. Nobody remembers his tumbling talents; many remember him as Otto Griebling, ersatz hobo. Hobo is an unfair and misleading word. He was true to the technical term for his role — "character clown." He was an ill-dressed, aging rowdy from the wrong side of the road, a blustery blowhard for whom life itself was one continuous boxing match. Him against them. Him against the bum fate he'd been dealt. He had no time for defeat. He wasn't going down, not Otto! He was up, out there hustling from dupe-to-dupe to make a legitimate impression. Out there getting himself into harmless trouble banging cymbals or slyly sneaking up on a woman entering the arena and the next moment slyly tucking his arm under hers and, by golly, having himself a real date for the evening. While it lasted. Until a laughing crowd disrobed the folly.

Many fans who admired Griebling's work (and younger generations who have discovered him on YouTube) believe him to be one of the all-time circus comedy legends. How lucky I feel to have enjoyed Otto's bawdy buffoonery when he appeared with the Ringling circus during its early indoor seasons. Simplicity of situation can produce some of the most amusing bits, Griebling demonstrated time after time. Bits you never forget. I never tired of his opportunistic chance-dating shtick. He encompassed the basic human aspirations stripped of social veneer.

I still see him clomping onto the arena floor with the attitude of ownership. This was his space and he would do in it what he damn-well pleased. Down the track he clomp, clomp, clomped in pursuit of incoming customers in skirts. We who had seen him before realized that he had only minutes to find a "date." Spotting a figure ahead, he accelerated his clumsy, big-footed gait, getting right next to her and slipping one arm under hers, and henceforth — finally! — being just another guy with a gal. But once the lady customer discovered her volunteer escort and broke free, Griebling's embarrassed look of surprise over the rejection was classic. What a perfect pleasure he gave the crowd; you didn't have to think anything through or concentrate on what you were watching lest you overlook some small item integral to an "overarching" theme. Griebling did all the work for us.

Another of his celebrated come-in bits was to go from person to person seated in the front rows, holding up a battered old batch of loosely strung together papers in his hand that looked ever so close to breaking apart. This was his excuse to intrude upon the public however he wished. I assumed that he was taking roll call, for he appeared to be checking off names. Many of those upon whom he cast his bombastically officious attention only reaped scowling rejection from the aging mischief maker. Years later, I learned from another clown, Mr. Sniff, that Griebling was actually playing postman, vainly in search of recipients for a bunch of letters he had in hand. You'd laugh at his overwrought expression of intense sincerity and dedication to job.

Characters they should be. Otto Griebling epitomized the essence of the American clown in its ascendancy before all of the pretty giggling painted-on faces replaced the older Ringling Joeys, whom Irvin Feld, shortly upon his purchasing the circus, derided as being over the hill. With everyone else of a certain older age in the circus that Mr. Feld now managed, he lumped all of the jesters insensitively together: "I wouldn't dare present a performer who might look aged or winded… The average age of my performers is twenty-three — all gorgeous girls and beautiful boys."

The older-guard Ringling clowns inherited by Mr. Feld were from a school that did not care one wit about whether they might offend or scare a moppet or two in the course of a day's play. Surely the invasively proactive Otto Griebling was one of them. His approach was plain and simple, the overbearing, in-your-face prankster who, down deep, envies the stars of the show or believes himself to be the show. They will do whatever it takes to grab the spotlights away from the actual performers, even if they have to make a shambles of everything, if they have to annoy the living daylights out of a pompous ringmaster or knock each other half dead in silly brawls.

If you ask me, please do, great circus clowning brings the spectacle supreme back to earth. Clowns remind us of the magic we are witnessing by being, themselves, so like us. A precious few mortals turn three perfect revolutions from springboard to chair, from trapeze fly bar to catcher's hands. Over a heard of elephants. And then there are the rest, those who, like we in the seats, can't. Can you qualify laughter? I suppose you can. There is the smiling sort kindly given to the hard working jester or to he who charms us with unexpected subtleties; the cynical kind awarded

Otto Griebling. TED SATO / AUTHOR'S COLLECTION.

a skit or a strut that satirizes political events or issues; and the warm big-hearted cackle freely expressed over the blustery shenanigans of an Otto Griebling.

Under the big top, the best of them bring an idiosyncratic persona to their work, be they hobo or fat boy, fidgety nerd or blasé eccentric taking a bath inside a motorized-powered tub as it rumbles around the hippodrome track. And that's Lou Jacobs, and that's a guaranteed rib tickler. Easy. Full. Joyously to the point. In modern times, these emphatically direct executions are the mark of a master mirth maker. Surely today one of the world's best is the Italian cut-up Fumagalli, who enlivened the Big Apple Circus in 2006-2007. Like Griebling, Fumagalli takes the tent, owns it immediately and is all you watch. He is, in fact, bigger than the tent, bigger than the ring, because his moves are big and bold. We don't need a dramaturge sitting by to explain to us subtext or scenario. It is all there on the surface.

Fumagalli's brother and partner, Daris, is the perfect foil. For Daris, we can tell, is just as amused by his partner's antics, just as desirous of slyly provoking him into comedy chaos, as are we. In a remarkably high-energy laugh-fest titled "Someone Please Set the Table," the two indulge in advanced slapstick, each trying to best the other in body whacks and all the variations upon. Somehow, timing and all, it is a simply well orchestrated caper especially to see Fumagalli getting whacked by one of his own backfiring props. And never to know how next fate may pelt him another one in the kisser. The sheer bravado of their delivery forms a perfect pleasure.

If, in their minds, the brothers are honoring old European clowning styles, they are honoring them with refreshing bombast, putting to brilliant use the acrobatic talents they possess.

When last I checked, and to be fair it was not recently, Old Europe wants too many set patterns. It wants the traditional comedy duo composed of the August and the white face. This does not hold true for Fumagalli, whose wildly shaped hair gives him only an ersatz August look, or certainly for his brother Daris, who wears no make up at all. They, among others, have broken a mold that may need breaking. I've seen a few comedy pairs in Russia that, likewise, did not adhere to strict customs. In the United States, fleeting have been the attempts by our home grown clowns to team up together and approximate the old world paradigm. The Pickle Family Circus, which during its brief tenure amused small grateful crowds throughout the San Francisco Bay Area and sometimes as far east as the Midwest, produced some of the best original clowning to be seen in the states. Bill Irwin, an early-day Pickle member, went on to a formidable career in musical and comedy shows on Broadway.

Another pure pickle delight was Geoff Hoyle, whose "Mr. Sniff" character kept us in steady giggles. Mr. Sniff came across as a clumsy kid who believed he possessed infinite powers to sniff out mysteries in the air, danger ahead. He did it all with a very long nose, sniffing his way in

Barry Lubin's "Grandma" illustrates the enduring value of character and of how a clown can infuse a performance with narrative threads.
COURTESY OF BERTRAND GUAY/BIG APPLE CIRCUS.

and out of improbable situations, sniffing suspiciously as he went, sniffing even if he didn't sniff. What fun it was to follow that sniffy snout of his.

Another modern-day classic is Barry Lubin's "Grandma" character, created while he worked on the Ringling show. A staple in the Big Apple Circus for many seasons, Lubin's work first came to the attention of the show's founder, Paul Binder, when the latter was taking in a performance of Ringling Bros. and Barnum & Bailey. Binder spotted Grandma riding a skateboard and it was love at first laugh. Lubin was soon lured into the Big Apple fold, where he appeared for 25 seasons, retiring in 2012. In later years, by contract he skipped many performances, sharing the role he created with a regular stand-in, Matthew Pauli, this rotating arrangement itself virtually unprecedented in circus history. But Paul Binder, who couldn't seem to live without Grandma, also couldn't seem to hold Mr. Lubin to a standard performance contract, and so he caved. Can you imagine any other producer allowing a regular stand-in for Otto Griebling? For Lou Jacobs or Fumagalli?

Lubin is at his peak as the envious copycat. For example, following the intrepid vase balancing work of Guiming Meng, Grandma, of course, insists on a chance to prove herself at the same trick. And how does she bring this off? With a very small flowerpot that still falls off her crown. In another Big Apple show, *Play On!*, during a mock dance competition between Grandma and audience volunteers, the old dame suddenly loses lung power and, out of a paper bag, pulls a portable ventilator, puts it pantingly to her mouth and gets herself a quick oxygen fix. So senior citizen. So simple. So very funny.

It's a pity that some of the best potential jesters never make it into the tent, but realize fame and fortune elsewhere. Think Jackie Gleason in greasepaint. That's what he was even out of greasepaint. Had the Ringlings been able to transfer him from stage to sawdust, what an overnight circus sensation he would have become. Gleason possessed true clowning instincts, the go-for-broke attack, same as Griebling had, same as Fumagalli does.

You will read about the three classic clown faces — White Face, all the way down to just above the neck; August, the more outlandishly made up face, as in Lou Jacobs, and the Character, a perfect example of which is Otto Griebling. In my book without borders, no matter how much or how little paint you apply, you are either talented or not talented, funny or not funny. Theories go out the tent whenever some off-axis eccentric stumbles in to make us laugh out loud. Please, let them all in.

I have seen comedy ring stars that defied all generic descriptions, I think. Then again, the word "character clown" could apply to almost any type, not just the hobo. One who fit this wide-ranging category was surely the gifted little guy named Karandash, whom I was extraordinarily fortunate to catch at Moscow's New Circus in 1979. By the end of his career, he had worked in the circus for 55 years, last appearing with it only two weeks before his death on March 31, 1983. Perhaps I read more into one of his bits than he intended it to mean. Nonetheless, here is what I read:

Russian icon, Karandash. AUTHOR'S COLLECTION.

A little fellow, who looks like he exists on a fixed income, with hammer in hand smashes to bits a single piece of wood, then has the audacity to take a bow. Acting as if he had just pulled Atlantis up from the ocean. Just like that. He did nearly nothing out there, and yet he extracted major applause from the house! From me, too. I was so startled by the minimalistic outcome, so mentally jolted and then amused by what Karandash seemed to be saying, that I still smile when I wonder if he was not lampooning how human beings will bask in hollow praise and acclaim for dubious achievements bordering on absolutely nothing? Under his human hood, Karandash struck me as wryly philosophical. What added to his appearance were the hushed sounds of shared reverence throughout the house for an artist so widely revered.

Our merry makers cum laude serve as emotional safety valves, helping to ease the tension that builds up inside us over the seriously hazardous stuff. They are hopelessly ground-bound, that class of would-bes who simply will not take "NO" for an answer, who will find other ways to re-invade the ring and steal as much time as they can, only to demonstrate once more why they are, excuse me for being so insensitive, losers. Failing to fly, they only enhance the cache of performers who really can fly.

Why many second and third rate joeys miss the mark is because they come with genuine acrobatic skills and spend too much time trying to impress this upon us. I say, if they want to juggle, juggle. This split focus usually dissipates the jester in the juggler. You can't, with rare exceptions, unless like Fumagalli you can turn your acrobatics into comedy gold, be both. Not if you are taking on the role of recurring clown. You are either an accomplished circus artist or a clown. It is, yes, quite often the case that a performer will work more than one act. And there is a natural cross-over between wizard to fool as the former ages into the latter. But the roles need to be delineated. Better to watch a fine performer, as was famously the example of Charlie Rivels, shade his aerial routines with comedy touches, than to witness a clown going off script to impress you with his grasp of advanced big top skills. I don't buy it. It blurs the roles between heroic artist and bumbling buffoon. And we are left with little of the contrast separating a gasp from a guffaw that gives the program depth and irony.

We do not need to know or have displayed before us evidence that the wise guy in baggy pants can also turn a double somersault. Just as we do not need to know or have displayed before us evidence, while engrossed in a stage drama, that the lead actor can also recite "to be or not to be" in five different languages, or that he also holds a degree in karate. When Otto Griebling performed, would I have enjoyed watching him work a tumbling act during pre-show warm-ups? Not unless he played it strictly for laughs. Otherwise, he would have broken character, and then we would have been forced to view him from two different angles. May I repeat the word "dissipate." Thank you. Now, do actors break character while acting in plays or films? I think not.

When I recall some of the clowns I have seen in years past parading about in drag, I pause to consider the fine line separating clown alley from plastic surgery. Perhaps, come to think of it, there is fresh comedy gold to mine in the classic botched up facelift job that renders the hapless victim, who had sought youth, a living mummy. Transvestite ticklers in clown alley leave me a tad on edge because they can seem more intent on flaunting their inner femininity than in giving me the giggles. It appears to be a serious business for some of these misunderstood souls. Among them, perhaps, are the ones who failed to make it in ballet and so, instead, settled grudgingly for dirt-cheap wages at the circus. To be professionally fair about this, there are the outrageously campy characters that amuse a sector of the audience that seems especially responsive to the fey shenanigans. Grotesquely extended eye lashes, for example, are a sure way to snare easy laughs, my own included. And the old pros like Lou Jacobs knew how to create an uproar out of donning overdone frills and feathers. As for the dreary rest for whom the circus is but a way station on the road to bigger, more impractical dreams, they should have stayed home or pursued a career in cabaret or musical theatre. Drag can become a drag real fast.

And then we have the modern-era "audience participation" clown, at the forefront of which looms the curiously acclaimed David Larible. This Polish jester has made an art in the eyes of his admiring fans by bringing into the act ticket holders, if that's who they really are, as opposed to shills. No circus funny face has done more to legitimize this bastardized form of entertainment, which really belongs in church recreation halls or frat parties. Larible's thing is to "select" individuals from the audience, prance them down into the ring and then engage them in party activities such as trying to juggle or pretending to lead a band, sometimes while blindfolded.

As the party unfolds, the clown is setting up his volunteers to be the butt of amusing outcomes. Example: they end up jumping rope not knowing the rope has been removed. Have you heard of Pin the Donkey? That's what a David Larible will give you, and, yes, some people laugh, and, yes, he has inspired a school of Larible spin-offs. Circus owners, you see, love all of the time you and your fellow audience participants take up when these party pranksters come a calling. It means fewer acts needed to fill the bill. On one of his recurring tours for Ringling, Larible consumed at least fifteen minutes in each half of the program. There are some of us who wished we had stayed home. In fact, one year I did, merely to avoid another David Larible show. All of which, no doubt, should leave you with a distinct impression that I do not favor audience participation. No, I do not favor audience participation, everybody will now please repeat a thousand times over. But let's get back to the show. I trust Mr. Larible's act is over by now?

Who wants to be a clown anyway? In the United States of America, traditionally the clown has been treated like dime-a-dozen Forty Second Street hoofers. Expendable. And too often has this given us yawning "amusement" in those spots where ideally we should be floating on giggles and guffaws. Too many American producers still short shrift comedy, making do with rank amateurs or with a token clown who comes in the package offered by a typical Mexican family. The default thinking is that all you need are some red noses and a few pratfalls to make 'em laugh. Many Shrine temples, in particular, are helping to decimate circus art and reduce it to new lows by allowing their members to don funny greasepaint and join the parade.

American clowns seem to be growing scarcer. You will see them still on the Ringling show because the Ringling show once ran its own productive Clown College, thanks to the marketing genius of the late Irvin Feld. The school's uneven legacy has, to be sure, turned out some younger talents whom you may find, now and then, on other shows. What Mr. Feld did so well was to make the idea of being a circus clown glamorous. His academy of amusement, which opened in 1968, appealed to thousands of aspiring youngsters eager to master the craft and audition successfully to go out on tour with the circus. Feld needed more clowns to both replace the older ones he was ushering out of the tent and to stock a second unit of the circus he opened in 1969.

Just to get into the school became a mark of destiny akin to making it through the early rounds of the TV show *American Idol*. Down to Sarasota, Florida, went the chosen few, there to be taught by pros. And there upon graduation, if they were lucky, to be offered contracts by Mr. Feld himself to appear in his circus.

What they all bore in common in the early years were pretty coloring book faces and a buoyantly acrobatic approach to their work. What they fell woefully short on was character. A good clown is much more than a cute face. The clown who engages our attention is a figure of discernible quirks and flaws. And those characteristics must come through not just in the make up but in the behavior. Clown College in theory was designed to rid the circus of the circus, that is, of its slightly creepy characters who amused your mom and pop. Scary clown syndrome, anybody? Yes, to some people. And we are not talking just children. In recent times, clown-o-phobes, as they are now properly called, have risen up to demand sympathy and respect. In fact, the trauma they suffer at the sight of a painted-on face is now ranked, according to experts, as "one of the top 10 phobias in the Western world," this from *The New York Daily News*.

The situation has become so dire, that the John Lawson Circus in Britain offers free pre-show counseling to anybody afflicted with "Coulrophobia," the psychiatric term for clown-induced terror. Quivering participants are encouraged to confront their fears before venturing into the big tent where creepy buffoons may lurk. They can dress up as clowns if they wish. No doubt, the medical-pharmaceutical industrial complex will soon convert coulrophobia into a full-blown personality disorder treatable, of course, by head shrinks, pills, and Dr. Phil.

Irvin Feld, kowtowing well ahead of his time, it would now appear, to a growing perception of audience ambivalence over clown alley's ominous oddballs and whacked-out weirdoes, seemed driven to root out all traces of strange subversive behavior. So Feld's funsters came out like giddy little children at play during recess, gift wrapped in giggles and boughs, as warm and cuddly as wind-up teddy bears. Far be it for Mr. Feld to rattle a single moppet suffering from coulrophobia or to offend any unamused adults with serious issues.

Clown College produced so much free press coverage that it became essentially a PR mill, necessitating the active turnover of clowns in order to generate fresh publicity. Even then, many who signed on to a first-year contract soon fell out of love with the romance of trouping and/or the insulting low wages they received. Some quit mid season their first season out. In truth, the school that Irvin Feld so flamboyantly established was never about building up a strong and enduring Ringling fun factory. It was about cheap bodies to fill floppy shoes and generate free publicity. It was about a circus with little patience for character, preferring instead to white-wash the alley and serve Mr. Feld's arching aesthetic: Young and beautiful.

In 1998, the college closed its doors. But its legacy lives on. Around ten percent of the graduates remain active in some form of entertainment, in the estimation of alumni Greg DeSanto, who clowned for ten years with Ringling, spent another five directing new Clown College graduates into the show, and, since 2010, has served as executive director of the International Clown Hall of Fame in Baraboo, Wisconsin.

Today when you go to a circus, you are more likely to be amused by a foreign face than by a Clown College graduate. The Ringling organization, however, still trains new jesters and presents original production gags, some of them amply amusing. Ironically, some of the best clowning produced under the Felds may have come out in the last ten years, since the school's demise. Among those who have graced this post-school category, there is the ambitiously creative team of Steve Copeland and Ryan Combs, who started out clowning for Ringling and are now featured with the Kelly-Miller Circus.

Our early-day fun makers talked a lot. And a lot more. The most famous of all was Dan Rice, who risked life and limb on occasion during tense Civil War days speaking out against slavery, hardly the normal banter for a tent show comedian. The circus fool's primary mission was to ridicule an authoritarian ringmaster. But not all "talking clowns" were very amusing despite rosy recollections of better days gone by. Not all days gone by were better.

The talking clown faded from view when one ring turned to three. Across the resulting hippodrome track that separated performer from

Steve Copeland and Ryan Combs perform their water gag at Kelly Miller Circus, 2011. COURTESY OF KELLY MILLER CIRCUS

patron, no longer could he be heard and so by default he lost his voice. Some die-hard fans mourned his passing for years. Others were relieved, as witness the words of one New York critic covering the first three ring circus in America, presented by Barnum & Bailey at Madison Square Garden in 1881:

> "There was a long line of clowns stretched through Monday evening and they were the best we ever saw, probably for the reason that we could not hear a solitary word they said."

Among the silenced, one ingenious soul managed to land a "genuinely funny" rating from the scribe:

> "He dressed himself as one of the ring hands, and confined himself during the evening to getting into the way of the others when they were spreading and taking up the carpets. He was a veritable busy body, always about to do something to help the others, and never succeeding in accomplishing anything except to get under the feet of his companions. About half the audience thought he was a genuine ring hand. This is the first new thing in clowns that has been introduced since circuses were first invented."

Maybe so. Maybe not.

One of the best comedic inventions to come out of the three-ring circus was the clown walk around. While the rings were reset between acts, a parade of elaborately costumed goof offs, each toting a clever visual contraption or guise, would amble around the track, stopping at intervals to amuse a section of the audience, and then proceeding onto the next. The visits moved so fast that you had to concentrate hard not to miss each clown's payoff just before he advanced on. And if one item fizzled, there was always the next. Most of them were funny enough, something like a good late light TV monologist delivering one zinger after another.

Out of this era came America's most famously recognizable clown face, that of legendary Lou Jacobs. He started tumbling with a Belgian act. In 1924 he was signed by John Ringling and brought to the States. Into the role of August clown went Jacobs after Mr. Ringling informed him that he would have to perform two acts, one on the ground, the other in the air. The sky-shy Jacobs instead defaulted to clown alley and never looked back. "That was one act," he told David Moore, "but that was good enough."

And more than good enough for a typical crowd. Jacob's most famous bit arrived in a tiny auto, before Volkswagen, into which he had squeezed his lanky 6'1" frame, unfolding it upon exit like a grasshopper springing back into shape. He was equally on top of his game circling the hippodrome in outlandish get ups. He once rode around the snow-less track on a pair of wheeled snow skis. Once paraded with a fishing pole slung across his shoulders from which only the head of a fish remained, a cat following behind answering the question. Jacobs smoked gigantic bigger-than-life cigars, and he romped outrageously in drag. He was still making 'em laugh at the age of 78.

Enter sadness. Enter a soft timid respite from everything else. Enter the remarkable anti-clown, Emmett Kelly.

He was a humble hobo, ill placed in a mammoth circus tent, yet so timidly unobtrusive as to be allowed by management to stay, to move at will during the program. He might be clutching in one hand an old head of lettuce, which he would peel away, one spare leaf at a time: his supper.

A "sportsman" for all seasons, Emmett Kelly makes his Ringling rounds in 1955. COURTESY OF TEGGE CIRCUS ARCHIVES, BARABOO.

He might come upon a lone peanut and wonder how to crack it: with a sledgehammer. Or go to a lone spotlight in the ring and humbly sweep it up and away.

A sedan, Kansas native, Kelly also pursued aerial acrobatics, on one occasion proving himself so awkwardly ill-suited, that his paymaster, Howe's Great London Circus, told him to stick to clowning. So Kelly did that, and within a few seasons he was longing to craft a whole new character. Recalling the sad-faced hobo he had sketched out while employed as a cartoonist for the Adagram Film Co. in Kansas City, Kelly resolved then and there to build a new persona based on that image. Against the resistance of the boss clown who dismissed the proposed greasepaint facelift as "too dirty, too scruffy for the circus," Kelly stayed the season in conventional white face. He also performed a double trap act with his wife, Eva.

By 1932, now trouping with Hagenbeck Wallace, Kelly slowly transformed himself into sad-face Weary Willie. The character gave his presence poignant relevance to the Great Depression. Audiences responded. In 1942, John Ringling North offered Kelly a chance to perform with Ringling Bros., where he would remain until the show's penultimate season under canvas in 1955. How sad, or sadly appropriate, that Kelly would never again appear on the Ringling show after it retired to the arenas.

I am sorry that I saw this great artist only once, and at the only Ringling circus I ever saw under canvas, in 1955. I am sorry, too, that it has taken me so long to begin to finally appreciate the one emotion missing from the big tent that Emmett Kelly gave it: pathos. And sorry to have misunderstood and undervalued the man's magnificent dramatic contributions to the world of sawdust and spangles According to writer John Culhane, Kelly described what he had set out to create as "continuity of character."

Unforgettable is my most poignant memory of Kelly, at the tail end of the Holidays spec. Following a glorious pageant depicting great days from the American calendar came the payoff float, and walking meekly behind it holding a birthday cake in his happy hands was Weary Willie. He looked so grateful to be a part of the grand procession, so overwhelmed by his good fortune: his own birthday cake. This little scene, which gave the entire parade such an emotional ending, was possibly the most touching moment I have ever experienced at a circus

Thinking back on how Kelly's "continuity of character" added human shadings to the performance, I must take issue, if belatedly, with the many fans who, as I have done, will too quickly dismiss Kelly, fans who hold Otto Griebling in higher regard. These two legends are much too different to compare. Each was a genius in his own right.

Amusement comes in many forms. Emmett Kelly's was quiet, unassuming, his comedic shadings full of a tender sadness that made them hard to laugh at. And so we giggled sympathetically for a poor soul struggling to make something of his limited existence but striking out yet again. In essence, he challenged us to be amused in the face of misfortune, and he left us laughing in the shadows.

So look for the clown, blustery or timid, who does not belong in the circus but can't stop trying to fit in, only to be left once more upside down outside the ring, the hopeless fool who brings a smile to your face.

9.

Animal Attitudes

Can it be a circus without animals? You surely knew I would invariably get around to taking up this subject of subjects. It is so today, so vexingly ever-present, weighing down your every footstep at or near a circus with yet a little more guilt, right?

Yes and no is my answer. It depends on your definition of the word "circus." All the word really means, down to the root basics, is a circle. Of course, it means much, much more than that, as witness its frequent use in many avenues of life for various and sundry purposes, from high-line entertainment to a denigrating description of the American political system.

As for myself, while I do believe that the spirit of circus as I define it is manifestly alive in Cirque du Soleil shows, there is a form of circus which I personally prefer. And so too, would it seem, does the world. This would be a rough approximation of what English horse rider Philip Astley eventually offered his patrons when he added clowns, rope walkers and acrobats to his equestrian exhibitions as a move to reverse declining ticket sales. I still believe that if any one moment in history defines "circus," it would be that moment. Circus as we have known it was literally born on the back of a horse ridden with commanding gusto by Mr. Astley, who continued to provide the center piece for the programs he presented south of Westminster Bridge in a spot called Lambeth Marsh at a place called Halfpenny Hatch.

The story is not quite that simple, however. We must also glance backwards upon the sometimes violent athleticism of Circus Maximus and of the various "circus" type acts that shared the same hippodrome track. The crude reality of those hair-raising spectacles did contain, and here our search for a beginning gets rather messy, the *seeds* of circus. Now, if Philip Astley had never presented a single aerial daredevil, one could argue that not he but Circus Maximus must stand as the most authentic foundation for what we have come to think of as circus, at least up until recent times. That is, if you can agree that the essential defining factor is risk taking. Buried deep in Maximus dirt, and in Astley sawdust as well, are the echoes of a living breathing form of realistic as opposed to theatrical entertainment which evokes the essence of circus, and which is why I embrace animal acts as being a critical component of the mix.

Here is H.S.H. Princess Stephanie of Monaco, who oversees the annual Monte Carlo Circus Festival competition, addressing the matter,

Monkey business in the old Soviet Union, produced by the Ivanovs.
AUTHOR'S COLLECTION.

and well worth a listen: "It's nice to have other types of shows and cabarets and all, but we must keep a little tradition. And for me a real circus is live animals and clowns, not only aerial acts or very choreographed acts; you need a bit of everything. We have to evolve, of course, but I think the most important thing is keeping animals in the circus."

In its bristling fullness, circus gives us a realistic portrait of humanity testing its self-acquired skills against the laws of nature, gravity, and equilibrium. Compared to artificial media (plays and ballets, for instance), the undeniable reality of a circus performance is more complete and compelling when it embraces the animal world as well. You ask why? Simply because animals are performers, too, creatures capable of being taught how to do certain things, just as children are. People take pleasure in the tricks they coach their pets to do — go out and bring back the paper; sit up, sit down; Stay there! Okay, walk! Go jump high and fetch the Frisbee. Go, Lucky, Go! Go chase the ocean waves and get the bouncing rubber ball!

The inevitable interplay between man and beast simply cannot be reversed or outlawed, and so it is only natural that these interactive relationships find their way into our circuses. How ironically wrong-sided, in my dissenting view, are the words of wild life science expert Rob Atkinson railing against the sight of bears riding bikes, tigers jumping through hoops, in essence accomplishing "nothing to educate the public or foster respect for animals." How is that, Dr. Rob? The very opposite argument can be made that children will gain a higher respect and appreciation for the complexity of learned-abilities in animal behavior. No?

When I was a little boy and Polack Bros. Circus came to Santa Rosa, I marveled at its performing animals. What fun it was to watch them mimic many human activities, like the little elephant Baby Opal standing on but one foot. So you have my okay during this non-PC chapter to enjoy any of the acts I may describe without fear of arrest for unlawful insensitivity to alleged abuse under the big top.

Yes, there were unseemly examples of animal exploitation and mistreatment in years gone by. How much? By today's standards, maybe a lot. Has it been cleaned up? By and large, it has. But things are still not perfect, and I do not intend to overlook some unpleasant realities that still lurk in the shadows, so please hear me out as I take on both the good, the ominous and the ugly.

First off, why should you reasonably expect circus animals to be treated with the respect they deserve? My answer is this: How can a circus owner dare afford to condone the slightest infractions knowing that at any moment, anyone in his employ could record damning evidence of abuse on a hidden micro-camera or a cell phone?

Given the incessant PR battle against circuses with animals by PETA and other animal rights groups, it's a wonder that any circus presents any animals at all. But virtually all of them still do. They do because you the customer want them. Circus owners are ever-responsive to public tastes and expectations. They are still operating in a free market.

The seasons of 2005-2006 may turn out to have been a pivotal turning point in the matter. Cole Bros. Circus owner John Pugh, tired of fighting PETA at city hall and elsewhere, removed his animals from the show. Like many beleaguered owners, Pugh decided to try a more Cirque-like approach, which meant an all-human program. He soon heard from his customers. Very soon. Very unhappy customers wondering what happened to the elephants. The kids missed them. The kids wanted them! Within a season or two, back they came. Pugh was emboldened by public response to stay the traditional course. Producers face enumerable threats, nasty attacks and all manner of harassment from a very small, very vocal band of do-gooder fanatics who can make tent trouping a challenge in patient forbearance. But the American public can also make its will known.

Over on the Ringling show, during the 2006 tour, owner Kenneth Feld heard from so many unhappy patrons wanting wild animals back, that midway through the tour he booked a white tiger display into the program. So far, Mr. Feld has prevailed in a couple of well-covered lawsuits filed against his circus alleging mistreatment of the elephants. He has made known to the media that the mighty creatures are a signature part of the show, going so far as to imply that without them he would lose significant market value. That is yet to be seen. Mr. Feld faces a difficult dance between, on the one hand, placating a major part of his customer base that favors wild animals while, on the other, alienating a growing segment of the American public that may shun circuses for the very same reason. Now it's a given, though hard to prove, that PETA's constant picketing of the show has driven down attendance figures.

At Polack Bros. Circus during my boyhood, the four-legged charmers played a big role. Not incidental but major. Besides the adorably nimble Baby Opal featured in the Besalou Baby Elephants turn presented by Peggy and Mac MacDonald, there were Klauser's bears and Roland Tiebor's trained seals, real hams at milking applause. Professor George J. Keller, a former art instructor turned big cage man, held amiable court with an amazingly diverse panel including lions, panthers, jaguars, cheetahs, pumas, muta lions, leopards and, yes, tigers. Oh, how I would love to see that assemblage in motion, or just sitting still, once more. Think of the affect it had on the eyes of a child. Think of what visions of natural harmony it inspired. Unrealistic? Well, there it was, quite real.

The smiling professor's teacherly ways with his charges made him an exceptional presence, more easy-going than the intensely melodramatic

Clyde Beatty with whip, chair and gun, dressed in white jungle attire and ready to take on the primal forces of nature.

The Zoppes with "Cucciola" (a 19-year-old, 41 pound midget charmer whose real name was Pasqualina Rizzi), sailed the sawdust atop three cantering horses. And there were monkeys on motorbikes, Victor Julian's pretentious poodles dressed out in fancy human-like attire. Some people

Al G. Kelly & Miller Bros. Circus. The show's 23 elephants were presented by tirelessly creative "Capt." Freddie Logan, one of America's finest animal trainers. Circa 1955. PHOTO BY SVERRE O. BRAATHEN. USED WITH PERMISSION FROM ILLINOIS STATE UNIVERSITY'S SPECIAL COLLECTIONS, MILNER LIBRARY.

today register acute displeasure over such displays. I thought the poodles turned out a hilarious satire on how human beings ridiculously overdress themselves in order to impress each other. Then again, maybe diamonds are a dog's best friend, too.

There were so many wonderful moments in the rings, pre-PETA, when we co-starred with our animal colleagues. Unforgettable are a dozen steeds gracefully encircling a dancing Gena Lipowska in soft symmetrical patterns to the music of "Stranger in Paradise;" is the impeccable mastery of a young Mark Gebel Williams pacing the liberty horses he inherited from his retiring dad, Gunther. Unforgettable, too, are the wondrously nimble elephant workouts I've seen down through the years. A trio of well-rehearsed pachyderm punks, such as those you might see at the Carson & Barnes or Kelly Miller shows, can charm the child in you. You don't need a huge heard to win the crowd anymore.

When it comes to bringing out a bear's inner bravado, the Russian trainers are masters at getting a bruin to play soccer, dress up as a ballerina, or, well, do almost anything that humans can do, but only funnier. 'Tis a pity the bear act over here is a thing of the past. Why? The imagery of the bear's head encased in a small cage to prevent injurious excursions into the audience is most repellent, I will concede. Added to this are the larger backyard space requirements mandated by the FDA for the proper accommodation of the animals. Just too costly and impractical for the average circus.

And still, the public is more for than against. And still, circuses present animal acts, if only dogs and horses, because they have the public on their side. One of the most unexpectedly pro-animal expressions I have come across gives me reason to believe that Americans may be coming to their senses on this issue and starting to take a stronger stand against the "anti" crowd. A middle-aged woman from Queens, New York, who described herself as an atheist, addressed our subject at the end of a board game party. When, by accident almost, the issue of circus animal acts arose, the Queens lady, without an inkling of my views on the subject, surprised, dare I say shocked me by taking a position the very opposite of what I expected to hear from her lips. She clearly bore the airs and trappings of a Bay Area liberal, and yet here she was, defending animal acts.

What swayed her the most, she disclosed, was to watch the reactions of a child watching a circus, of how much joy and inspiration a child would manifest while the animals performed. The woman is ill-at-ease with the PETA class, believing they are dead wrong. And, as it turns out, she is far from isolated in her sympathetic attitudes. More and more, the public may be starting to answer back to the protestors: Enough is enough.

The more radical crusaders are being exposed. Some have been convicted of criminal actions, such as setting fire to circus tents and to laboratories that use animals for medical research.

To be completely truthful, a history of abuse is there, and it need not be shunned in order to stack the deck or white wash the argument. Penning a piece nearly fifty years ago on the plight of circus elephants, prolific author Bill Ballantine, who spent many seasons clowning in and around the big top, wrote freely about bull hooks and their forceful application against errant elephants: "If the beater gives up for lack of courage, strength or energy, he never again will be able to control that particular behemoth. In this case at least, the elephant never forgets." That last assertion, which may have more circus press agentry than scientific investigation behind it, is infinitely arguable.

Furthermore, Ballantine discussed the pain that can be caused by the mere tap of a bull hook against a sensitive area: "The idea that you can't

Wry Russian animal humor in the ring. Circa 1979. AUTHOR'S COLLECTION.

hurt an elephant because it's so big and powerful is a popular misconception. Among bull hands, elephants feel even a fly or mosquito on their hides so they feel the hook all right. The trunk is especially sensitive. Any injury to it results in exquisite agony."

Whatever the merits of Ballantine's sobering assertion, the routine handling of performing elephants in times gone by that subjected them on occasion to pain and injury has been virtually eliminated, we would like to think. The animals, we are assured over and over again by circus owners, are regularly monitored by FDA inspectors. And, of course, there are the observations of the public itself and of journalists, ever ready to report on questionable incidents rising to the level of possible abuse. As far back as 1961, when the issue was hardly an issue it all, one honestly outraged *San Francisco Chronicle* critic had plenty to say about the observable abuse of

"Uncle Heavy" who worked five hogs and a piglet for James Bros. Circus in an act titled "Pork Chop Revue." During set up, while the trainer was unloading his animals and a couple of boys stopped by to watch, he yelled at them to "Beat it!" And during the program, noted the scribe, "His disposition was about as sweet in the circus ring where he beat, kicked, and cajoled his hogs through a series of dreary stunts."

A young Mable Stark. USED WITH PERMISSION FROM ILLINOIS STATE UNIVERSITY'S SPECIAL COLLECTIONS, MILNER LIBRARY.

Consider what animal man Terrell Jacobs, who billed himself "world's greatest subjugator of savage jungle beasts," had to say on the subject: "You are training them to do things adverse to what nature intended and you must be patient, kind and understanding as acrobatic parents are throughout their own child's training…kindness and patience must be the golden rule of all animal training."

Through the 1920s, Ringling Bros. and Barnum & Bailey moved powerfully forward in, around, and above three rings and two stages, and it moved on aerial power and on animal power. Horses ruled the rings then as they had at the dawn of Astley's circus. From the primal thunder of the elephants to the spine-tingling poetry of high-flying stars, down to the foolish pranks of the clowns below, the circus gave you the world from earth to heaven. It gave you the yin and the yang of human existence.

So, yes, I'd say that animals are very much a part of the complete circus.

We and they share the same planet, and this alone is remarkable. So why not share as much of it interactively as we can with each other? Circuses are getting better reviews these days as government inspectors file favorable reports and as surveys refute the claims of the activists, who would go so far as to remove every guard dog from every blind person on the planet. The British parliament, itself leaning decidedly in favor of outlawing animal acts, commissioned a study to compare the general welfare and health of circus animals to their counterparts in zoos and permanent compounds, hoping it would buttress their position. To the chagrin of the Lords, the study, which they financed, concluded that big tops were no worse a place for monkeys or lions than were zoos. The official findings also took issue with a recurring PETA complaint about elephants being chained to stakes for periods of time, finding no evidence of mistreatment.

Some owners will tell you that the animals actually enjoy performing. Romantic nonsense? In time, the laugh may be on the cynics. Scientists with open minds and hearts are learning more and more about the brain functions of animals. The idea of "animal emotion" has now advanced to serious study, all of which gives me faith in my own admittedly idyllic views. Have they, in fact, feelings like us? A small but expanding school of scientific investigation into the issue is beginning to earn some grudging respect. Wrote Michael C. Bradbury in *The Seattle Times*, "A growing number of scientists agree that animals are conscious and capable of experiencing emotions, such as happiness, sadness, boredom or depression. A few scientists even see the possibility for higher emotions like love, jealousy, spite."

There are circus trainers who will have none of this, who believe that an animal is an animal, period. Others, like tiger trainer Patricia White, hold firm to an opposite view: "Have I 'loved' some of my animals? Absolutely. Have they 'loved' me back? In some cases, in their own language, in their own lion-tiger-dog-horse-animal way, I'm sure of it."

Which brings to mind the sight of a guy and his dog one Sunday morning, he on a bike, the mutt trailing behind. Both had a backpack. I expressed my amusement over the matched luggage. "He loves it," said the guy.

One example cited of animal emotions are rats, who "enjoy" being tickled. Giggly rats, anybody? Ringling Bros. and Barnum & Bailey, are you listening? Opines Bradbury, "If animals have sex only to propagate the species, they would not spend or waste energy on sexual activity when there is no hope of producing viable offspring. Yet they do."

Our earthly neighbors also depart the biological script in other human ways. Bradbury quotes one scientist: "Most biologists today also recognize same-sex interactions as being part of the normal, routine behavioral repertoire of the animals that engage in them."

While I watch a YouTube clip of former Kelly Miller Circus trainer Casey McCoy presenting three hind-leg walking tigers, I marvel at how naturally willing and compliant they seem to their trainer's mild-manner touch. They bring off an impressively unusual sequence of moves: First, one tiger rears up on its hind legs and walks backwards across the ring, placing himself between two seated tigers. Now, all three occupy identical upright positions. Then, all together, they rear up onto their hind legs and walk across the ring with creamy unison. The gingerly interplay between them and the easy-going trainer epitomizes, I believe, how animal acts are being reconstructed to satisfy contemporary expectations. Into this atmosphere, Clyde Beatty would be hopelessly lost.

These exceptional images may tell you why animals not only belong in the circus but why the crowds miss them when they are not there. Without them, you have a party without the champagne, a picnic without the ball game. And without them, too, claim the dissenters, circuses are deprived the opportunity to further mistreat and exploit them.

Okay, putting aside my poetic perceptions, here is where our discussion must take a rather ugly turn. The story is far from resolved, nor will it ever be as long as hard evidence surfaces on YouTube videos implicating circuses for gratuitous animal abuse and/or mistreatment. And not yesterday but today. In the year 2009, a disturbing stream of footage made on the Ringling show by an undercover spy for PETA exposed, at the least, a callous insensitivity to a group of elephants backstage being readied to go on. Bull handlers are seen striking the elephants with bull hooks for no apparent reason, and shouting profanities at them. These images that circulate freely across the internet provoke justifiable outrage, and this in turn only fuels the fire of public dissent, turning more people away from the circus.

"Now, I always take PETA's claims and campaigns with a grain of salt," wrote blogger Cliz Biz. "They are an extremist group and while I applaud their mission, I'm not always down with their tactics. But after viewing the video in question, I have to agree that something smells very bad here. What you see in the video (taken by a PETA spy) is two or three macho men whipping elephants for no apparent reason. The animals are merely standing there, not misbehaving or acting out. These men not only whip the animals, one of them yells directly at one elephant, 'F.. k you, fat ass.'...the expletive somehow reveals a depth of sickness here that cannot be PR'd away."

Feld Entertainment issued a press release claiming that the footage was "deceptively edited," but then subsequently refused to explain how it was deceptively edited.

Others in the circus community were outraged. One was blogger Crash Moreau, a stunt man and circus fan who challenged Ringling to take immediate action:

"First, anyone involved in the tape should be (like Donald Trump said on his TV program "You're Fired") fired with no exception. This does not happen for any reason. Second: Ringling should bring up charges against all of the ones who were beating on the elephants and the judge should throw the book at them, PERIOD."

Such troubling revelations of inexplicable animal abuse, doubly inexplicable on a circus that has ostensibly done so much to do the right thing, are what place mountains of growing resistance in front of all circuses with animals. And they are why you are seeing fewer animals in the show these days, and why, at some day in a future season, you may see none at all. Pray that season never comes. Pray the Felds can prove how the YouTube video *was* "deceptively edited." If it can't, it has a lot of explaining to do. And while it may continue to be found innocent in courts of law as it was in early 2010, the video expose of apparent animal abuse will only further alienate the public, not just against the Ringling show but against other shows as well.

Given these odious public relations setbacks, it is little wonder why some shows have shied away from animal acts or cut back on the type and number. In 2005, the Shriners in Sacramento, California made known their intent to forgo animal acts. They said they just wanted to try something different, maybe a little more in line with modern trends. But something happened to their resolve on the way to the circus. During a fairly mediocre, ostensibly all-human program, about mid way through the first half came a bursting cacophony of happy restless barks — a cavalcade of rambunctious doggies scampering up and down slides, running through barrels, skipping rope, jumping around and over each other, walking wires. They were Moore's Mongrel Misfits, trained and presented by Bob Moore, a nephew of the late Sonny Moore who worked a similar act on the Polack show over fifty years earlier. The audience came alive that day in Sacramento with more natural enthusiasm than it displayed at any other time in the program. Almost all circuses these days at least feature a dog, if not half a dozen.

Will the world's most successful big top ever relent on its no-animal format and allow a dog or a kitty, maybe even a horse or two into one of its rings? Don't count it out. The man who founded and runs the modern-day phenomenon, Cirque's Guy Laliberte, seems forever open to exploring new modes of presentation. He has produced a diverse range of touring tent shows, and he's enjoyed staggering success with

From shelters to circus rings: Luciano and Gladys Anastasini's Pound Puppies were all rescued from their homeless fate. COURTESY OF BERTRAND GUAY/BIG APPLE CIRCUS.

his permanent Las Vegas attractions — among them, *O, Mystere, Believe, Zumanity,* and *Love.*

Lucky for us, Laliberte and his young co-founders never struck a strident no-animals-in-our-show manifesto onto their moniker as did the Pickle Family Circus during its brief peak years. In fact, Cirque du Soleil has flirted with animals on a few occasions. One of its first programs included a duck that bobbed back and forth. On another early show, a snake is said to have coiled a little. When it toured in Europe with Switzerland's famed Circus Knie, the Knie animal acts stayed in the lineup. Cirque's Madison Square Garden theatre production, *Wintuk,* includes puppet dogs who "perform" tricks. Does this alone not constitute in spirit Mr. Laliberte condoning the concept of performing dogs? If he believed that no dog, indeed no animal of any kind should ever be forced into such a role, would that not make him a virtual hypocrite by fostering the likeness of such a reality in puppet form?

Here's your answer. His mind is not completely closed on the issue and so it could happen, and I have living proof of my assertion in Las Vegas. There at the Luxor Hotel and Casino, his Criss Angel illusion show, *Believe,* makes use of a live elephant. The only risk here is that if the scathingly reviewed *Believe,* projected to run for ten years, flops out early, Laliberte may consider that mighty mammoth a curse and fear ever again having anything to do with an animal.

Still, one of my long-term dreams is to see how the magical Montreal monster just might integrate a horse or a dog into one of its touring units; or, more radical yet, how it might give a wider range of animals equal prominence in the show. They have the resources and they have the imagination to make it happen in a very interesting Cirque sort of way. They also have the respect of the public to forget and forgive were they to come out with a complete circus that failed to click at the ticket windows.

Can you imagine populist mobs storming the Grand Chapiteau from Montreal were it to promise something *this* different? Were it, indeed, to honor the indisputable roots of circus art and take us back. Now, there is yet another untapped market for the great Laliberte to seize, caress and conquer. And if the Cirque King needs to take a more safe and incremental approach to a full scale menagerie revival, I can see him having a high time of it with a boisterous brigade of clever, audience-stealing little charmers. Who knows, they may open his eyes to a bright new day. And Cirque may never be the same again. After all, is that not what Cirque down deep is all about?

Send in the dogs!

10.
Ring Spoilers

Your circus ride, the performance, is flying high. Every act a winner. The stream of action fluid, varied. The audience is lapping it up on waves of shared delight. And then, that bright buoyant balloon waving happily in your hand suddenly…pops.

Show comes to a halt. Silence. House lights on. Out comes a man with good news for everyone!

"Ladies and gentlemen! We are happy to be able to bring to your town a one-time only opportunity made exclusive to our circus from Peterson Peanuts!"

There it is, again. Yes, the old peanuts pitch. The promise that some bags contain a prize inside! Special offer, holding the performance hostage, good for only three minutes! Buy now! How do you feel? Go ahead, let it out. So do I.

Now, if you sense a rant coming on (you should) and wish not to be dragged through schlocky showmanship riddled with sub-par artistry and overbearing concession grinds, you might want to skip ahead and meet me at the next display. If, however, you view circus as a legitimate art form, please allow me the chance to make my case. I told you at the outset that the journey would not be all grassy lots and star-studded shows.

Why am I taking on such an innocent little disruption? Here for your consideration is my best illustration why: Attending a performance of Circus Vargas in the year 2008 was something akin to sitting down at a fine French restaurant, first entree magnificent, only to be interrupted every five or ten minutes by one retail distraction after another: man off the street with pet alligator offering to take a picture of you sitting on it between the main course and desert; another fellow running up to your table, shouting "ARE YOU ENJOYING THE MEAL?" and not getting out of your face until you shout back, "YES!" And still, another character approaching your table, wanting to pull you into the kitchen to teach you how to be a star chef for an additional fee. After this going on half the night, you leave exhausted and irked, fighting to remember why you ever went there in the first place.

Think of how you'd feel were this to befall you inside a movie house while engrossed in a good film. Let's say the film is *Psycho*. During the shower scene, the screen goes dark and out steps a lady onto the stage to offer you the chance of a lifetime: to have your picture taken in front of the ancient 1922 popcorn machine in the newly restored art deco lobby. How psycho would you go over *that*?

At Circus Vargas, the ringmaster just happened to have with him a pet boa constrictor. At one odd break in the program when nothing seemed to be happening, I looked around wondering why. On the other side of the tent standing in front of a section of seats, the man with the big slinky snake was showing it off to some patrons. Then came an announcement to the effect that during intermission, anybody who wanted to could have a photo taken of themselves with the snake. What the announcer failed to mention was that it would cost them $10 a shot.

Now, here's my theme: These tediously time-consuming commercials do absolutely nothing to advance the program. They only deflate whatever momentum may have been built up, dropping us back to ground zero. I have a theory that people as a rule are being turned off by these boorish diversions. Maybe that is usually why, when I've been to Circus Vargas in recent years, we of the spectator class amounted to very few.

You are apt to bump into these irritating grinds on smaller circuses, most of them desperately in need of every last penny they can talk you into spending. Corner the show owners who allow the money changers in their tents, and be prepared to hear them explain to you, as did vet concession veteran Dick Dykes a few chapters back, "Without the concession sales, we could not afford to stay on the road."

You, the customer, have a right to be an understanding adult and to appreciate what they are telling you. You also have a right to stand up and holler back, "But not during the show! Stop it already! I've been Peterson Peanut-pitched to death and I'm not going to crack 'em anymore!"

Can you imagine attending a play or ballet and having to endure a similar interruption to the program while a few clowns walk up and down the aisles peddling whirly birds? Only at a circus. And that brings us to the worst insult of all, the enlistment of clowns to hawk the merchandise. I am, if you will bear with me here, trying to honor the premise that clowns are artists too. Agreed? For any funny man or woman who takes the job seriously, what denigration they must feel; no wonder we have so few American fun makers any more. No wonder so few newcomers last in the business. Doubtlessly, many if not most of them fled the sawdust for lack of pay and respect, their spirits worn down by having to make ends meet working concessions. Can you imagine this happening in any other avenue of entertainment?

When Steve Copeland and Ryan Combs joined on with Kelly Miller in 2009 they suffered a mild shock upon learning that they would have to sell coloring books during the early part of the tour while awaiting the arrival of a Mexican clown who would then handle the task. Copeland did not hesitate from venting his discontent over the issue on his popular blog, and when at last he was freed of the duty, he expressed happy relief.

Many circus owners view clowns as a natural boost to coloring book sales because they offer kids a chance to shake hands with the man in big floppy shoes and get his autograph. This pathetic circle of survival does nothing to honor the art of circus comedy. The comic's primary purpose is compromised and distorted every time he holds up a coloring book (although some cynical owners may actually see *that* as his primary purpose), and the public is left with a muddled impression of the clown's role. Just another vendor with a painted face? Nothing should convince you otherwise. This expedient practice is an affront to any true self-respecting artist.

None of those activities should ever be allowed to transpire while the show itself (stress *show*) is on. They rarely if ever occur at high-end circuses. You the customer have every right to feel dissatisfied and to register your displeasure with management. Of course, now if your children were ushered in on free passes and only you had to purchase a ticket, unlikely is the chance that you'll complain. The owners bank on your tolerating this wearisome status quo. So even though you may feel the urge, as I have on occasion, to douse a seat vendor with a tray of snow cones for blocking your view of the ringmaster showing off his snake, you probably remain silent and let the grinds proceed. More probable are the odds that you'll never return. Worse still, that you'll judge all circuses by the one you've just sat through and never give any of the others a chance. You'd be surprised at the growing number of people who have not been to a circus in many moons.

Our bottom feeder big tops will work as many retail angles as they can get into the program. For instance, the modern-era photo concession sends a company member with camera into the tent to snap photos of kids and parents in the seats. They are informed that the photos can be picked up during intermission. Even then, photos not claimed may hasten a return visit by the photographer during the second half of the show through the seats in an effort to make the sale. All of this can pose just another irritating distraction from the performance, especially when the photo vendor blocks your view while he is trying to talk the subjects into buying a picture they may have not requested in the first place. These labored pushes for additional revenue do nothing to enhance the show's stature.

The only thing I have yet to witness is the passing of a hat through the crowd.

Stop a ball game with the bases loaded top of the ninth to offer fans that rare chance to bid on Florida homes in foreclosure? Interrupt a Broadway musical to sell discount organic avocados?

When Carson & Barnes played San Francisco in 2008, bringing to the city the last tour of the last under-canvas three ring circus in America, that season its program unfolded with speed, pep and pace. With polish and confidence, crackle and spark, and it kept moving, and it fairly reminded me of the Ringling show during the sixties when its performances fairly sailed with precision and pizzazz.

This terrific Carson & Barnes attack lasted until mid-way through the first half. It lasted through six or seven tightly linked displays. Then came too much of what I've been talking about. First to crash the show: a Peterson Peanut pitch. How I yearned to grab hold of owners Barbara and Geary Byrd by their tone-deaf ears and shake some showmanship into them. If only they had stuck to their better artistic inclinations all the way clear through to the end. If only they could, just one shining season on a hill, break the concession habit. If only.

You have every right to expect *a performance* through and through, not the Home Shopping Network under the big top.

How might these disruptions affect the public's perception of circus art? On a subliminal level they do nothing but demean and diminish the potential impact of the show. Need we re-enroll in Entertainment 101 to remind ourselves that, in any of the performing arts, every move, every gesture and pause either advances or retards the action. This may seem all too obvious to have to mention, but mention it and re-mention it over and over again I must. Even for the single mom wishing to give her kids a little amusement, although she may feel lucky and grateful to have gotten in on such generous terms (freebies for the moppets), she is not likely to overlook the unwelcome specter of gratuitous merchandising. She may pass along to her friends a mixed reaction. Or a negative "don't go." People talk. People blog and twitter and tweet. And yelp! Anybody out there wonder why some circuses are playing to fewer souls year after year?

Just to be ridiculously fair, I must acknowledge the uncommon mortals who claim to actually enjoy these older-fashioned spiels. One such mortal is veteran circus fan and bookseller Paul Horseman, who declares unapologetically his affection for that which I find onerous, ignoble, intolerable, exasperating! "I've attended and loved mud shows all my life. The pitches, concert [after-show] announcements, banners are all part of the ambiance." One thing is certain: If you can come to embrace the Paul Horseman school of patronage, you will suffer fewer let downs.

Okay, leaving those sinfully irresistible big top edibles aside, let's examine another form of ring spoiler, the borderline stuff that passes for "entertainment" which some of the more cynical among us refer to as "filler."

Where to start? At the top of the infamous heap of sub-standard human achievement, I'd place the house hula-hoop act. As a rule of thumb, these exercises in veiled belly-dance titillation belong in the dime-a-dozen league of circus "acts" that almost anybody can execute. In fact, most every Mexican family plan comes with a set of K-Mart hoops. Heck, you or I, with a little practice, could twist and twirl. You only have to show your navel, not much more. Maybe twice in your lifetime if you are lucky, you'll come across a "hula hoop" routine that actually merits respect rather than a gawking deference to mid-section skin. When exceptionally spun, the hoops are set into clever motion, closer to juggling in non hula-hoopy ways, thus redeeming the hoops of the hoops. At Circus Chimera a number of years back, a Russian lad named Dimitri Timchenko handled his hoops in so masterful a fashion as to work them as a fine juggler working clubs or the smaller hoops long associated with juggling.

Where next, circus "act" from popular culture? Ball and jacks? Badminton practice? Spin the Bottle? The ultimate in part-time filler passing for "entertainment" is the leaden trek of a clown into the audience to spot and recruit somebody willing to be made the butt of an impromptu comedy bit. But wait, I've already had at this lame excuse for professional entertainment in my blast, back there, at the David Larible school of clowning. Okay, if you really prefer watching your neighbors become a part of the act, go for it, I suppose. I do not go to the circus to see Pin the Donkey, and neither should you, for you are allowing the producer to retard the pace, rhythm and unity of the show and weaken its grab. Where, may I inquire, have you ever seen your neighbors pulled into the show other than at a circus? The ballet? The concert hall? A Broadway musical?

Audience participation in and around the ring need not be totally outlawed. It must be confined, as it was in the older bolder days, to seconds rather than minutes. Or to professional shills working polished setups. The gifted comic bike rider Justin Case, who toured with Ringling's wonderful one-ring *Boom A Ring*, works what must be a shill into his act. The guy is instructed to lie down on the ground, and then Case proceeds to ride a unicycle between the man's legs and arms, at one point perilously close to his most delicate body parts. We cringe at the thought of...

King of pin the donkey: Audience participation clown David Larible having fun with a "volunteer." COURTESY OF TEGGE CIRCUS ARCHIVES, BARABOO.

and then Case proceeds to jump his bike over each of the man's limbs while making hilarious innuendos about what might happen were he to mis-peddle.

Of other bargain basement turns, surely the tired spectacle of a motorcycle being powered up an inclined wire is a standout. Usually the driver is male, and usually he has with him a female passenger. At the summit of their gas-guzzling climb, over and over goes the bike with the "performers" clinging to it. Whatever skill this takes does not translate into a performance to remember. Perhaps the most dismissive observation that can be made about this display is that, ironically, for all of its macho allusions to courage and danger, it is in reality one of the *safest* of all circus acts. Take a good scorching look, if one sputters and roars your unfortunate way, and tell me, please: Just how do the passengers face imminent peril?

I'd much prefer a retro return of the old Barnum & Bailey somersaulting automobile, that spunky little coup that was gunned down and up a curved ramp into a mid-air loop-the-loop, landing, if everything held together, on a receiving ramp down which it rumbled to a thundering stop. Now, that truly thrilled the masses, as it still would, I feel certain, today.

At the higher end of bogus circus "thrills," there are those ever-present (on nearly every show today, it seems) billowing silks, referred to by some as "fabrics," by others as "tissues," and by Ken Dodd as "the bed sheets." Younger generations of aerial dreamers who prefer self-expression to genuine risk-taking have taken to the fabrics with a zeal for story telling. Younger women are particularly drawn to this new form of self-help trapeze in which it can seem as if they are working out their issues on the tissues. In which emotion can play a larger role than barbaric daredevilry. Although, sad to report, there is a dangerous irony at work here; the overly choreographed performer can get lost in his/her emotional expressiveness aloft and lose contact with the critical application of gymnastic skill so vital if one is to remain safely airborne. A disturbing number of younger fabric aerialists are taking falls causing injury or death. In lesser hands, a fabrics work-out can be rather humdrum, lending to a sense of just more padding to an already lean program.

However, I've seen a few artists take the form to marvelous new levels combining ballet with complex acrobatic maneuvers. The Chinese, prominently featured in recent Ringling shows, are also infusing the form with elegant invention, producing a number of male-female duos that blend superb athleticism with evocative romantic interactions. They have their own lovely term, "sensual silks," for these exhilarating aerial ballets.

Many of the Mexican families employed by our cash-starved circuses will bring a wide roster of "acts." A few might impress. The rest may amount to little more than pleasant fare prone to please the first-time kid-goer. This stuff, too, borders on filler. For most of its eight-year existence, Jim Judkin's since-shuttered Circus Chimera relied on the Chimal family. Between its various members, Chimera was able to furnish as many as six or seven numbers per show. Star of the family was Alex Chimal, a charismatically creative juggler who also scored moderately well working a low wire display. Other Chimals worked the fabrics and the hoops. Together, they offered elementary Russian swing and teeterboard turns.

Truth be told, from Mexico we get the very good down to the very not so good. We might get the next star trapeze thriller, for from Mexico, most of them hail. And because these multi-talented families usually bring with them ambitious youngsters, you are just as likely these days to watch one of them attempt the "triple" on the flying return and miss it. And not try it again. Chances are, it's in the show primarily to authenticate a melodramatic announcement by a ringmaster for the purpose of advancing the illusion that you are patronizing a grade A circus.

You, too, can be a circus star! Most hula hoop workouts are considered just another from of revenue-saving filler. COURTESY OF TEGGE CIRCUS ARCHIVES, BARABOO.

Typical of the smallest Mexican troupes is Circus Osario. It pitches a little tent, installs a couple of decent seat wagons containing plain bleacher-style planks, plugs in a rinky dink sound system and gives a program that lasts a total of one hour including a 20- minute intermission. When I caught up with the show in Petaluma, California, it was about the weakest package of "acts" I have ever seen. With the exception of a showmanly contortionist who managed to squeeze himself into and out of a tiny glass box, filler all the way.

Nobody wants a free ticket to a bad concert.

There is, of course, a difference between filler and the genuine article, and it will be up to you to decide which is which. Obviously, the child watching that motorbike whiz up the wire may be naively impressed. And obviously too, a certain segment of the crowd may fall for a beautiful young aerialist expressing herself on the fabrics.

Interestingly, probably not by sheer coincidence do all of the shows out of Hugo, Oklahoma (Carson & Barnes, Kelly Miller, Culpepper Merriweather) tend to bear the unmistakable markings of a show out of Hugo, Oklahoma: pony and elephant rides for sale; show-stopping concession pitches (not meant in the flattering sense); extended intermissions to handle the grind for more of the same; filler attractions from the Mexican family plan; and recorded music. When John Ringling North II purchased Kelly Miller in 2006, he talked of adding "a little Ringling magic" to the program, yet he stayed this pedestrian course. The idea of a Ringling condoning the sale of concessions by a clown struck many of us as unseemly. To his credit, however, as I've already mentioned, North II relieved his two mad caps, Copeland and Combs, from coloring book duty in 2010. Smiles all over their blog.

But five years into his promising tenure producing performances of above average quality, North had still not shaken off completely the intrusive noise and dust of low-level showmanship, which worked against the modest manifestations of "Ringling magic" he had managed to import. During the 2010 performance, an overzealous barker treated a stock peanut pitch as a matter nearly of life and death, staging a mock one-minute countdown while exhorting the crowd to buy "before it's too late!" The desperate spiel, which had all the subtlety of a diesel truck blasting through a summer tea picnic, was certainly the most offensive example of promotional hysteria I've yet suffered.

After Carson & Barnes rolled up its three-ring layout for good in Tucson, Arizona, on October 5, 2008, insiders voiced a hope that owner Barbara Byrd would be inspired to rescind her concession-heavy operation and improve the quality of the performance. Nothing of the sort transpired in 2009. Ms. Byrd merely reduced the size of the tent, settled into a solo ring showcase and continued merrily, or warily, down the same-old, same-old mediocre road. Mr. Peterson Peanut still enjoyed premiere placement in the program. If only — let's dream — Carson & Barnes were to make its programs more exciting and *continually* engaging, potentially a favorable word of mouth would grow, turnouts would increase, and there would be — surprise! — more happy bodies in the tent with money to spend on hot dogs and burritos. And, yes, on Peterson peanuts too, but available, please, *not* during a tasteless show-stopping spiel.

On a more promising level, by 2011 the Byrds revealed an obviously sincere determination to give their customers a wider and deeper spread of talent. It surely contained at least two outstanding acts that could hold their own in any circus in the world. Unfortunately, the same show also contained second and third-rate performers cast in a grating production format that did nothing to dispel a lingering carny-circus impression. At the performance I caught in Northern California, there may have been, at most, a couple of hundred people in a tent capable of holding easily eight or ten times that many. About the same number I'd noticed in the seats on my previous two visits to the show in earlier years.

We need only look to a trio of touring tent shows that appear from all accounts, and from my own experience attending them, to draw large crowds: Cirque du Soleil, Big Apple Circus, and UniverSoul Circus. None of these companies stop their programs to sell. None of them arm their clowns with coloring books. None of them subscribe to the Mexican family plan. And, by and large, you will not see the bottom tier filler acts on these shows. However, I need to make one thing very clear, lest you buy into an unintended black-and-white comparison. No, I am not saying that "they" are all good and the "others" are all bad. The leading circuses, too, may disappoint you now and then, just as, now and then, a Hugo syndrome show may leave you perfectly pleased, eager to return.

I've identified most of the leading ring spoilers, certainly the more egregious ones, hoping to turn you into a more discriminating patron. You need to be aware each moment why your interest is up or down.

And finally, there is yet another dubious offshoot to the dime-a-dozen operations, and that would be the infiltration into the performance itself of the interactive midway. This has caused a blurring of the line between "circus" and "carnival". And it may cause you to wonder whether you are not, all at once, at a county fair. You will feel a jolting shift away from the performance as you notice that in and around the ring itself, the apparatus of a small roadside kiddy fun park is taking shameless shape. Line up, everybody, for a chance to taste the magic, to be a clown, to ride an elephant and sample the circus up close.

Intermission!

11.
Intermissions Without End

Did you come prepared? Ready to weather the invasion of carnival rides and diet-busting fun food? Possibly you got your kid to sign a pre-show nuptial agreement, "I will not torment you with repeated badgering to buy me anything I see for sale at the circus."

We're not yet free of the circus world's most avaricious agenda. Remember, it was you who freely entered the tent. You who must endure the moneychangers inside. Consider my just-vented rant against their performance-disrupting effrontery as but a cautionary warm-up to the crass trade-talk tone of this next inglorious chapter. But here we must go, for here, too, are many circuses with increasing frequency taking you. Once upon a season, they could not take you here because once upon a season they did not go here. No, they ran the show straight through, first fanfare to final bows.

When it toured under canvas through the mid-1940s, the Ringling-Barnum show was a one-act rush packed inside two lickety split hours. It did not offer a fifteen-minute break in the middle of the show until 1946 when Robert Ringling, then in charge, brought the first intermission to Madison Square Garden. The move made sense to New Yorkers, for the Garden offered ample restrooms, and the interval favoring food and Mother Nature had long been a staple, of course, in Broadway playhouses. So, too, with most Shrine circuses that were presented indoors.

Under canvas, the Ringlings continued running the program straight through without a break, even when the running time ballooned well beyond the two-hour mark. This trend led to customer discomfort and occasional impatience. The absence of easily reachable restroom facilities made circus going a challenge. Tent show seats back then, including the gloriously modern Art Concello seat wagons with skimpy-sized thin-framed chairs, were not designed for long sits. You'll recall Ringling's overly long 1955 program hastening the early exit of patrons at some of the performances. No matter how good you are, too long is too long.

The intermission became a regular feature on The Greatest Show on Earth in 1957 when it abandoned the tents for the arenas. And from there, the practice would eventually be adopted by most of the nation's under-canvas troupes as well. Owners discovered a lucrative new way to maximize concession sales. The food, ride and souvenir fests consumed more and more time, only increasing customer demand to Buy! Buy! Buy!

Spin the bottle, to your left! Ride the elephant, to your right! A scene from intermission at Jose Cole Circus, 2004. COURTESY OF TEGGE CIRCUS ARCHIVES, BARABOO.

And then the carnival arrived to exploit a captive customer base.

This little interval gradually ripened into a cottage industry of its own, with more ways to sell things getting tossed into the mix, until it would consume sometimes, believe it or not, up to an hour on some of the Shrine dates. The resulting orgy of merchandising overkill has become, arguably, one of the reasons why fewer and fewer Shrine Temples are producing an annual circus anymore. Among a number of things that irked and alienated Shrine audiences, the protracted intermission proved especially galling. Consider:

A survey of audience members exiting one Shrine circus in 2000 addressed the "poorest circus features." At the top of the list, 56% of the respondents answered "intermission too long." Next in line came "too many commercials (pitches), 47%; "Show too long," 44%; "performance started late," 42%; "Unnecessary Shrine ceremonies;" 40%; "concession prices too high," 38%. Most of the respondents, we can reasonably assume, were sympathetic Shrine supporters. Had everyone been equally forthcoming, likely these unflattering numbers would have been higher yet.

And still, the Shrine potentates who condone these irritating intervals that parade as part of the circus experience don't seem to be getting the message. At least, give the Yaarab Shriners of Atlanta, who claim to produce the largest Shrine show in America., credit for their honesty in advertising exactly what it is they are up to these dreary days; They call themselves "The Yaarab Shrine Circus & Carnival," and they offer the public a wide range of carnival rides approaching a full scale county fair.

In the midst of all this activity that can go on and on and on, you may start to wonder, where did the circus go? To be historically fair, some of these staples have always been a part of the scene, but they were previously confined to the midway outside of the tent, which is where they still belong. Came the Felds, who developed the interactive "All Access Pre-Show" Ringling open house, heretofore covered. But there are no rides for sale at the Feld parties, just the incentive they instill to purchase very expensive souvenir program magazines or coloring books for young autograph seekers. Other shows have adapted the Feld model by loading their intermissions with a similar spirit of interactivity, albeit with pay-for-play amusements.

We are still, yes — sorry to have brought you here — sledging through the trenches of big top survival. A dirty little secret that applies to the majority of American circuses at one time or another is that, down through the decades, they have devised all manner of revenue-enhancing strategies, from common larceny to sophisticated marketing. The arc of veiled holdups began with the infamous insertion of pickpockets and short change artists onto the midway and into the tents. Gone, don't fret that! From there, minus the thievery, it moved into the boiler rooms, set up to serve one or another of a dozen worthy causes. As Arthur Concello put it to me in his inimitable fashion, "When grift went out, the phones came in." He was directing my attention to a racket long-since either outlawed in certain cities or legislated into quasi-respectability. Through the 1970s, a number of aggressively operated shows made out like bandits at the phone banks, preying upon local merchants to buy blocks of circus tickets for free distribution to kids in need, the profits to support a named charity. Lovely deal made with a circus devil.

Exit the boiler room. Enter the concession pit. Faced with mounting lawsuits and public outrage over flatulent telephone solicitations (most of the money not going to the charity), showman turned to the saturation of free or discounted kid tickets, banking on concession sales to make the difference. That has led to a steady increase in the number of concessions offered and the time allotted for pushing them upon captive customers.

Which brings us full circle to where this untoward chapter began. Never will you be as captive to a circus's concession wing as you will during

Shameless con man: Ben Davenport, photographed with his daughter Norma, operated Daily Bros. Circus as a high-pressure grift show.
PHOTO BY SVERRE O. BRAATHEN. USED WITH PERMISSION FROM ILLINOIS STATE UNIVERSITY'S SPECIAL COLLECTIONS, MILNER LIBRARY.

the time-out jamboree that separates the two parts of the show. You are now squarely on their sawdust. And at this fiscally risky juncture in the program, I feel a fiscal duty to offer you a free primer on how to mentally prepare for what may transpire. You might leave your credit cards and cash at home, for starters. You might, prior to leaving the house, have your kid(s) sign that pre-show pledge promising stoic silence in the face of blaring barkers.

Nobody denies a circus the right to sell and market anything it wishes. Pony rides. Elephant rides. Clown face paint-ons. Tarot card readings. Re-birthing exercises. But there is a *time* and a *place* for everything on the lot. The line between performance and pitch is breeched every time a vendor invades the ring. Even during intermission. The proper place for these recreational amusements is out on the midway. Yes, tell that to a struggling show owner and get a blank look in return or maybe a tactful explanation. They are crusty souls who have a particular genius for sheer endurance. As long as they can stay on the road, no matter how, they are unlikely to stop hawking glitzy junk food, overpriced souvenirs, bungee bounces, pony rides, *et al*. And as long as you, the ticket buyer, accept the arrangement, it will go on for as long as there are enough of you out there to keep the show on retail life support.

The public, however, does not forget. And the "public" is largely influenced by the parents who take the children to shows that themselves are the worst offenders of intermission time.

In its most flagrantly prolonged form, the intermission has turned itself into an open-ended party, and you may find yourself wondering when the show itself will ever resume. Forty-five minutes later at a Shrine circus party, you are now cursing the carnival that came to town. You are reaching the point of philosophic inquiry, about ready to convene a symposium of like-minded circus captives, ready to pose a question for open debate above the carnival down there: Is *this* why the circus is dying?

The Shriners, many of whom themselves love dressing up in Bozo attire, are rarely if ever denied the chance to "amuse" by the producers they hire to stage the shows they sponsor. And so, the Shriners are not only harming circus art by their self-willed participation in the show, but they are also committing additional harm by the obscenely long intermissions they foster and tolerate. Can you say, "sixty minutes"? Yes, *sixty minutes* is not unknown in the world of the new and disappearing Shrine Circus.

Concedes media relations man Ben Trumble, "The Shrine show that takes an hour-long intermission to sell elephant rides may make money, but it drives the parents around the bend."

Probably the greatest harm caused is that, the longer the intermission, the less connection will you feel between the two parts of the program.

That is, if you *are* sufficiently engaged by the program when the crowd takes a break to storm the fast food counters or line up to ride the menagerie. Sometimes, a rousingly active intermission can bring an under-responsive crowd alive. At Carson & Barnes these tedious days, I've observed this phenomenon, wondering if the audience found more excitement during the interval than they did over the actual show itself. Certainly, the children come alive over a chance to be hoisted onto the back of an elephant and feel it carry them around the ring in lumbering circles. And have their picture taken with a clown.

But the parents who sponsor all of these unexpected drains on the wallet can leave the tent acutely disillusioned. Such was the experience for a gentleman from San Diego, Marcus Bethea, who took his wife and children to Carson & Barnes Circus at a Southern California date in 2009. They had been charmed in on free passes for the kiddies. The father lived to regret it.

Popcorn, cotton candy and whirly birds add critical revenue to circus coffers. Seen here is the concession stand inside the Ringling's menagerie tent. Circa 1924. PHOTO BY CHARALES CLARKE. USED WITH PERMISSION FROM ILLINOIS STATE UNIVERSITY'S SPECIAL COLLECTIONS, MILNER LIBRARY.

"I was very disappointed in this show. This was the first time since I was little to see this show. My kids loved it. My wife and I hated it. Everything is very expensive, and not worth the money paid. I spent over $200 for cold pop corn, a little bag of peanuts and one ride on a camel in one little circle, same on an elephant, and supposed VIP seating in plastic patio chairs. I was very disappointed. But it was for my kids. But I will never do it again. I was thinking Ringling Bros. Barnum Bailey would be better but now I am scared of any kind of circus."

Back to Circus Vargas and that snake owned and rented for photo ops by ringmaster Ted McCray. During intermission before a packed tent in

Hollywood, McCray announced that, for $10, anybody could come down to the ring and have a photo taken of themselves with his snake draped around their shoulders. Since the show did not include a single animal in the lineup or offer animal rides that season, the concession seemed blatantly out of place. It bloated the intermission, stretching it out to nearly 25 minutes. We in the audience had to sit, watch, and wait while Mr. McCray took his sweet time accommodating every last customer.

The question begging to be asked here, and so I shall ask it, is why an intermission at all? Moviegoers sit through films that easily consume a couple of hours, if not more. So why not a circus? If the two parts of most shows were placed back to back, allowing in some cases for judicious cuts, the running time in total would be less than two hours. Circus Osario's two paltry parts amount to a mere forty minutes. Ninety to a hundred minutes is actually a good amount of time for a well-paced performance.

When Carson & Barnes used to run its program non-stop from start to finish, as did most of the tent shows, it clocked in at around one hour and thirty or forty minutes. The waning attendance turnouts that have plagued Carson & Barnes, and other such shows, in recent years do not speak well for the drawn-out intervals that corrupt and cut up mediocre programs into pieces, rendering them even more humdrum.

Remember, you who desire ideal memories, that the ring is a special place. How can you help preserve its dignity? Simply by refusing to let them hoist your child onto a pony or camel. By saying no to the man with the snake. No to the bungee slide. No to it all. Let the circus vendors spiel and deal on if they must, just so long as they do it away from that special place where ring stars hold court. Let that be what we leave the tent remembering. And then, might a new generation of children grow up to revere the circus rather than dismiss it as corny or outdated or something for little kids, subconsciously linking it in their sullied memories to all of the irrelevant amusements that came attached to it, like so many annoying TV commercials messing up a good movie.

They might even go back. It can still happen when the show is good.

Exit, please, pandering circus owners and Shriners who should know better. Re-enter, before it's too late, the *circus*.

By the way, is intermission over yet? I could go for another order of garlic fries.

12.
The Thrill Might Be Gone

Let's talk dangerous. Let's courageously recall a time when daredevils were daredevils, when the ever-present specter of death stalked the big top

Here on YouTube (you really ought to check this one out) is the stylishly blasé, scantily clad Tiny Kline, star of Ringling Bros. and Barnum & Bailey during the 1920s, grabbing hold of an "iron jaw" with her teeth and getting whisked along a wire strung high over New York city traffic during rush, rush, rush hour. She is taking a circus short cut from one side of the street to another, a fearless flapper whirling herself around and around as she commutes all alone up there in the vacant air, her expressive leg movements hinting of a late night Charleston. Down below, thousands of New Yorkers are gawking up at the circus siren for whom a sudden loose tooth or collapsing crown could spell a fatal detour onto cars and crowds. She's not merely a stunt mistress. She's a sassy show lady, a bona fide daredevil not rigged to the unflattering safety wires you'll see being worn by too many of her counterparts today.

Upon her touch down across the busy Gotham street, circus celebrity Kline is greeted by the cops waiting to arrest her for sky commuting without a license. She is, nonetheless, unassumingly delighted with her clever accomplishment. "At last, I found a safe place to cross Times Square!" says she, dashingly liberated new American dame, now covered in yet-to-be-liberated fur. "I'm saying, Hello, Broadway!"

And we're answering back, "Hello, Ms. Kline!"

What an era of elegant courage to have lived through. Possibly the greatest of all American circus decades. Certainly for high thrills it was. Another roaring twenties Ringling flapper was wire dancer Bird Millman. She, too, once elevated herself to skyscraper status by strutting her stuff across a rope tautly stretched between two Manhattan towers high over midtown madness. In one celebrated photo, the self-absorbed Bird appears almost heady with a sense of air-born infallibility, as if she were dancing through a late night party and having too much fun to go home and turn out the lights. Ms. Millman leavened her balance with but a single Parisian parasol. She literally danced on top of the world.

The intrepidly free Bird Millman rigged to safety wires? She and her like-minded aerial associates would sooner have danced across the Grand Canyon blindfolded in the middle of a snowstorm than submit to

Singing wirewalker, Bird Millman, on a New York city rooftop working a publicity stunt. USED WITH PERMISSION FROM ILLINOIS STATE UNIVERSITY'S SPECIAL COLLECTIONS, MILNER LIBRARY.

performing with safety belts strapped around their mid-sections. These "lifelines," as they are today more euphemistically called, in previous eras were confined to training sessions for apprentice performers. Back then, no self-respecting circus artist would dare be seen, let alone be *allowed* to by any self-respecting circus manager, strapped to such a rig. Nor would an audience tolerate the sight of it. Amateur would-be, back to the learning barn!

All of which may sound to your ears like a rather harsh way for my getting you properly into this chapter. Are you, may I ask, deriving any genuine thrills at the circus these dithering days? If you aren't, chances are the dispiriting sight of safety wires is one big reason why. Either that or something no less regretful: You are seeing fewer and fewer sky acrobats than did your thrill-expectant parents half a century ago.

Let's return to that hypothetically inferior show which just used up another 20 or 30 minutes for intermission. Think back upon what it's given you so far, and ask yourself, did any of it *thrill* you? Okay, now ask yourself another question: Knowing what you know now, would you rather have stayed home and watched Judge Judy read 'em the riot act or Dr. Phil smack his lips over yet another "learning" episode from garden variety infidelity? Are you now regretting that you skipped *Law and Order* for hula-hoops and this?

Have heart. Circuses still know how to bring out "the big one" just when the crowd is yawned out, popcorn stuffed and ready to call it a binge. The best producers know how critical are last impressions in not only satisfying customers but sending them out of the tent ready to talk up the show to others, the others being prospective ticket buyers for the next show. At a circus program shrewdly assembled, if your breath is to be taken away, the point of impact should come closer to the end than to the beginning.

San Francisco Chronicle columnist Gerald Nachman once cracked, "By intermission, I craved an elephant or tiger and those tacky Shrine Circus souvenirs of my youth — chameleons on a stick, terminally ill turtles, glow in the dark flashlights…"

Nachman was reviewing the intermittently cerebral *Saltimbanco*, a Cirque du Soleil creation, finding a certain something to be seamlessly desired. "Indeed, the most satisfying moments are total Barnum throwbacks: two be-spangled women…who perform truly death-defying tricks on a midair swing, forming geometric patterns with erotic love overtones."

The circus, this book will not deny, seems forever to be marching further away from a sordid and titillating thrill show past into a more saintly and humane future (read "ballet"). I've mentioned how the diabolically pandering Circus Maximus went for the jugular. Its sadistically violent exhibitions in which Christians were alleged to have been served to lions drew thousands of heartless voyeurs.

From Rome to Ringling, by then the public had learned to substitute the dreaded *possibility* of human misfortune for the sure spectacle of mayhem and gore that it had practically demanded of the brutal Colosseum games.

Non-homicidal daredevils replaced sinister chariot thugs. And our hearts learned to pound in more civilized ways. The circus advanced from guaranteed blood spilling to spine-tingling risk. Today, some people are repelled by the linkage of the word "circus" to the word "Maximus."

"That was not circus!" they, and even I, would protest.

Truth is, to the millions of spectators who poured into the Roman Colosseum, *that* was circus. Just as, to those of us who today favor the status quo with animal acts, it is the circus.

By the turn of the last century, Barnum & Bailey were raising a crowd's collective blood pressure by sending a spunky woman at the wheel of a small auto, as previously referenced, down the loop-the-loop ramp to turn a vehicular somersault through mid-air. Crude. Gutsy. Graceless. All those things. A little daring and, granted, perhaps a tad skillful too, if you were the dame driving the blasted jalopy. Far less legitimately artistic, for sure, than Tiny Kline's jazzy iron-jaw cameo across Times Square. Aerial specialists taught themselves how to merge peril with poetry. In turn, we the audience witnessed performances both very real and symbolically metaphorical: life can be, in fact often is, both beautiful and dangerous in tandem.

When the performer advanced from stunt trickster to graceful aerialist is when the circus came into its own.

The reigning question of the moment should be: How far from the element of authentic risk-taking can tomorrow's artists retreat before meditating themselves through naval-gazing choreography into irrelevance?

Many of our top headliners have hailed from the distaff side: Millman, Leitzel, equestriennes May Wirth and Dorothy Herbert, aerial thrillers Rose Gold and La Norma. And how appropriate that it should have taken a woman to recognize their work as epitomizing that which most distinctly sets circus apart from all other entertainment models. Here is English scholar Helen Stoddart on the subject:

"Circus is, above all, a vehicle for the demonstration of taunting danger and this remains its most telling and defining feature. Physical risk-taking has always been at its heart."

Addressing the same issue nearly 80 years ago in his book *The Circus From Rome to Ringling*, author Earl Chapin May observed, "Circus performers are just as keen about their calling and just as tempted to exhibit artistic temperament as are opera singers. The principal difference between the two schools is that circus performers are daily risking life and limb while opera singers risk their voices."

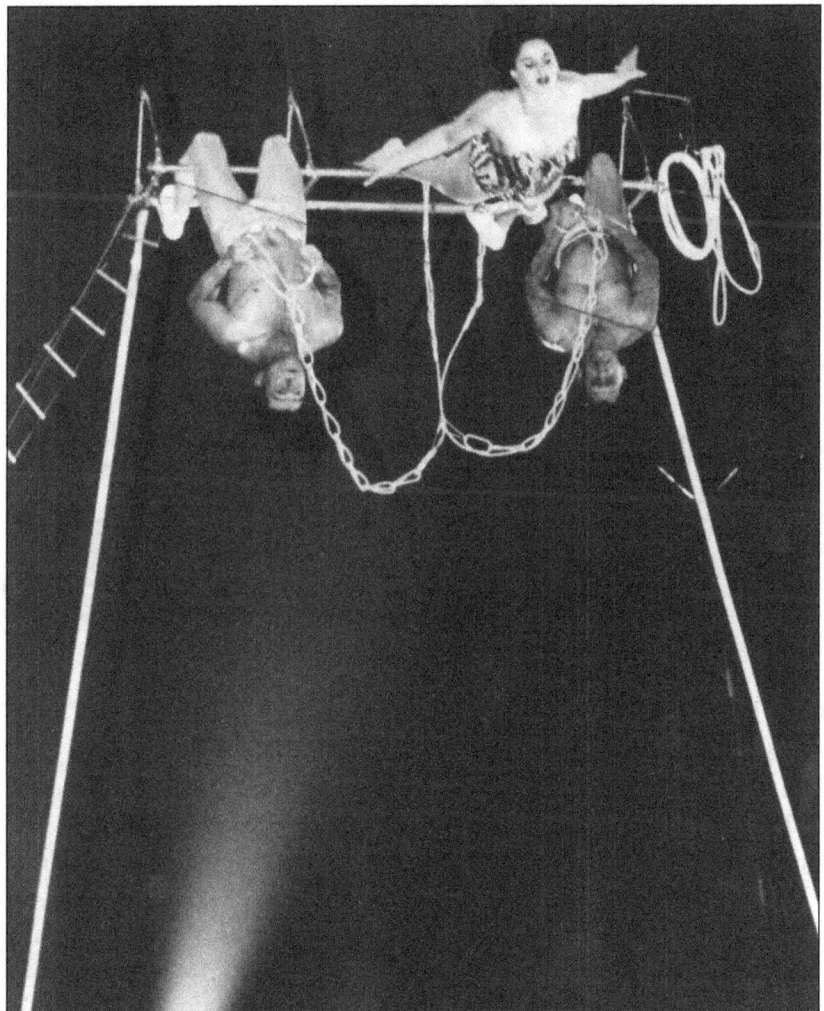

Like many foreign artists imported by the Ringling show, after European sensation Rose Gold served out her contract, she switched to Polack Bros. Circus, whose single-ring focus drew the appreciative patronage of many circusgoers. USED WITH PERMISSION FROM ILLINOIS STATE UNIVERSITY'S SPECIAL COLLECTIONS, MILNER LIBRARY.

Most of us buy tickets hoping to be astonished. Even to be frightened a little by something unexpectedly ominous. Could be inside a wild animal cage. Could be on top of a large rolling globe spinning precariously up a narrow ramp. Those feelings of apprehension lurk in the subconscious, and they are the forces, I suspect, that lure us back.

High wire diva Josephine Berosini, a mid 1950s headliner, produced

Josephine Berosini at Madison Square Garden, 1955. PHOTO BY TED SATO/ AUTHOR'S COLLECTION.

quiet audience apprehension performing all on her own up there, dancing over the steel strand one way, riding a bike back the other, and at the midway point standing erect atop it. A solitary maneuver that tightened hearts and quickened pulses. Another wire treading teaser was Harold Alzana. While jumping a very short rope over and over again, he'd suddenly turn it twice around his body before landing back on the wire, and you felt your heart skip an extra beat. One of the simplest-looking tricks, and yet one that in a split second evoked the primal power of circus. All it takes is the right split second to experience spangleland's classic power.

La Norma flew high and wide from a swing ("single trap" they say), expanding her arc with each pass until diving recklessly forward, taunting fate to take her as we gasped, but sparing herself in a split second by the bare skin of her heels gripping the bar.

They execute the seemingly impossible before our disbelieving eyes. They *were* and *are* circus. They were skill and courage, grace and stamina and control. They filled us with dread and respect and awe, and we bought the ride, traveled it vicariously, and when the trick was landed, we landed it too. And felt a rare exhilarating release from the precipice. Symbolic? No, real. Not a movie. A circus. Call it big top catharsis.

Too messy for a contemporary crowd to handle? Or is the fade-out of fearlessness why the crowds have drifted elsewhere?

By virtue of casting the performance into more dream-like settings, John Ringling North softened the edges a little, whether or not this was a conscious goal of his. In this more surreal atmosphere, North's favorite aerialist, Pinito Del Oro, herself naturally surreal, appeared to be blessedly lost in a self-absorbed fantasy. Standing on a free swinging trapeze, sometimes with only one foot, Del Oro sustained her balance while swinging both back and forth in the conventional mode, then unconventionally from side to side, and finally in circular arcs. The effect was almost hypnotizing. She had transformed herself from daredevil into a dream figure taunting gravity. Hers was one of the most memorable circus acts that I have ever seen for it was so atypically understated, almost mystical.

Make no mistake; what Del Oro did up there was deadly dangerous (she survived two falls). Now, had she performed her act with a mechanic attached to her body, everything I have told you would be null and void. Who would have felt what I have just recounted feeling? Would you?

Did Lillian Leitzel ever feel nervous working her act, asked a reporter interviewing her in 1931, only hours before her death from a fatal fall in Copenhagen.

"Yes, of course," replied arguably the greatest circus star who ever lived. "But you have to continue your act and to fight the trick that has teased you until you can master it. It is the only way to fight fear. The secret is concentration — when doing your act you will only think of the tricks to be done. I can wake up in the middle of the night scared to death by the thought of not being able to remember how to do a specific trick. But during the act it comes naturally."

It was not through any fault of her own that Lillian Leitzel fell to her death a few hours later. Her rigging failed her.

Today, when you spot a wire strung to the backside of an aerialist, what do you feel? I lose respect. I feel a yawn coming on. I know that, at their best, whatever a shielded performer might do can certainly be theoretically interesting. But "interesting" is no substitute for thrilling. Nothing they accomplish can produce absolute value as long as a mechanic is in place to spare them from falls or assist in their execution of difficult tricks they have not mastered and likely never will. Not as long as they can count on a safety harnesses to compensate for insufficient skill or courage, for the failure to practice and perfect. These inevitable perceptions diminish our sense of imminent danger and leave us only academically impressed.

For you who've followed me closely on this issue, you will by now know that the emasculation of aerial work can easily be traced back to the Soviet Union. Following the Bolshevik revolution of 1917, an intense nationalistic cause to craft a more distinct Soviet circus art led to significant changes in how the public came to view the performer. The use of safety wires was mandated for all. And a new protected class of aerialists who wore them, whether they agreed to or not, did redeem themselves to a degree by the sheer brilliance of their innovations.

And so audiences in Russia, and gradually throughout the world when the Moscow Circus began to tour internationally, were conditioned to overlook the safety belts routinely worn by the artists and to concentrate more on the esthetic qualities of their respective work. They, and then we, made a bargain in the key of ballet: Let the trapeze artist become a sophisticated ballerina in the air, as safe as are her counterparts on the stage. Relieved of the fear factor, audiences would derive a more thoughtful pleasure by turning their attention to the complexity and originality of the routines. This was a central argument advanced by Soviet intellectuals.

In a unified context *in which all* artists abide by this rule, it is easier for a typical audience to accept the secured performer. However, in the West, where one act may perform cold turkey and the next with lifelines, the glaring disparities only add to our skepticism and discontent. For, if one star has the skill and the resolve to go it alone, why not all the others? This clumsy dichotomy came to a head on the Ringling show in 1976 when the Tzekovi high wire troupe from Bulgaria walked on double wires while rigged to mechanics. The cumbersome display of really nothing at all begged the question: what exactly is the point of having a group of protected performers work so high over the ring? Why not have them work on a low wire close to the ground without mechanics, where they can sustain a little integrity? This was the Soviet circus at its most embarrassing.

Secured aerial acts that are misleadingly advertised as "Dangerous! Thrilling!" have encouraged an influx of younger performers who might otherwise have shunned the circus altogether as being too risky a calling. And this trend has thrown open the tent flaps to theatre and ballet types eager to incorporate their theatrical inclinations into the (safer) circus programs. They take fewer risks, spending instead most of their time aloft posturing expressively and losing themselves in the silky folds. So determined are they to separate themselves from what they disparagingly call "old circus," that they have even invented a new form called "static trapeze." Not to disparage back, I'll grant them the possibility that their creative endeavors may influence if not revolutionize aerial action.

Without the mechanic worn by the woman at the top, this theoretically outstanding turn presented by Peckulin's Group in the Soviet Union might have been a genuine thriller. AUTHOR'S COLLECTION.

It may surprise you to learn that some American circus owners today tend to favor the lifelines, and will openly defend their use. So, increasingly, do circus performers of not just the aerial class, some arguing that, given the low pay, it would be recklessly irresponsible for an artist not to perform risk-free. Indeed, from upper management down, aerial art is gradually being gutted of its blatantly visceral thrill factor. Writes Big

New thrill in the circus skies: A "sensual silks" routine performed at the Charming Shanghai Acrobatic Show, 2010. PHOTO BY BOYI YUAN.

Apple Circus founder Paul Binder on his blog, "Safety must always be the first priority. Circus performers place a premium on safety. They're artists, not daredevils."

Not exactly so, certainly not once upon a recent time when the word "daredevil" was a highly respected term among the circus going public. A term that defined the very essence of big top drama. But daredevilry still now and then dares a crowd not to look away. At the moment, aerialists seeking maximum movement through the air continue exploring new forms to express both poetry and peril. I've mentioned the Chinese and their sensual silks. And on the ground as well, they are demonstrating the capacity to keep alive at least the illusion if not the reality of risk taking. During a performance of the Golden Acrobats in Berkeley, 2006, a very showmanly young hand balancer working the old chair-staking routine gave us reason to feel fear, hope and admiration. As he added, first one, then another and yet another chair to advance his eerie elevation, we were treated to a subtle display of old-fashioned bravado.

Just when you thought he had gone as high as he should go, there came that look on his playfully taunting face: should I add just *one* more chair? Should I increase the danger and prolong your trepidation? From his perch on high, this slyly humorous entertainer smiled down upon our mounting sense of unease. We were on edge; not he.

What charges our emotions during such a performance is a feeling that only through skill, careful calculation, steely concentration, resolve and bravery can the artist stay the course and avoid the unthinkable. Every moment is in the balance as he moves higher and higher on a stack of precariously connected chairs. A metaphor for life, I'd say.

Now ask yourself, would you feel the same tension and admiration were the young showman strapped to a safety harness?

With a mechanic, it is virtually impossible for the artist to succeed purely on skill, even if technically he does. In fact, he does not have to succeed at all because a lifeline will be there to spare him from accident or worse in the event that he slips or loses contact with his rigging. And so, these unsightly symbols of protection rob the performer of the opportunity to prove that he possesses indisputable skills, and they render his act semi-impotent.

In direct contrast to the Chinese chair guy, the same year Cirque du Soleil brought out its new touring show, *Corteo*, to the San Francisco Bay Area. You could glance up at a pretty young ballerina walking across a "high wire." She was tethered, every antiseptic step of the way, to a thick white rope affixed to her backside. You might have wondered, as I did, if Cirque was not mocking the dangers inherent in real circus as old hat or crudely inhumane If, indeed, they were striving subliminally to deconstruct your appetite for the real thing by manipulating you into accepting a harmless image. The day I attended, nearly one-third of the seats were empty.

When Cirque returned to San Francisco two years later with its compellingly real *Kooza*, gone were the lifelines. And gone were all the ominously empty seats. Present were two genuine thrill acts heretofore mentioned, both shrewdly spotted near the end of the program. One was the high wire troupe working on double wires; the other, the two guys working the wheel of death with a reckless jaw-dropping flair.

And that's what the Montreal magician-in-chief, Guy Laliberte, is smart enough to include in most of his touring shows most of the time.

The company veers between these authentic thrillers and the more intricately choreographed aerial routines. Since the Cirque founders took their early cues from the Soviets placing ballet over big top, they too tended to avoid the kind of tricks that open our eyes wide and set our hearts into overdrive. Laliberte has also asexualized his shows, possibly a conscious effort to both mystify them further and reach lucrative world-wide markets that are breaking up and splintering off into a wider range of sexual role-playing. This too contributes to the emasculated circus.

No matter how modern or exotic or androgynous or asexual the circus may become, audience turnouts will further recede when the thrills disappear. Most of us are drawn to the show hoping to watch our fellow human beings accomplish incredible things through the application of skill and concentration. Those are the attributes of human nature on display, and we exult in witnessing what they can achieve. With them we identify. We become the flyer, the wirewalker, the chair stacker. Sharing in their victory, our sprits are empowered.

Tomorrow may deliver a resurgence of accomplished daredevils from unexpected quarters. Currently, we are looking east to the Middle Kingdom, which for years stayed put mostly on the ground, content to perpetuate juggling and acrobatic traditions. A low wire act now and then. This, I am delighted to report, is changing, and we in the west are the luckier for it. The acrobatic troupes over there are taking firm hold of the swings and the webs, hoisting muscle, might and agility aloft to prove themselves as flawlessly adept and inventive *over* the sawdust as they have been *on* it for ages. The daring young Chinese man on the flying trapeze has arrived.

He arrived in the form of the Shanghai Swingers, who dazzled UniverSoul Circus audiences in 2005. He arrived in the form of a fearless foursome, the Yunnan Flyers, who infused the woefully weak Ringling circus in 2006 with heart-pounding audacity. These young daredevils combine a Russian swing device with a single trap destination. Their gripping finish has each man in succession flying off the Russian swing to lock arms and legs with the guy he follows. They end up forming a four-man human chain anchored to the trap bar. Artistically, when I saw the number they were on the rough side, which only made it more amazing. And that's how I hope they stay. Too much ballet might have diluted their raw virile attack down to a dull, lifeless perfection. We can see and feel their rambunctious desire to succeed. And if that quality in and of itself is an act, what an act it is. Bravo, Yunnan Flyers, bravo!

Now, *that* is circus. *That* is the true pulse of the big top. That is why you go, and why you will go back.

Ah, those inscrutable Chinese! What sly showoffs they are becoming How utterly nerve-wracking they can be when the circus of risk gets into their cool blood. When even Buddha himself may be cringing down upon the big top in a transcendental tremble.

13.

Some Big Top Broccoli, Ma'am?

Too easily do we belittle storytelling over sawdust (and I plead guilty here), failing to acknowledge the role it has played, if only in cameo form, down through the annals of circus history. In fact, character and plot have forever existed in the shadows, however subtly. They have existed in the form of spectacular pantomimes and pageants, in sly narrative interjections between performers, and surely among the clowns, masters of bawdy satire. So let's give the controversial matter a little provisional respect. You might say it returned with a subtle burst, about twenty-five years ago, in a challenging new manner both abstract and strangely affecting. It returned before the show in which it returned even began.

The ring stood empty, silent. In through an opening in the tent wandered a humble throng of strange-looking innocents. Their masked faces distorted, their eagerness child-like, they delighted in their chance discovery.

Then into the same ring burst a troupe of circus artists who proceeded to take the strangers under their wings. Some were turned into performers, one of them, the ringmaster.

They had been welcomed into a tent of startling creativity that was about to reshape conventional circus acts into a rare bohemian spectacle. And when the show was over the visiting innocents were returned to the humdrum reality from whence they had come, some given a souvenir token — the ringmaster, the red hat — before being waved off.

Simple enough? Easy to follow? Amazingly, by program's end a very touching little situational story had brought us to our cheering feet. A circus had moved us in unexpected ways, combining an intimate human premise with a fresh approach to staging circus acts, all of which spelled the stunning difference between a very good show and a groundbreaking hit. And once it got seen beyond its Canadian borders, overnight the world took note. Acclaim soon followed, setting the clever troupe onto a glorious path it doubtlessly had never quite imagined traveling.

Appropriately, the show was named *We Reinvent the Circus*. The company itself — Cirque du Soleil.

Without those average-looking mortals becoming a part of the show, I might not be writing this chapter. In fact, this book may have taken a very different, more traditional path. The young troupe's audacious originality proved to be revolutionary, perhaps too revolutionary to some who would view it as counterproductive to the cause of circus art. We could spend hours debating the vexing definitional issues it raised. Let's just spend a few pages here.

We Reinvent the Circus marked an extraordinary occasion for me personally, as I believe it did for many people. I had never before been so engaged by a storyline or story angle inserted into a ring program. So strong was the show's immediate impact on the Los Angeles critics and audiences when it appeared in the city of angels in 1987, that within no time at all other circuses were trying to imitate aspects of the Cirque style. Today, you will see, at the minimum, traces of that style at almost every circus you attend. It may appear in a performer's manner of entrance; in the artful interchanges between an aerial duo, or in a line of tumblers dressed to resemble not tumblers at all but figures from another profession.

The company's sensational debut in the city of angels sent shockwaves through circus offices from Montreal to Moscow, Moscow to Monte Carlo, Monte Carlo to Shanghai. The critics swooned. The critics raved. This is new! This is what we've been waiting for! This replaces a tired old format in need of a brilliant new make over. This is where the circus should go!

Well, maybe. Don't get too carried away too easily. You out there, "the customer" (sounds awfully ordinary, doesn't it?) may regard yourself as the beneficiary of something fantastically new and exciting. Or you might feel more like a hapless victim deprived of a number of elements you look for in a "circus." It depends on your level of engagement under the "Grand Chapiteau," as the French call a tent. Whether you like it or not, a new producing esthetic dominating circus offices around the world is banking on your not settling for the same old menu of unchallenging brainless amusement. No. No. Down deep, you now harbor a need to be fed a little big top broccoli along with those sinfully addictive other things. Translated into the show, this means that a mere triple somersault across a horse or into the arms of a partner is not enough. Been there, seen that. No, the circus has gotta convey a touch of "to be or not to be" while walking its high wires. Gotta juggle its fifteen clubs like a mad scientist tossing test tubes about in a fit of research mania. Gotta scale its "Wheel of Death" like Woody Allen being chased by a screaming string of ex-girlfriends.

Now, please tell me if you will, did you really grab that free kid's pass at the drug store check-out counter hoping to catch an evening of great theatre under a tent? If not, perhaps you need to be re-educated. A lot has happened since your grandparents went to a circus expecting to

The Living Statutes, a feature in the early half of the 20th century: This 1924 display on the Ringling show — billed "The plastic art in a novel environment!"— depicted a series of historical themes. Over the years, subjects included The Dance of Life, The First Americans and On The War Path, The Spirit of Flight, and Victory. PHOTO BY CHARLES CLARKE. USED WITH PERMISSION FROM ILLINOIS STATE UNIVERSITY'S SPECIAL COLLECTIONS, MILNER LIBRARY.

have their emotions played with by acrobats swooping bravely through space; by macho men cracking whips at snarling big cats. Cirque du Soleil, which completely shuns the latter, is the leading modern-day trend setter; another elephant in the room, of course, are the vociferously disruptive animal rights groups bent on publicly fingering every last one of you who dares gulp down popcorn or shovel trivia into a cell phone while dogs dance in tutus, elephants in hula skirts and children are allowed to take shockingly insensitive pleasure in such barbaric spectacles. Shame on you all! PETA's brainwashing drives, a form of subliminal aversion therapy, have produced a new class of anti-old-circus snob. These insolent, haughty, disdainful, overbearing agitators infest city council chambers with disproportionate power to influence laws against performing animals.

What has *this* to do with the *storyline* angle, you are asking? Okay, I didn't mean to go off point. But I had to for a reason. I'm onto a Big Theme here, if you'll bear with me. For one thing, by importing touches of theatre into the show, circus owners upgrade their intellectual imagery. They make themselves look less carny. More egg-heady. When you read about aspects of "the human condition" being addressed in a circus show, you are more inclined to think, "Oh, the people who run this circus are more theatre like so they must be better educated. Yeah, I bet they are more sensitive to the animals. They wouldn't dare abuse one, not them. No way!" Indeed, one of the critics who embraced Cirque du Soleil's first American tour in 1987 called it "the thinking person's circus." Many others felt the same way, and that fatal act of heightened validation may have doomed the idiot's delight circus that entertains you without recalibrating your brain cells.

And ever since, virtually all circuses have dabbled in the Cirque style of narrative- and theme-based action. They too have tried to enshrine their big acts with big ideas. To hire writers to script the show. Might work. Usually, it comes up a bust. But they are still working in this hazy direction, and can we blame them for wanting to stay with it? After all, the public tires of the predictable. Give it something new, like a rolla bolla performer playing the role of a city plumber in Cirque du Soleil's *Wintuk* (good) to a Soviet artist playing a surly prostitute in the New Pickle Circus's *Circumstance* (iffy).

When you spot a lone female ascending a long flowing fabric, she might be on her way to another spiritual workout above the ring, to something that may resemble a self-induced trance in which, heck, for all we know, in her mind she is playing Blanche in *A Big Top Named Desire*. Overeducated moms and dads from the Boomer brigade may then satisfy themselves that this circus must be politically A-Okay because, well, look at how close they are to ballet and theatre. Read the program notes; they are into some deep, deep stuff! These performers are *intellectual, educated, progressive*, not like those others. No way are *their* animals being mishandled by some lowly high school drop out who probably pushes drugs on the side, not to be confused with the college graduate who pushes drugs on the side.

So, give them a little broccoli and *then* they'll buy your cotton candy and wild animals and all your other old-fashioned diversions, which is why they came out in the first place. They just needed a redeeming reason to indulge.

Sorry to burst your Berkeley bubble, but the act itself does not depict a specific human condition other than the remarkable set of skills necessary

Poetry set to circus: Ruslan and Liudumillia, staged at the St. Petersburg circus in 1979, climaxed with a celebration featuring four standard acts. AUTHOR'S COLLECTION.

to complete a trick. The interrelationship of two aerialists — how they move together, part company and reconnect — is another basic demonstration of all the physical attributes necessary when two people set out to form geometric patterns between and around each other in space.

Of course, the element of drama can be viably introduced. There is the impressive example of the staging of *Ruslan and Liudmila* at the Leningrad circus in 1979. Russian director Alexei Sonin, previously from the world of ballet, ingeniously dramatized the famed Pushkin poem through illusions and circus action. Acrobats were cast as gladiators and trick riders. To illustrate how deftly Sonin merged circus and theatre, during a fight between Ruslan and his romantic rival, Chernomor, the former, astride horse with saber in hand, slashes away at his enemy's long and tangled beard, but crashes to the ground in vain. Sans horse, he grabs hold of Chernomor's horrendous growth with one hand, grasping his saber in the other, and is flung high into the air where the two resume a terrifically exciting struggle. The pantomime's happy ending joins a celebration with four standard circus acts. This was an evening to remember, so much so that I returned for another.

For the most part, however, technical mastery in the aerial arts thrives more on harmony than adversity. It is difficult enough to execute a routine of control and coordination; introducing the element of conflict restricts and coarsens the artistry, for the shape of conflict is terribly asymmetrical. Aerial work is the very opposite. And great aerial work in and of itself offers a totally satisfying pleasure neither superficial nor gratuitous. Karl Wallenda spoke of the performer needing to be an "actor" too; I wish I had pressed him more on the idea, as it was to me that he made the statement. I have long considered that what he was saying was that to be a star wire walker, you need to *look* and *act* like a star wire walker.

Were our circuses more richly endowed with exceptional aerialists, they would likely spend less time on ethereal allusions to the inner soul in crisis.

How tastes change across the decades. Nearly one hundred years ago, in 1912 the Ringling Bros produced an elaborate opening pageant, *Joan of Arc*, which involved a cast of hundreds. Alleged to have cost a staggering $500,000, a probable overstatement, the epic was met with critical delight, and relief. Ironically, the reviewers are said to have termed it "a welcome change from dangerous thrillers…" Actually, *Joan of Arc* in flames strikes me as just another thrill act. Maybe the critics were fooled once again.

These then-popular productions, termed "specs" (but not derived from the word "spectacular") actually approached theatre and grand opera for they were most definitely narrative-based. Some circuses sold librettos illustrating scenes from the drama to customers upon entering the tent. For a time, many of the smaller 3-ring concerns also presented specs.

But the pendulum could swing back at any time to favor a full-scale return of "dangerous thrillers" over the current glut of audience participation, third-rate make-do clowning and mediocre aerial work that together can leave an audience vaguely discontented. There is no substitute for tough tumbling and fearless flying.

The earlier American one-ring troupe, which had neither the room, muscle, cast size nor wagon space for a *Joan* opera, relied for dramatic shadings on the interplay between ringmaster and clown, as previously I've noted. You can still spot residual echoes of that classic encounter pitting authority and buffoonery in some of today's programs. For instance, under the Kelly Miller tent in 2009, Steve Copeland and Ryan Combs raised laughter as gold prospectors getting in the way of the show and onto the nerves of the man in red, John Moss III. All of which ended up with two shovels getting confiscated and two goofy gold diggers being handed bows and arrows. And, only a little later, the ringmaster returning, amusingly unaware that he was now wearing an arrow, one end protruding from his front side, the other out his rear. Very funny.

Our inaugural circus affairs, confined to wood amphitheaters permanent or hastily thrown up for the occasion, followed closely the British performance format that emigrating Scottish equestrian Bill Rickets introduced to Americans when he established the first circus in Philadelphia in 1792. Included on the eclectic bill were dramatically enacted historical pantomimes, thus turning the ring into a primitive theatre-in-the-round. Ropewalkers and tumblers shared the sawdust with full-fledged thespians or circus troupers passing for such.

As we moved into the three-ring era, itself a colossal gift, welcome or otherwise, from Barnum & Bailey's Greatest Show on Earth in 1881, now the owners had vast amounts of additional performing space to fill, and fill it they did with not just three rings of acrobats and animals but with themed pageants that preceded the regular performance. Owners competed with each other in cast size, costumes and music, addressing such far-flung topics as *Columbus Discovering America, The Durbar of Delhi, Pilgrimage of Mecca,* and *Cleopatra,* to name a few. They boastfully advertised the enormous up-front expenses incurred in mounting these productions. Scenic effects were elaborate. Directors from opera were enlisted. The "cast" would include dozens of canvas men dressed in subsidiary roles. Nearly every available staff member from prop hand to rope walker donned costume or camouflage. To the eyes of Robert Barbour

Johnson, a circus fan and writer who essayed an in-depth story on the history of circus "specs" for *The White Tops* magazine in 1955, these big top epics, which consumed up to a half hour before the circus acts where whistled on, "had absolute three-dimensional reality! The audience sat all around them, so close that they could almost reach out and touch the participants. You could smell the animals, hear the actual armor clank and the draperies rustle...It gave an astonishing feeling of actuality." He even welcomed the unbathed aromas of chorus roustabouts, for they lent an aura of blunt reality removed from the theatre. Citing an example, he explained:

"The whole point is that the REAL Julius Caesar most certainly also hadn't had a bath for a week, most of the time needed a shave, and was certainly as worn and battered looking, during his campaigns, as the canvas man. It was the only true realism ever attempted in historical presentation. And the fact it wasn't intentional, but accidental, only made it more convincing." This same enthusiast, I should note, also acknowledged widespread amateur acting and off-key vocalizing among the players.

In his research, interestingly Johnson traced the spec's possible lineage back to a French ritual, which evolved in the late Middle Ages, celebrating a monarch's entrance into a city. The rituals, he tells us, were one of the "important causes" of the French Revolution. They were not theatrical illusions, however, but real life pageants produced on stages to depict any number of historical, biblical, or fairy tale themes (one called *Adam and Eve*), concluding with an outlandish procession into the city. That climactic parade seems a clear forerunner to what expansionist minded American circus owners offered the public in years to come.

In fact, this gives Johnson cause to link that nascent French form to the much smaller one ring historical pantomimes that showed up in the first modern circus programs of Philip Astley's in London, Franconi's Hippodrome in Paris. From there, across the ocean they came in 1793, a distinctly dramatic form that would explode in size, stature, and opulence under American three-ring big tops at the turn of the last century. They endured in full force until 1919, when the Ringling and Barnum & Bailey shows were merged into one, though other circuses continued producing them into the 1930s.

The Ringling brothers had dominated the field for a number of years when they operated simultaneously both their own circus and the Barnum & Bailey title, which they acquired in 1907. Each spring on each show they either premiered a new opening spec or dusted off the previous year's opus for another tour of duty.

Upon his attending a wildly successful mounting of *Joan of Arc* at the Hippodrome in Paris during the winter of 1911-1912, John Ringling pushed onto his four brothers the idea of adapting the story into the opening pageant for the coming season. Ringling was awed by the sight of Joan being burned at the stake. According to his enthusiasm, it "amounted to a sensation and was the talk of Paris." In a letter he wrote to Al, he described a climax that he felt sure could be staged at their spring indoor engagement in Chicago: "...as the smoke and flames came up around Joan, she made her getaway into the bottom of the funeral pyre, and in her place there was a very finely gotten up dummy, dressed like Joan of Arc, and two angels came down from the top of the building on wires...This could be done at the Coliseum in Chicago and would be a great effect."

Brother Albert's reply conveyed the acute reservations of he and the other brothers, believing that such a spec should instead end with the coronation of King Charles. "I doubt whether the burning scene would take so well with the majority of our patrons. It might perhaps be looked on as sacrilegious."

Whatever version the brothers agreed to, John's primary push prevailed. The following spring while actively at work on *Joan*, Charles wrote to John in New York. "Al says that we will try to work the ascension in if we can. Of course you know that our drop curtain at the coliseum comes out to the edge of the balcony, and we would have to work this from a position in front of the drop curtain as we can not draw her up through the balcony floor. However, I believe this can be worked out alright and shall try to assist Al in getting away with it, which he seems agreeable to."

Ringling's *Joan of Arc* was a critical hit. It certainly gave audiences a heavy dose of big top broccoli up front before the regular circus features — the fun stuff — took over.

When John Ringling North entered the picture 26 years later, in 1938, the opening spec was a thing of the past, having been replaced by what is more correctly termed "The Grand Entry," a parade of gilded floats and costumed characters representing, but not limited to, exotic locations or epochs in history. According to the fussy Johnson, defending the thoroughly dramatic nature of the true "spec," the North parades and all others like it were not "specs" at all, even though fans and insiders continued to refer to them as such. Now, the goal was just to create an enormous splash of color and animation at the outset, to show off the livestock and performers en masse in extravagant attire. North immediately went to work reshaping the parades. He generally avoided history and politics and he certainly avoided religion, no thank you, Joan or Jesus. Instead, he favored distant locales and colorful stateside settings. The aura of place took precedence over allusions to history. "Jungle Drums," the 1950 closer, with a haunting original score by Henry Sullivan, cast the elephants and showgirls in African garb. Dramatic interactions? Not really other than what the audience might fancifully read into the choreography.

Among the many spectacles produced under North's aegis, to name

Jerusalem and the Crusades, the Ringling brothers 1903 spec, boasted a ballet of "ninety five young women" and drew turn away crowds to the three-week Chicago opening. So popular was the production with critics and crowds that it was brought back in 1904.
USED WITH PERMISSION FROM ILLINOIS STATE UNIVERSITY'S SPECIAL COLLECTIONS, MILNER LIBRARY.

a few, there was "Ballet of the Elephants," "Old Vienna, "The Circus Ball," "The Glorious Fourth," "Rocket to the Moon," "'Twas the Night Before Christmas," "The Good Old Times," and "Rock! Ringling Rock and Roll!" Although these festive offerings could hardly be called dramatic pageants, in a panoramic sense they stirred the emotions with their humorous interactions between familiar figures from history and popular culture. For examples, we got a little Walt Disney, and we got a little of the equestrianship at "Queen Antoinette's Gay Court."

The show injected a moderately effective touch of story telling into the 1967 performance with Richard Barstow's modern version of the Lewis Carroll classic, aptly re-titled "Alice in Topsy Turvy Land."

Surely, one of the most daring departures for a circus spec, credit, once more, Richard Barstow, did not, unfortunately, last beyond Miami, Florida, the first stop on Ringling's 1964 tour. That year, the big production

Years later, only the parade remained, and virtually every performer took part in it. The boy riding the Showboat float in Ringling's 1953 spec, Candy Land, is the show's young star, xylophonist Mr. Mistin, Jr. With him are Linda Lawson, left, and Carmen Slayton. PHOTO BY SVERRE O. BRAATHEN. USED WITH PERMISSION FROM ILLINOIS STATE UNIVERSITY'S SPECIAL COLLECTIONS, MILNER LIBRARY.

splash, which brought the first half to a close, was "Welcome to the Fair." Designed as a spangled salute to the New York World's Fair, the parade ended on a soaring spiritual note, with Harold Ronk singing Rodgers and Hammerstein's immortal "You'll Never Walk Alone." We may never know how the song affected the Miami audiences. We do know how it affected Henry Ringling North. Directly after arriving in Miami to follow the show on its annual tour, North stepped into the arena while the parade was in motion, the band was playing the *Carousel* hymn, and Ronk was, as he would later recall, "having enough trouble wallowing in it." North stopped dead, his face flashing disbelief.

He called Ronk over during intermission. "That sounds like a funeral dirge!" he complained. "This is supposed to be a happy affair. All those long-faced Europeans and you singing you'll never walk alone."

North called for Merle Evans, the bandleader who regularly accepted and played specially created production scoring handed to him by Barstow.

"What's the matter," said Evans. "Don't you like it?"

"No, no no! We can't turn people away hearing a song like that."

Against Evan's initial resistance (for all we know, he may have actually liked the number), North kept pressing his case.

"Well," relented Evans, finally, "we'll just play 'The Greatest Show on Earth!'"

Who can say for sure how well the number may have clicked with circus crowds along the way? How different things might have turned out had Henry's brother John been on the scene at the time to overturn Henry's hasty rejection. In retrospect, it seems both bold and respectful of Barstow to have enlisted the soaring song in a circus parade; after all, are not faith and hope among the sterling attributes of character that define and inspire circus artists to the summit of their excellence?

Circus companies by now had retired their respective operatic choruses of "actors" and "dancers" to concentrate on fast-moving costumed processions sprinkled with simple dance steps and feel-good hoopla. Narrative was yet to re-enter the picture, full force. The Russians added little day-to-day vignettes to the individual act. In Moscow's New Circus in 1979, a man named Zhenya stole the show showing off a group of misfit bulldogs and poodles dressed as beach-going vacationers out for a day of fun and sun. Into the ring he drove his charges on a small wagon hooked to an automobile. He parked it next to the public toilets, one marked "HE," the other "SHE." One very restroom-ready male dog ran into the wrong lavatory. That drew a warm and full laugh.

Into the park, next, came a water wagon pulled by a white horse wearing a pink cowboy hat; talk about wry Russian humor. On top of the wagon rested a large bird. The sunbathing mutts made a mad dash for a drink of water, stopping short of a collision to form, ever so politely, a proper queue. But, as is usually the case at such a mad convergence, a bully latecomer crow barred his way to the front of the line. A light rain began to fall, prompting the beach goers to take shelter under an enormous umbrella, after which they made an early exit. Just enough conflict and comedy to give the act a decidedly charming theatrical dimension. This dramatic approach influenced deeply Cirque du Soleil's first artistic director, Guy Caron. His eyes were opened to how standard acts could be redirected into character-driven vignettes when he saw the Moscow Circus perform in Montreal in 1970. He was fairly blown away by the epiphany.

And that was it. And that was and is how history is made and remade. The Soviets realized a high mark with the Flying Cranes, who spent five years in rehearsal, and whose routine was directed by Vilen Golovko to depict the spirits of fallen soldiers ascending to heaven. Like ballet, it is tempting to read many feelings into the abstract movements, or to ignore those movements altogether and simply enjoy the exquisite athleticism. Some will point out that the underlying thematic matrix adds an emotional depth that is subliminally felt by an audience whether or not it follows a stated scenario. Through the intersection between aerial execution and historical allusion assumed to be active in the minds of the artists, perhaps something distinctly surreal may occur. Had we not been apprised beforehand of the drama said to be embedded in the Cranes' intricate maneuvers, would our reaction have felt less meaningful? I'm not so sure. I do know that for those who were affected by the death of so many valiant young Russian soldiers during World War II, it is impossible to imagine them not feeling a deeper degree of connection.

And yet, at the other end of a hypothetical argument, we are witnessing a flying trapeze act through and through, without dialogue and with virtually no dramatic pantomime. We have little to connect to the drama behind the number. The English author Anthony Hippisley Coxe might argue, as was his wont, that a circus performer does not, indeed, cannot "act" a role but must "work" his trick. And yet this has not stopped Cirque du Soleil from trying. And trying. And trying our patience. In fact, the keenest media critics routinely grumble over obtuse allusions in Cirque press materials to character and plot. Reviewing *Zarkana* at the Radio City Music Hall in the summer of 2011, David Rooney of *The Hollywood Reporter* spotted about a dozen good acts but complained of their getting "stretched, padded and often distractingly undermined by copious dollops of performance filler.... From the elaborate frames that wrap the stage to the constant wash of imagery over the rear LED wall (floating eyeballs, writhing snakes, you name it) to the carnivalesque jumble of costumes and the bombardment of overbearing, high-decibel music, *Zarkana* is burdened by inorganic clutter and sensory overload. All of which just pulls focus from the undisputable skill of the circus acts."

Which is another way of arguing that circus is a silent form which expresses itself in physical feats. And a "trick" does not in and of itself convey any aspect of human existence other than to symbolize the miracle of human achievement. These demonstrations are infinitely universal; anybody in any place around the world will share an almost identical feeling of exhilaration when a flyer throws so many somersaults into a catcher's waiting hands. Staging Polack Bros. Circus in 1953, the great conceiver of aerial production numbers, Barbette, sent the showgirls aloft to execute movements from various rigs. None of these numbers were intended to evoke a particular human crisis or address pressing global issues.

That same fine Polack season, Barbette veered off the ordinary path by inserting into the show the little ballet about which I've already enthused, "Carnival in Spangleland." In effect, this delight added genuine pathos through the spectacle of a lovely ballerina being fought over by two clowns, set to the haunting music of Morton Gould's "Pavan." Credit Barbette's staging savvy for the delicate item being shrewdly sandwiched between two guaranteed crowd rousers, the horse-riding high jinks of the Zoppes and the mid-air excitement of the Nine Ward Bell Flyers. It came and went like a gentle breeze blowing a fresh delicate tone across the ring.

Cirque du Soleil, whose Guy Caron was smitten by the Soviet approach, has made an art form of the *entire* show, doing with it what the Russians had done with individual act. The company's directors devise an overarching theme or situation and go to work finding ingenious ways to integrate the component acts into the structural mystique. Sometimes it works, or seems to. Sometimes the contextual effects can feel heavy and belabored and a little too contrived. Some Cirque editions, like the cerebral *Coreto*, can feel trivially light and fluffy and a little too precious. Others, like *Varekai* or its cousin, *Kooza*, are red hot, invincibly compelling packages.

Without these intellectualized formats, indeed, minus all of the thematic preparation that is said to take place well before and during the long rehearsal process lasting up to nine months, it is tempting to wonder if the organization, so entrenched in its ways, would risk losing the mystical atmosphere and staging ingenuity that has set its work apart from all other circuses.

There is something else to consider here that merits a theoretical excursion into the subconscious mind of both the creator and the intended recipients sitting out in the audience. Perhaps even the introduction of a new concept, which I shall call "subliminal structure." Hear me through, if you will.

Let us say that, during the planning stages for a new show, Guy Laliberte and his creative colleagues share among themselves a feeling, more

Barbette's mini ballet, "Carnival in Spangleland," presented on Polack Bros. Circus in 1953. AUTHOR'S COLLECTION, COURTESY OF ROBERTA YOUTAN KAY.

abstract than dramatically fleshed out, for a story or thematic thread, a cerebral force if you will, such that they can chart its progression on a graph, assigning pivotal developments from act to act. So that, in their minds they are able to embrace a narrative shape that we the audience may never fully understand and may not even begin to grasp, but yet are able to be moved by on a subliminal level, feeling, indeed, a subconscious connection to something deeper than the mere tangible action of the circus performers. In this manner, it is possible to argue that such abstract plotting, though no where near as dynamic on the surface as the actions in a play or film, yet gives the layout of acts a greater sense — or illusion — of emotional progression.

Other less lucky producers, confined to shoe-string budgets, have too tried, each in their own way, to capture a touch of the Cirque mist. A few have even tried to gain notoriety by lampooning its excessive quirks, but most are somberly in thrall and prone to mild forms of imitation. Cirquesita, a Sarasota-based family show, set out to pay tribute to one of its late members, Desi Espana, who died following a fall on the Ringling show in 2004.

"What is new about Cirquesta," wrote the *Sarasota Harold-Tribune's* Kate Spinner, "is its combination of circus gaiety and the depth of a storyline, one that delicately nods to family tragedy." We are told that the story "enters the dreams of a boy whose mother passes away before fulfilling her promise to take him to the circus."

Which is fairly typical of a circus storyline these days. Usually, somebody wants to join up, a slight upgrade, I suppose, over the old horse act that would recruit a "volunteer" from the crowd, hook her to a mechanic and let her try riding without falling off and left dangling through the air anchored to a safety harness. This funny little diversion rarely failed because it was usually very brief and very funny once the volunteer slipped and the mechanic went to work.

Critics in more liberal circles tend to give higher marks to experimental shows like the youthfully charming *Traces* or the theatre-heavy *Birdhouse Factory*, both of which began life under the sponsorship of San Francisco's New Pickle Circus. These efforts showcase the talents of the young, eager to take the form in new directions. Both *Traces* and *Birdhouse Factory*, critical darlings, have struggled to find wider patronage beyond a few publicly funded venues in the larger metropolitan areas hospitable to avant-garde troupes. They are ambitious hybrids that appeal to small niche markets. You are encouraged, nonetheless, to patronize them all, for out of such innovation may come an exciting new form taking the circus forward or even, inventively, backwards.

Now, if you want a subversively dramatic "circus," I'd recommend Circus Oz, should it ever stumble your way. I'm not sure, to be honest, what exactly it is. A circus? I'd say not. Anybody, remember, can call themselves a circus. Oz trades on circus action in the irreverent act of lampooning what is left of it. Oz is character-centric, and so you may find yourself at a Samuel Becket version of the Not Greatest Show on

At last, now entering the tent! On your feet, ladies and gentlemen! The unique mystique of Cirque du Soleil, passionately evoked by select members of Michelangelo Nock's Cirque Equinox. Tim Tegge is the clown. Circa 2002. PHOTO COURTESY OF TEGGE CIRCUS ARCHIVES, BARABOO.

Earth. And you may find it very funny. It can be. Its performers have plenty of attitude, even those who are not very talented. Half or more of them can seem half smashed or drugged out of their minds and just might actually be.

You are witnessing an Aussie take on the end of the word as seen through the eyes of a certain class of young acrobats who can't make up their minds whether they wish to be legitimately good or, rather, subversives in mock sequins thumbing their noses at traditional acts. Actors? Some are, but they can't bring themselves to the end point of where they are going, which would be, hilariously, to tumble the entire big top into comedy shambles. They want to be too many things, and so, ultimately, they are nothing more than a sporadically wacky troupe of intensely free spirits. Perhaps the best way to sum them up is to quote their witty little robotic dog who runs around the stage in heat, seeking bare skin to lick, cracking, "Yeah, I know why you really came here. You want to check out my balls."

Most media critics who do review circuses still harbor a guilt-free taste for the solid older fashioned staples. We are talking about genuine circus acts. Cirque du Soleil's *Wintuk*, an annual holiday show at the Madison Square Garden Theatre beginning in 2007, came with a situational premise: Boy deprived of snow longs to find snow, and this sets him on a journey. Drenched in the usual Cirque special effects, *Wintuk* was met with critical dismay by the New York scribes, who complained of a lifeless affair, albeit one gloriously redeemed at the very end by the release of an artificial snowstorm over the 5,600 seat auditorium.

"Too much time is wasted in setting up the story," wrote Scott Lipton in *TheatreMania On-Line*. The next season, another more satisfied critic found what he came hoping to find in the individual acts themselves.

That is what a typical reviewer will end up defaulting to — authentic performers who supply core content. And yet, following Soviet traditions, the directors did find ways to give some of *Wintuk's* performers character roles to play. Alexadre Monteril, for instance, by profession a rolla bolla artist, took on the part of a city worker repairing a malfunctioning singing lamp post. *Variety* deemed the disguise a plus, dubbing it "something more than just another balancing act, and quite an amazing one at that."

Kenneth Feld, who is notoriously successful, or so it would appear, at running Ringling Bros. and Barnum & Bailey, has also succumbed to story telling. And, like the others, his narrative interpolations are sometimes so obtuse as to render themselves nearly mute. But he seems unable to let go of allusions to character and plot, even though he and his co-producing daughter, Nicole, speak out of both sides of their mouths when the issue is put to them by inquiring reporters. Well, yes, they seem to say, our audiences have told us that they really don't care too much about story lines. And from there they segue into a pitch about a new story angle in their latest show.

Ringling's 2006 edition, the drastic make over with video screen and only half a ring, wrapped itself up in — Surprise! — the tale of a family wanting to join the circus. Its impact was minimal. A couple of seasons hence, the Felds, still unable to break a habit which they admitted had left audiences yawning, were now pitting a clown against the ringmaster in a tug of wills over who should get to blow the whistle and run the program. This little beef did generate some fun gags that tickled the moppets on the morning I saw the show in Oakland. Some of the kids were even apparently following the ongoing feud for power. So, yes, credit is due for a siimple story line that clicked with the younger set.

Might a storybook circus ever register so dramatic an impression as to send the customers to their cell phones after the show, excitedly dialing up friends and urging them not to miss it because the characters were *so* good, the plot *so* hot? "What a play! I was blown away! You gotta see this circus before it leaves town!"

Have you ever called up a friend to rave about a gripping tale you just sat through under a tent?

Okay, here's how to judge the effectiveness of big top broccoli. Look for clarity and brevity. And I must repeat, *brevity*. A clearly defined circus-compatible tale can be told in brief encounters sprinkled throughout the program. Something like the gags in a good clown production number spread out at intervals over the entire evening. And ask yourself at the completion of the show, how much did the "story" parts add to or detract from your experience? Go with your gut feeling. You need not feel as if you have just witnessed Pirandello's *Six Characters in Search of a Producing Clown* to feel that your time has been well spent and you can talk it up to your friends with unequivocal fervor.

We might wonder if ever there will come a day when we are handed a libretto upon passing through the marquee, preparing us to better understand what we are about to witness in the abstract language of body movement. I'd say, forget trying to penetrate deeper meanings. Enjoy the timeless pleasures.

Still, you might some lucky season inside a small tent, as did I in Little Tokyo when Cirque du Soleil came to Los Angeles the first time, discover the next big breakthrough in the ever-changing world of sawdust, spangles and special effects. A breakthrough that could challenge a new generation of producers and performers to match its brilliance. And you may find yourself cheering the artists, young or old, for infusing the show with fresh ideas and holding you gratefully in thrall.

In fact, recently I experienced such a breakthrough, possibly the first since my trip to Little Tokyo in L.A. nearly twenty five years ago. This one struck me, of all places, at a seaside resort. Yet how appropriate. Back to the basics. Inside a tent not far from a beach, I marveled at a circus so tightly put together, so fast-paced and expertly staged, so wonderfully entertaining that I felt overjoyed and reassured to see the big top reasserting its ageless magic, totally unencumbered by any story line whatsoever.

They called it *Boom A Ring*, and, surprise, it was produced by none other than *Ringling Bros. and Barnum & Bailey*. At Coney Island.

Hold the broccoli. A *circus* is back in town!

14.
Rising Stars, Falling Stars

Might you prefer your circus in the flesh or through a dreamy mist? Personal or collective?

We've been seduced by the geniuses of Cirque du Soleil into an abstract realm that itself may eventually become passé. A realm more surreal than real. And then what? Back to Roman sweat and gusto? First, let's follow the current course for as far as it can hold our fixations. Try pulling up a YouTube video of Zhang Gongli, who as of this writing performs with Cirque's *Kooza*; You'll discover a chair balancer in possession of a flawless physique whose controlled hand stands, set to a hauntingly spare soundscape, lift the act to a new level of breathless perfection. To be sure, a very *abstract* perfection. This display represents the outer limits of the new circus where mood, music and atmosphere share equal force with human dexterity.

Zhang Gongli is a perfect example of what may one day replace the more active elements long associated with circus fare, such as raucous acrobats and free-swinging flyers. Or maybe not. When a performer vanishes into the act so that his movements approach the robotic, audiences may turn away feeling a lifeless disconnection from humanity.

Gongli, whose slow-moving contortions are symmetrically pure, is a marvel in his own exalted right, and I would like to see him perform in person. The afternoon I took in *Kooza*, he did not appear. Word was that he, very human still, had taken a fall and was recovering. So we are up against a paradox: How many Gonglis would be too many for a circus? Might one be more than enough? *Kooza* gave us, as I've told you, a terrifically visceral last half replete with genuine risk-taking. The creators up there in Montreal may well realize that these more slow-moving sequences have a place but do not form the heartbeat of a successful campaign.

It is all very wearying, this trying to predict where the circus might be headed, especially when your typical audience still expresses its strongest regard for the big tricks that fuse big turbulent emotions. So let us proceed debating an issue that knows no end: What, really, *is* circus?

Of course, we still desire that journey into a mysteriously wondrous place where the impossible can happen. But now, the place may be replacing the face. No wonder that Paul Binder and Michael Christensen, co-founders of New York's own Big Apple Circus, have forever harped on their mantra about the artist needing to make immediate and "joyful" contact with the audience. I think I am finally getting it. Perhaps they cling to this belief as a necessary antidote to the abstract leanings of Cirque du Soleil. Messrs. Paul and Michael have also tinkered with masks, once when they hired Cirque's first artistic director, Guy Caron, to direct their show. But the tinkering was soon tinkered out of the script, not very long into a strained rehearsal process during which Big Apple performers began to look miscast in the wrong ring. Paul and Michael developed a mutual concern that too much heavy makeup would drive a wedge between artist and audience. And so, off came the Guy Caron add-ons. Back to being human went the very human Big Apple stars.

Not that Big Apple Circus was completely opposed to makeup and flashing lights. Or that it might not at some future date reconsider a more radical departure from the status quo. Now that Paul Binder has retired from artistic control and handed the reins over to his long-time assistant, Guillaume Dufresnoy, it will be interesting to see how closer to the Cirque phenomenon the new director might take "New York's own circus." Mr. Dufresnoy's first offering, *Dance On!*, was one subtle sensation, brilliantly directed, lacking only in sufficient aerial power. The new Big Apple impresario revealed a promising flair for selecting international artists of the highest caliber and casting them in a finely honed performance structure. *Dance On!* reaffirmed the company's well-earned reputation as a national treasure. America's number one circus? At the time of this writing, yes, I would wholeheartedly affirm.

Atmosphere in one form or another does matter; although the Cirque directors clearly place more attention on the mask than on the personality behind the mask, artistry still prevails, as it must. Out from the mist of *Kooza* exploded a captivating young juggler, a juggler so incredibly accomplished, powering himself through a repertoire of tricks linked seamlessly together, that I sat there mesmerized, wondering if he was not the greatest I had seen since the great Francis Brunn took my breath away at Polack Bros. Circus when I was but 10 years old.

Who was *that* juggler, I wondered. As is the custom there, performers are not introduced by name. In this instance, the mystery of the juggler's identity only added to his other worldly mystique, making me wonder if he per chance had been imported from some distant galaxy. So, yes, there is most definitely something to be said for ambiance. Later, I dug through the program magazine, which does not make it easy at all to identify individual artists. Mug shots of them appear in tiny rows; under each photo we learn nothing beyond their name, skill, and nationality. They are really part of what the troupe's founder and lead guy, Guy Laliberte, refers to as a "collective." Okay, I thought, so look for the word "juggler" under the photos. These dedicated performers would get more respect on the Wanted wall at the post office:

Anthony Gatto.

His name, Anthony Gatto. Just another performer in the world's most successful, some would argue most artistically advanced circus? Apparently, Mr. Gatto would rather work with a world famous "collective" and settle for a mug shot in the program than go out with Ringling Bros. and likely draw more attention, certainly major coverage in the program magazine. Into the superior mist of a new world elusively forged, many artists would apparently rather go.

Program magazines today, in general, are less and less informative about the individual artists. Some shows have discontinued printing them, which is a shame, especially when those same shows do not offer customers even a one-sheet handout at the door listing the names of the acts they are about to witness. You are kept in the dark. Ringling Bros. and Barnum & Bailey no longer includes a running order of the acts in its floridly oversized program magazines, which can cost twice the price of the cheapest ticket. Presumably, this vagueness covers for changes to the show. Cirque du Soleil confines the mug shots to a separate stand-alone insert in the program, presumably making it easier to revise the performance and replace performers without having to reprint the entire magazine.

All of which has done nothing to build up and help establish reputations for individual ring stars. What a striking contrast to the day, fifty or sixty years ago and before, when circus stars were household names, earning headline attention. For instance, the ongoing drama inside Clyde Beatty's wild animal cage — when next might one of his ferocious lions break rank and go after *him*? — generated plenty of press coverage. During the American three-ring heyday that peaked through the 1920s, such circus celebs as Bird Millman, Jorgan Christensen, Dorothy Herbert, the Cristianis and the Zachinnis, May Wirth and Alfredo Codona, among many others, enjoyed national name-recognition. Perhaps none quite so memorable as a diminutive female dynamo who spun giddy one-armed planges, tossing her body over her shoulder repeatedly from a single web high over center ring. A woman who took the crowd with her. A woman who gave the circus what rare mortals give it — skill and showmanship, personality and joy. My mom, once writing a letter to me, ended it on a high and happy note: "I saw Lillian Leitzel years ago. She was wonderful!"

Then, too, most of these performers worked dangerous or excitingly

Contortionists at the Flying Acrobatics Show in Beijing, 2010. AUTHOR PHOTO.

difficult acts and they worked them when Americans flocked to big tops in huge numbers, ready to embrace more messy and dangerous programs.

Today if you drop the name Gatto or Gaona, even Gunther Gebel Williams to a friend, chances are you will draw a blank look. Who they?

When the wire-walking (*not* the "flying") Wallendas opened at Madison Square Garden in New York, in 1928, they received an unprecedented ovation, in the words of equestrian director Fred Bradna, recounting that astonishing moment in his book, *The Big Top*:

"They made the biggest hit of any death-defying feat ever displayed under canvas. Their thrill was cumulative. Even their warm-up exercises looked impossible at the dizzying height of seventy feet." While performing their greatest trick — a four-person pyramid involving two bicycles — Bradna wrote that "many a strong man in the audience looked away to relieve inner tension."

"Even before the troupe had reached the safety of their pedestal, the Garden was in an uproar of whistling and stomping of feet...In forty years I never heard an ovation of half the decibels. The great circus stopped for fifteen minutes while the audience clamored for another bow. Finally, I went to the Wallendas, and told them what had happened, waited outside while they dressed, and escorted them to the center ring."

Spectators still sense an outstanding performance in their midst. Or, perhaps I should say, a remarkably acceptable performance, for not all the acts that thrilled yesterday's crowd may fare so well in today's market. Animals still charm and amuse the children and some of their parents. But they are tricky propositions with audiences that have been unduly conditioned by PETA to fear and fret possible abuses taking place outside the rings. Forces of popular culture, doubtlessly emboldened by the example of Cirque du Soleil, have helped hasten their demise in some quarters.

As for the aerial stars, even here we are treading on precariously shifting ground; it is no longer a given that your average ticket buyer will be as eager as he was fifty seasons ago to be thrown into a panic by the courageous abandon of flying daredevils. I've given you, I trust, a few reasons why this may be so. And so, perhaps, the action in the air is shifting to a new school of aerialists who take a more intellectual approach to their work, sometimes, to be sure, accomplishing noteworthy ends.

So circus art advances in certain of its genres while retreating in others. There are fewer family horseback riding acts around, unless they are all hiding out away from American patronage and scrutiny, but we have a plethora of finely polished contortionists and equilibrists who garner well-earned respect. Less single trap performers, perhaps, but a welcome abundance of gifted jugglers. The Germans may not be turning out as many riveting show stoppers. The Chinese may be taking up the slack, and not just on the ground where their acrobats have excelled for centuries, but now, more and more, in the air as well. While La Norma and her like seem to have vanished, the Shanghai Swingers and their like are, hopefully, on the rise.

We don't see performing seals or monkeys any more, not on U.S. soil. We do see a surfeit of wonderful dog acts. And from the Soviet Union, we are getting those marvelously sly and slyly adept kitty cats. The humdrum hula-hoop has dumbed down shows. But ensemble jump roping routines are a major hit when executed by ambitiously adept jumpers.

To be sure, not every "icon" from a "golden" age deserves lasting iconic status. There are the sacred cows of circusdom that live on in hallowed memory; some of them still enjoy adoring reputations for questionably flawed acts. Surely one is Unus, the man who "stood" on his forefinger.

I have never quite been able to rouse myself as have others over his performance, primarily for the reason that, structurally, his act turned anti-climactic the moment its featured stunt, the one finger stand, was consummated. And that moment arrived at the very beginning. You see, Unus worked with a secret pistol-shaped hand-gripping device inside his glove to make possible what really *was* impossible. The well-concealed

A new urban beat for the Big Show: The King Charles Troupe were a hit with Ringling audiences in the 1970s. COURTESY OF TEGGE CIRCUS ARCHIVES, BARABOO.

gimmick necessitated the stunt being executed first so that the rod could then be secretly retracted in order for Unus to complete his program of easier tricks not needing the aid of gimmickry.

By not working your greatest feat, real or no, at the conclusion of your routine is to render it structurally feeble. All acts must build to a climax. Unus built backwards from the payoff to his apparently less-arduous items. I would have urged the performer to contrive a method of momentarily disappearing from view, just long enough for him to install the hand device up his sleeve so that his act would crest on the show-stopping one-finger stand. In order for so hyped a feat to be effective we need to feel a tension rising toward its highly anticipated execution. On this critical count, Unus failed.

Still, would I go see him again? Only were he on a good show. Shortly after the dawning of the man who stood on his forefinger, a number of other hand balancers were duplicating the stunt, and we had numerous one finger stands, all of them making each other that much less remarkable. And by then, I suppose, audiences suspected that the trick was only a trick. Even John Ringling North, who chased Unus all over Europe to sign him, hinted at this much during a 1955 telecast featuring highlights of the show which he co-hosted: "It's one of the most popular guessing games on the circus."

To understand how circus has changed, one need only compare the act of Unus to that of Zhang Gongli. The more flamboyant and diversified Unus also manipulated hoops around his arms and legs while balancing by one hand on the tip of a cane; Gongli concentrates on effecting subtly shifting body positions as he builds the stack of chairs beneath his alternating one-hand stands. The one is validly circus; the other, closer to athletic balletic. At his best, Gongli's slow motion workout instills in us a quiet sense of wonder.

The Chinese troupes that favor nameless ensembles of meticulously crafted tumblers and jugglers, hoop divers and pole climbers, are another unintended contributor to the demise of marquee icons. Can anyone out there tell me the name of that entertaining chair balancer with the Golden Dragon Acrobats, whose sly showmanship made him a virtual *star*? No name anywhere in the promotional or program materials could I find, nor could I extract an answer from the producing organization when I e-mailed it. Perhaps even they do not know. Just call the guy comrade 2000-A-34.1. For that matter, can anyone out there name a single Asian artist you have seen at *any* circus *anywhere*? They come to the states in groups named after cities or regions. They inspire us with their velvet-smooth mastery, and they leave as anonymously as they arrived. Yes, there are the rare exceptions, the solo artist who either gets a ringmaster's preface or more than a mug shot in a program magazine. That is, if she is lucky enough to go on tour outside the country.

Credit the Big Apple Circus, almost alone in its appreciative focus, for putting names and faces on the outstanding Chinese acrobats it manages to land. Recent notable examples would include bowl balancer Guiming Meng; the breathlessly perfect Nanjing Duo performing the "Pas de Deux;" and multi-talented slack wire marvel Cong Tian, the later a winner of Silver Clown awards at circus festivals in both Paris and Monte Carlo.

It is even worse inside China, where a program magazine may well publish mug shots with names, but fail to specify each performer's particular skill, thus leaving you in the dark when you try linking act to artist.

Almost impossible. So I asked Tian Run Min about this. Why do the acrobatic troupes refuse so basic a credit to each of their members?

"They don't," he ruefully agreed, seeming to share my frustration. "No, they pay much attention to the whole group. They don't like to train the single act. They don't build up just one or two artists to become more famous."

Breathless balance: The Nanjing Duo. COURTESY BERTRAND GUAY/BIG APPLE CIRCUS.

Is this a national policy?

"I can't understand," he conceded. "For the other disciplines of the performing arts, like the Peking Opera, that's the tradition. They build up the name."

He suggests it could simply be directorial vanity. "I am the boss. I must be more important than the artist."

Another modern development that has not served well the performer seeking fame and respect are the incriminating safety mechanics about which I have already, I know, said more than enough. But more I will say. They deprive the artist of the respect for indisputable talent that we would otherwise feel, and without a felt respect, there is scarce motivation to remember a name.

Those are some of the changes that are pushing big top entertainment closer and closer to dance-acrobatics. This only adds to my teeterboard thesis, that ever since the advent of Circus Maximus the form has been evolving into progressively more refined versions of itself. One day it might well join forces with or be absorbed by the ballet, and then it will no longer be a "circus" at all. And perhaps every last despicable trace of that thing that raised blood and dust in the Roman Colosseum will be gone, gone, gone forever.

But seasons come and seasons go, and the balance of artistic power and influence is forever shifting, so I must again turn back the clock, acknowledging how the Chinese of late are discovering aerial arts and bringing renewed energy, creativity and gusto to silver cables and bars. And let me note how a typical crowd that yesterday entered the tent with reservations over dancing elephants may tomorrow be missing them and, the next season, rejoicing in their return.

Another problem can be the producers themselves, who misread an audience or refuse to listen to what they are hearing, who pigheadedly pursue stubbornly held views of what a circus should be. Altogether, the image of an audience seeming to be sold on second rate fare (hula hoops and fabrics, etc) can motivate show owners to present more of the same. Fact is, a crowd comped-in on free tickets may not reveal honest reactions to what is being offered it on the cheap, and so the owners are ill-served by their own misperceptions of customer satisfaction.

Changes in content and programming may also help explain why the public does not feel as excited about going to a circus anymore. Gone are a number of amusing exploits that could make a program more interesting and varied — horizontal bar acts, single trapeze flyers, monkeys and bears. Gone are the horse acts of dressage and the massive liberty horse drills

Contemporary Chinese ingenuity: The acrobat adds a kick ball trick and supporting acrobats beneath to a standard rolla bolla at the Flying Acrobatics Show in Beijing. AUTHOR PHOTO.

that, in seasons gone by, populated rings with festive animation. In their place, yes, perhaps there are more fine jugglers, more ground acrobats from the Orient, but are they sufficient to fill a widening void? I take heart in a troupe of high wire walkers from Columbia, the Topastras, recreating the legendary 7-man pyramid on the high wire that was introduced by the Wallendas over sixty years ago. This sensational feat, even with lifelines, has been duplicated by only a precious few groups. In 2009, the Topastras, not apparently mechanic-free, toured with Cole Bros. Circus of Stars. And a younger generation of Wallendas is also recreating the legendary pyramid. But not until they can cast aside their tell tale security lines can they truly claim to be authentically reviving past glories. Without the element of true danger, a high wire act renders virtually lifeless its tepid reach.

Overall, it seems as if there are fewer performers out there competing for a spot in the show. If this, indeed, is the case, then the producers have less from which to draw. And that gives you, the consumer, programs of diminished diversity and depth. Programs rounded out on second- and third-rate wares. And by this time, I need not designate the types. Now, on the other hand, if you'd rather see hula hoops and motor bikes than a line of high-flying gymnasts scampering lickety split down a ramp to a springboard and flinging themselves into revolutions over elephants, well then, there you have it: your dream circus of today.

I prefer a thriller over filler. And we are far sooner to witness a resurgence of the flying trapeze than the return of Clyde Beatty or Vladimir and his Russian bears. After all, humans are or should be beyond the reach of PETA's wrath. They can do exactly as they please — unless a group of do-gooders are able to make a case against humans risking life and limb 50-feet above. In England recently, a loony labor law was passed requiring that flying trapeze performers all wear hard hats! Pray this madness does not visit our stateside big tops.

The history of the flying return display, of late in rueful decline, may turn out to have chartered the rise and fall of the circus that grew out of Philip Astley's equestrian and variety show in the round. It was Mr. Astley, as you who have taken notes will recall, who added clowns and rope walkers, tumblers and jugglers to his horse riding exhibitions as a move to revive a waning customer base. The date was around 1772. Sixty-seven years later in Paris, an ambitious acrobat named Jule Leotard got an idea for a new kind of aerial act involving two swings. Between each he turned a single somersault after flying away from one en route to catching hold of the other. Something quite extraordinary was born in France that would eventually captivate American circus crowds as no other feat did.

Leotard's brainstorm was slow in reaching majestic maturity. It would take other people with more complex dreams. Twenty years later, in 1879, another air-breaking event occurred in Paris when Eddie Silbon sailed through two somersaults into the hands of a catcher. This brilliant addition of the second flyer as catcher gave wider wings to the act, making possible the triple. That trick was first turned not by a man but a woman, her name Lena Jordan. She thrilled a group of Aussie spectators in Sydney, in 1897. And it would take a dozen more years before a male performer could duplicate the extraordinary feat. In 1909, Ernest Clarke earned the honor in Havana, Cuba. Tony Steel added half a turn to the trick when he made it three-and-a-half down in Durago, Mexico, in 1972.

When the quad? If the quad? A great classic flyer named Miguel Angel Vazquez, all of seventeen years, achieved the circus miracle of miracles before a Tucson, Arizona audience at Ringling Bros. and Barnum & Bailey on July 10, 1982. What a greatest show on earth it was *that* night. Headlines around the globe celebrated the Miguel's historic achievement. Some declared him the best athlete in the world. This lithe human meteor, this circus star of the universe, spun 2,630 quads during an unprecedented 14-year span that may never be equaled. Although there have been a few other flyers who also turned the quad (the Flying Cranes, for one), none can begin to match the phenomenal success rate achieved by Miguel. He took the circus to its highest summit athletically and artistically. Through the excellent eighties he flew. And through the eighties, you might say that our American circus lived out its last great decade.

The Prince of flyers caught his last quadruple somersault on November 12, 1994, while appearing in Germany with Circus Krone. He continued flying for another 10 years, some of it amidst the indifferent atmospheres of Las Vegas venues. And then, as they all must do, Miguel Vazquez came down. He came down in 2004 at the age of 38. Since then, when we examine a seemingly slow decline in trapeze art, it seems as if the circus has given up on its highest aspirations. At Circus Vargas, its headline act, the Flying Tabares, are as likely to give you all flash and no substance, as they are to demonstrate why they won a Gold Clown at Monte Carlo in 2004. A triple? Don't count on it. Of my four visits to Circus Vargas, only once did they attempt it. Nor can I recall them taking on the universally common passing leap.

There may yet be hope. For the first time in nearly a quarter century, the quad was given fresh wings when Ivo Silva, Jr., of the Flying Caceres, landed his first during opening week with Ringling Bros. and Barnum & Bailey in Tampa, Florida. The season: 2010. Will Silva establish a continuity approaching that of Vazquez? So far, the trick has eluded him as if, like a heartless lover, teasing him for a night only to leave him in abject sorrow for all the days to follow.

Mention the name Vazquez to friends. Think any of them will know who you are talking about? No, they will not have a clue. Not unless they are from the vanishing class of circus fans who can tell you about the

The last great flyer? Quad God Miguel Vazquez returns to the air during a workout in Las Vegas, 2010. COURTESY OF PHILIP WEYLAND.

summers when big tops played to thousands rather than hundreds. When circus day paraded down Main Street and caused schools to close. When Con Colleano danced like a toreador on fire across a tightly strung low wire. When May Wirth turned somersaults through paper hoops on the backs of cantering horses. When the Wallendas inspired a 15-minute standing ovation at the old Garden.

Now, if a Chinese acrobat were to spin four somersaults from fly bar to catcher's grasp, given the country's classic deference to modesty and group identification, would the world even know? Not unless the artist were to be presented with just respect on foreign sawdust. So beware the occasional challenge to search beyond the mist when you can't see the face.

Anthony Gatto to Francis Brunn. In a boyhood blessed with world-class big top stars, I beheld Brunn in his prime, as I would, over fifty years later, Gatto in his. The one proudly announced with Polack Bros.; the other, anonymously with Cirque du Soleil. These are the rare artists who cast searing imprints of perfection deep into your soul. If you let them. So deep that you are left with a lifetime of haunting memories and high expectations. And those memories and expectations call you back to the big tents time and time again. Back hoping to experience the same thrilling satisfactions that turned you into a believer in the first place.

Be careful. It can become a religion.

15.
Last Impressions

*When you're down and out
lift up your head and shout,
there's gonna be a great day!*

A ringmaster's vocal chords rose high and glorious. A parade of circus stars from nations far and wide streamed out onto the hippodrome track. A presidential election year was at hand, reason as good as any to celebrate democracy in action. And so marched the sure-gaited performers, bringing to a triumphal close one of the *greatest* greatest shows on earth I'd ever seen.

The audience swelled in euphonic agreement, a rare show of unity at the time, 1968, when the nation was politically at war with itself. Somehow, in a three-ring setting, two sentimentally rich themes, circus and patriotism, clicked in tandem, a double whammy topped with spangles and a rousing old Broadway show tune. What a finale that was. We had just witnessed high-spirited Tito Gaona turn three perfect somersaults on the return trapeze and then, upon dismounting to the net below, bounce back up high enough into the circus sky to end up sitting, spunkily erect, on the catcher's swing! The Flying Gaonas were now safely back on earth swirling their capes, taking their victorious bows while the audience cheered, while roustabouts hurried in to strike the net. Silver poles came crashing down. Blaring trumpets went sailing up. Windjammers scaled the tumultuous notes of a heroic fanfare, and in came the last parade. The ringmaster, Harold Ronk sang of Gabriel's imminent warning…of his high-soaring horn that would be heard by everyone far and wide.

Down and around the hippodrome track marched the entire company. "There is a brotherhood of man!" declared the vocalizing Ronk. Come November, the country would be returning to the polls to elect a new leader, thus a grand finale titled appropriately "Democrats and Republicans."

Into the rear ranks thundered 18 prodigious pachyderms, on time, on pointe, precise and powerful. Circus all the way. Up into a screeching long mount they roared, each behemoth placing his big front feet onto the back of the one preceding him, each joining in to lend stature and force to the ambulant spectacle, to herald a thousand angels in the sky.

The crowd rose from its seats into a spontaneous burst of gratitude, awe and applause, cheering one remarkable show.

"All out and ovah!" once shouted the sawdust orator after the last act. "All out and ovah!"

And, oh, what a show it was when three rings overflowed with action, the seats with happy fans. When the man in red sang, "…there's gonna be a great day!"

Bringing the 1968 edition to a climax, Ringling Bros. and Barnum & Bailey pulled out three knockout features from its bag of tricks, any of which alone could have sealed the deal: top flight trapeze act, fast moving parade, and rousing allusion to the American storyline.

"Storyline" you ask? Under Richard Barstow's straight-ahead direction, Ringling-Barnum got about as close that year as a circus could get at the time to narrative allusion. The angle here was the upcoming presidential election, a thematic springboard that joined jubilee song writing with circus pageantry, itself a campaign. Indeed, the circus has never been as good at telling stories as it has at living them out in the present tense. So what they gave us in '68 was a triple decker climax: flying act, parade, and Broadway style tribute to Americana.

The smartly paced program brimmed with inventive staging. That year's aerial ballet "Winter Wonderland" unveiled an invigorating new concept described in program magazine syntax, "Adroit Aerial Achievement." Lads peddled bicycles aloft, very Barbette-like, to power a carousel-rigging track from which the glamorous "North Starlets" performed on separate webs. As the ladies moved in circular patterns, Ronk sang "Love Makes the World Go Round" and thousands of bubbles sprinkled down through the rigging. The house fell into shared sighs of pleasure.

"Carnaby Street" brought out the elephants fancied up as "Hipsters and Mod-Maids," set to a mod beat by the band that referenced the rowdier refrains of the psychedelic sixties. It was a gas, man, a gas.

We all love a parade. Always have, and always will. And perhaps no other avenue of the show world is as naturally endowed as is the circus to produce showy walkarounds shamelessly contrived to tug at the heart strings. During the heyday years of the great *American* circus, most shows staged a daily street parade, the sole purpose being to drum up consumer interest and get the masses on Main Street out to the ticket windows on show grounds. Out with billfolds open, ready to pay for a seat to "the big show." The passing sparkle of feathers and sequins, sunburst wagon wheels, roaring lions and screaming trumpets surely constituted the most elaborate advertisement ever produced by the show world.

These bombastic come-ons symbolized American pride and vanity: we were bigger and better, richer and smarter and more beautiful, so we liked to believe, than any other place on the globe. Not until the late teens of the

Circus Maximus, the Ringling way. Estelle Butler rides Roman style at Madison Square Garden when hippodrome races ended the show.
COURTESY OF TEGGE CIRCUS ARCHIVES, BARABOO

last century did the costly daily rituals become too costly and impractical to continue. Other factors spelled their eventual doom. For one, city fathers grew intolerant of street damage inflicted by the rumbling red wagons. Circus owners embraced any and all excuses to send their parade paraphernalia back to the barn for good. Into the 1920s, the "grand free circus parade" gradually faded from view.

Ringling's 1953 finale, "Americana, U.S.A." PHOTO BY TED SATO/AUTHOR'S COLLECTION.

The parade got moved, well, *some* of it did, into the tent where it became the Grand Entry. And this concept evolved into the more sophisticated "production number" or, in popular parlance, "spec." John Ringling North paid it discriminating attention when he recruited Miles White to design the entire show and John Murray Anderson to direct it. Under North's bohemian bent, the old horse-jumping feats and the "Roman" hippodrome races that had by arch tradition finished the program were phased out. In to replace them came the themed finale, sometimes entailing complex aerial apparatus.

These closing spectaculars, which at their most elaborate practically rivaled the show's main specs, traversed a wide spectrum of conservative subject matter, from American holidays ("The Glorious Fourth" in

1949) to exotic locales ("Jungle Drums" in 1950), the latter touted in program notes, "A Weird Wild Tom Tomic Jubilee in The Fantastic Land of Mumbo Jumbo with Native Girls, Boys and Elephants." They could excite. They could enchant, as did the surreally beautiful 1955 closer, "Rainbow Around the World." In that radiant instance, Miles White's shimmering hues were an embracing treasure, indeed, the undisputable star. You left the show feeling subtly entranced by something very special. Something atypically mystical, not unlike the calming atmosphere imparted at some of today's Cirque du Soleil shows.

Advancing into modernity, one of Kenneth Feld's smartest proclivities as Ringling producer is to know how to end his circus with sure-proof flash. He does not speak a subtle language as was Mr. North's occasional leaning. Mr. Feld, as did his late father Irvin, seems happy to flaunt a flair for addressing the critical end point with a blast of color and narcissistic parading. He evidently knows how important it is to send the customer away on a sight show high. Certainly, Feld's epic 1996 closer, "Ariana," must rank as one of the greatest endings ever to any circus anywhere. Astoundingly operatic in shape and scoring, it remains a puzzle to me why this incredible build-up to "The Human Arrow" failed to generate lively discussion among fans and scholars who pretend to study and follow the ongoing evolution of circus art. What a gripping score. What a gripping onslaught of choral pageantry. Credits, please!

Music: Doug Kastsaros
Lyric: Lindy Robbins
Direction and Choreography: Danny Herman
Costumes: Arthur Boccia

Ariana today? With what circus? The Shriners? Where? Under the Big Apple Circus tent? On that black ringless parking lot that now passes for a Ringling set? The Ariana I saw required three rings and the encircling hippodrome track to accommodate its engrossing cinematic sweep. At last, here was a new form of spec expanding to dominate a huge indoor arena, boldly compelling in costume designs, original scoring, and old-fashioned big top hyperbole pushing shamelessly the melodramatic extravagance of grand opera.

One ring, I'm afraid, and you should be too, will not suffice. Not for Ariana. As our U.S. circuses have reverted back to single-focus formats, the outlandish workarounds have nearly disappeared. They are, by default, relics of the past. How do you stage a grand procession around a single ring, assuming you are even logistically able to? In most of the newer tents, one side of the ring butts up against the performers' entrance, thus eliminating the possibility of a march encircling the entire ring.

So you are left, if you wish, to spread your parading sentiments inside the ring itself, which is decidedly restricting. If you are a producer who operates indoors, of course you may bring on the parade full force —

A splash of exotica concludes the Flying Acrobatics show in Beijing, 2010. PHOTO BY BOYI YUAN.

assuming you still (unlikely) employ a decent number of performers to make it look like a real parade rather than a token ceremony. A parade without many bodies is no parade at all.

The Felds can still set the cast in marching motion if they wish. They too, however, are handicapped by their amorphously truncated settings which range from totally ringless to one or three rings in a variety of ever-changing configurations. Where to parade when you haven't a clear parade route? Still, Feld Entertainment has the resources and the talent to end the show with flashing sparklers, exploding confetti and arm-waving hoopla. Just what the doctor still prescribes for sending the customer away with joyful memories. And the Felds are masters at reinforcing their principal claim on the public's patronage, for they own the most famous slogan in their field: *We* are the greatest show on earth. This message is often embedded in special ditties composed for the opening and closing segments. Which introduces to these pages a fourth way to finish off the performance, with an arm-waving self-testimonial by the performers themselves.

But Feld overkill can also ruin what otherwise might be a perfect surge of action down the final drive. And is that not what we all really desire, *one* rousing climax? The wildly uneven *Barnum's Funundrum* offers a perfect textbook example of how a series of acts ill-strung together can each, inadvertently, feel like an anti-climax. Indeed, rarely have I witnessed so oddly disjointed a succession of misfires. Let me explain as best I can:

At the Oakland arena, when I attended the show in 2010, early in the second half of the program, following an outstanding flying trapeze act presented by the Caceres, though marred by the spectacle of the star flyer falling woefully short of turning a quadruple somersault, a gradual exodus of dozens of people from their seats began. And this minor migration of customers continued on through the rest of the program. Here, we need to ask ourselves, why?

One reason might have been the sledgehammer showmanship at work throughout the performance, principally the exhausting contributions of an overactive ringmaster named Jonathan Lee Iverson. In this overcharged edition, he came across as a human hurricane of sorts, laboring for a circus whose producers evidently believe that the more you can drop the words "we are the greatest show on earth!" the more you will impress your client base. I would argue the very opposite, that so prestigious a phrase should be uttered with confident restraint; otherwise, its impact will be diluted down to a cheap TV ad slogan.

Another possible reason for the early exits: Perhaps by this point in the program, those fleeing the arena felt sufficiently entertained and considered the trapeze turn to be probably the show's highpoint, thus deciding to get an early head-start on avoiding a traffic jam out in the parking lot.

"Ladies and gentlemen!" bellowed the overzealous Iverson, trying to dissuade the deserters, "we have so much more to do!" Not an appeal to flatter your product at hand. At another point, Iverson addressed the crowd, as I have never before witnessed a Ringling crowd being addressed by any announcer: "How are you enjoying yourselves so far?"

That final stretch may have been purposely laid out to maximize impact. To the contrary, however, it proved more enervating than exhilarating. After the flying act, came eight elephants who cavorted about in a mini-production number. Then a sword fight, and then some crack Russian springboard acrobats working on stilts to boffo effect.

Following this came a colorful parade of performers. Now, at last, it felt like the Big Moment was finally upon us: the highly heralded entrance of baby elephant BARACK, born on January 19, 2009. This would have made a properly suitable climax to a circus honoring in its subtitle the showman who brought Jumbo the elephant to the United States.

Incredibly, no. Through more walkouts, this circus still had "so much more to do." From triumph to triviality we fell, next subjected to one of the lamest so-called "thrill acts" that a show can foist upon the public: a motorbike up the inclined wire. And then, a rambunctious ensemble of trampoline bouncers in semi-disarray.

Finally, the *final* finale. More arm waving, costume art and Feld fireworks.

Other shows that must make-do on limited budgets can still produce a memorable last blast, albeit with less eyeliner and solar mist. They only need a little imagination to bring everybody out for one last bow. Dime store sparklers will stand in for stadium pyrotechnics. In fact, theoretically it should be much easier and far less costly to stir up a crowning flourish when you only have one lone circle to fill. Here is an opportunity to fill it well. Call it one-ring lavish.

Otherwise, under littler tops the show is likely to wrap up with a simple walk-around full of smiling faces. The more artistically ambitious shows *(Boom-A-Ring,* a prime example) may wrap up with another burst of performers simultaneously reprising elements from their acts. This can form a splendid climax, nothing more needed, thank you Mr. Feld, and please, not another song about how great you think you are.

The Big Apple Circus has its closing frames down to a T. The old Pickle Family Circus wound things up with the "Big Juggle," utilizing practically everyone on staff. This is how the new student-based Circus Bella completes its lively show. For all of its maddening artistic shortcomings, Circus Vargas gets the closer just as perfectly right as it does the opener. But then, at the very end it blunders back into grasping overkill by having its performers march out through the front door only to stop and stand there, waiting like a group of needy starving artists for adulation and flattery and autograph requests from departing customers. The strained ritual was doubtlessly concocted to sell more program magazines. There they stand, waiting to be fawned over and told how wonderful they are. And we, the intended fawners, are forced to pass them on our way out. This places us into the uncomfortable position of feeling guilty if we do not pause through the sieve of smiling faces to offer praise, sincere or feigned. There is a needy air about Circus Vargas, advertised every time the ringmaster turns to the audience to ask, "how are you enjoying the show so far?" And then advertised at the exit drill. I have twice been compelled to register a complaint with a non-performer concerning a heralded flying trapeze act of posturing showoffs who essentially did nothing.

I'm sure that's not what they were standing out there hoping to hear from anybody.

Circus Bella's closer, 2009. AUTHOR PHOTO.

Actually, there is no *one* or *right* way to end a show. Have I mentioned that a strong act — say, the trapeze — can give an audience the perfect send off? Some of the best programs manage to stir up climactic fervor in this fundamental fashion, although most of them today still bring back the company for bows. Cirque du Soleil's *We Reinvent the Circus* put the frosting on the cake with a Chinese bicycle act. In their best years, Circus Vargas gave its patrons the elephant long mounts, Polack Bros., three trapeze troupes of the Ward-Bell Flyers performing simultaneously side by side.

More recently, the Chinese in China concluded one of their best shows, ERA Intersection of Time, by sending eight motorcycles into the globe of death. *Eight.* What might have seemed a crass exploitation stunt in other circumstances, in this instance achieved searing thematic heft, serving as a metaphor for the show's theme. Through it, I envisioned the country's new-found infatuation with motor power. In a sense, the evening had come full circle from a hand cart to what seemed like a thousand Yamahas roaring through a faceless neon night. It felt almost hypnotic.

Company bows at ERA Intersection of Time in Shanghai, 2010. PHOTO BY BOYI YUAN.

When a very small tent show faces the end point, is it better to skip a company encore and avoid reminding the audience of what a slender program they have just tolerated? Circus Osario took it on the chin and hauled out all six or seven of its performers. Nonetheless, there is something to be said for that one last opportunity to re-strut your spangles and smiles. A beguiling group portrait may help annul memories of individual let downs. And the flash of flesh seductively attired is, to some, a circus in and of itself. So let's take another gawking glance at the good-looking acrobat we just couldn't take our eyes off of. Please do send us out on a high and happy note, if you know what we mean, and we just might overlook a lot of things.

Circuses need to surprise and amaze clear up to the last image, the last note. Cirque du Soleil prefers neither the big parade nor the big act for its final ring fling. A show usually slows down poetically, referring back in pantomime to the original story premise, as they did so poignantly with *We Reinvent the Circus*. And as they do with *Kooza*.

So, there you have it. You have just been to a circus. Maybe one of the shows I've been discussing in these pages. Are we here already? But please, don't go anywhere yet. Imagine back, if you will, to your immediate feelings as you left the tent or arena. Imagine yourself taking a snapshot of those emotions you felt. Were you totally swept away? Partially? Did you leave lighthearted or doubtful? Elated and amused, or yawningly glad that it was over? Warmly entertained even though you had misgiving over parts of the program? Naggingly unimpressed? Peeved? Ripped off? Was it too abstract? Too pedestrian? A bloody masterpiece?

Try to recall exactly how you felt *then* more than what you are thinking *now*. Tabulate your exit emotions into a quick grade from A to F or 1 to 100, and don't quibble with yourself. Go with your inner gut. I need your honest summary feelings upon exit. Bring them with you to our next chapter. And bring a pencil and pad.

We'll need to discuss them in greater detail. I am about to try turning you into a circus critic.

16.
High Wire Critic

Emotions — basic, immediate, from the gut, uncensored by friendships or rivalries, editors or press agents, bribes or gratuities — emotions honest and raw give birth to a circus review.

Have you the pluck to write one, let alone try getting somebody to print it?

Big basic emotions are what a big basic circus stirs up inside us, swirls around and tosses high. The job of the performer is to rouse, rivet, surprise, astonish. The job of the "critic" is to honestly report on how well they succeed. If the entertainers are on their game, in touch with the moment and bristling to impress, you are more prone to feel connected and sold and therefore more fired up to file a positive notice. Of course, at the other end of the spectrum, if you must suffer a schlocky experience you should be prepared to fearlessly say so, and this will mandate your elaborating on the specific reasons why. It is no more acceptable to toss out innocuously gushing platitudes, the mark of a suspiciously puffed piece, than it is to issue vile invectives, no matter how clever and witty you believe them to be, without substantiating your reasons why.

Whatever it was you felt just then, that should form the critical underpinnings of the review you are about to compose.

Don't "think" at first. Feel. Feel. Feel. Dig deep into your fresh memory of what you've just witnessed and ask yourself as you review a mental list of the acts: how did each of them affect you? Most important of all, how consistently engaged were you, such that you hoped the course of action would continue non-stop? How many memorable tricks brought off by the performers spring to mind? Were you left fully satisfied? Only partly? Hardly at all? Left feeling so high on circus art that you already have a good feeling about checking out the next circus that comes your way? Or simply, be truthful here, wondering why you came in the first place and how you can be first off the parking lot? Be frank in answering these questions and then in allowing your answers to form the foundation of your appraisal. Otherwise, beware, you are not going to turn yourself into a genuine critic. Honesty to yourself, to what you feel and believe, is the first lesson to be practiced in your conversion from fan to judge. And the more you practice it, the easier it will be at the outset to form and reinforce correct critiquing habits. Really, it's something you have to teach yourself. You must value it enough to embrace it fully, as in full time. Part-time will not do. You are either true to the core of your emotions or not true at all. "Probably" or "sometimes" does not count. The subject is not complex. You either are or you aren't. Equivocation does not a critic make.

Why do I stress *emotions*? Because emotions bear a clear truth that need be honored and drawn upon if you are to craft an authentic notice. Your mind can in any number of ways deny or contort, glorify or denigrate that which you have just experienced, and this too often happens in the deceptive service of spinning for a friend or a company with whom one has hidden business interests, or issuing a purposely negative review out of personal spite or envy in a veiled attempt to harm the achievements and reputation of a rival or of someone against whom you are seeking revenge. Your emotions do not lie; they are what they are, period. Your intellectually nimble mind can lie in a thousand ways.

The first thing in your preparation is to commit to an exercise in reviewing from the gut. Your gut. You can always back out later if the drill induces vomiting, resurrects a Twinkie addiction or leads to suicidal dread of social disenfranchisement. Okay, let's start.

Make a list of every act in the program. Remember, the "acts" are the all-important building blocks upon which you will develop a sense of how to evaluate them in total. Now, go down the list, recalling how each act made you feel while you were watching it. Put some kind of a mark next to it, Could be A to F; 10 to 1; an asterisk (tops) or dash (not good). You can use words like "so so" or "outstanding" or "average." "Great" will also work. So will "lousy" or a lot of other words I won't mention here.

This list will serve as your anchoring guideline. You should continuously refer back to it as a safety check against placing too much emphasis on staging elements. While flashing lights and neon navels can be a plus, they should not blind you to the primary content. For instance, this list should help you avoid blasting the program merely because one of the costumes reminded you of your grandfather's long johns, or heralding the show as "ground breaking" because they played your favorite song (the one that spins you into painful ecstasy over that person you met on Craigslist who stole your iPod). As you consider all of the production elements from music to pacing, it is vital that you stay focused on the collective strength of the *performers*.

So, you now have a list. Take a good look at it. These are your individual act marks. From these, you should gain an overall sense of the company's collective talents. Face the truth of it, and don't' be surprised if your scores vary widely from artist to artist. It happens more often than not. Rare is the circus without at least one redeeming performance; rare is the circus without at least one unredeeming clunker.

Next, compare the first half of the program to the last. About the same, overall, in quality? Or was one part obviously, according to your marks, superior to the other? Tracing your scores may produce a graph tracking emotional highs and lows. You might discover a directorial progression at work. Possibly connections. Give this some thought.

Now, consider key production elements. First of all, music: Think back and try recalling how effectively each of the acts was scored. Equally important is the music's overall impact on the entire program. I am still moved, whenever I think back upon the Flying Acrobatics Show I saw in Beijing, by the haunting original score composed by Guo Feng. Indeed, it is well worth repeating here: Of all the production elements a circus has at its disposal, none possesses quite the same power as does music to join a disparate assemblage of performers. A score created by a single composer stands a better chance of imbuing the program with the illusion if not the reality of cohesion and thrust.

And the very opposite can happen. Prime example, the original score for the Big Apple Circus's 2009 opus *Play On!* In its well-meaning deference to music in a multitude of forms, that year's curiously uneven offering ironically reaped the unintended consequence of *disunifying* the action. I could never quite get a grip on the show. For instance, a gratuitous rock number was made even more annoyingly irrelevant by the failure of director Steve Smith to relate it to any real circus act, which might have been revelatory. Too eclectic can be as unsatisfying as too familiar.

Your judgment call on music will be your most personal call, for we each respond the strongest to the tunes we prefer. There are ever more types of music to draw from these days, and this expanding reality is likely to increase as a wider array of cultures assume larger influence in popular entertainment. So perhaps the best you can do is to determine if the scoring matched the dynamics of the respective acts. On this one consideration alone, you should be able to make a fairly objective call, however much the score failed to move you personally.

You are encouraged to resist conventional expectations. Let's say you are watching a flying return act and you believe it is most suitably served by a waltz. The band may instead render something slower or something jazzy. Right or wrong? I'd say try letting the music influence your perceptions. You could be pleasantly surprised. Your viewing attitude may shift slightly. At Ringling's 2010 edition, *Barnum's Funundrum*, which offered some of the best original music I've heard in years, during the tiger act one lone trumpet player serenaded us in an unexpectedly lyrical fashion. What a beguiling revelation in alternative scoring. Something completely different can imbue a standard circus staple with a fresh edge, forcing us to view it from a new angle. Our perceptions may be challenged such that we discover things we had previously overlooked or under appreciated.

Here is another illustration, and from yet another tiger act, this one presented by Germany's Judit and Juergen Nerger at Cole Bros. Circus of Stars in 2011. The slinky smooth exhibition progressed with remarkable fluidity and restraint, the animals moving seamlessly between their tricks. What made the display particularly memorable was the hauntingly relevant music, free of old school bombast, which combined familiar refrains with contemporary scoring, each lyrical passage addressing the action with a rare embracing sensitivity. All together, the calm animal movements, the mood and the music produced one astonishing display.

On the other hand, there are those annoying occasions when music can sound clumsily irrelevant to the action at hand. For instance, a group of jugglers tossing clubs to a mournful ballad may strike all but a precious few as woefully off the mark. Not every new twist works. Stay open, nonetheless.

Any way you hear it, given our widely divergent tastes and consequent responses, circus music is the most difficult element to rate. Both the Russians and Cirque du Soleil have shaken up the charts, in effect challenging our notions of what a group of musicians under a tent should sound like. Because both producing entities have reached for balletic effects, they are more inclined to foster serious symphonic or contemporary new age scoring.

All of the above having been said, you must remain true to the emotions you felt while each act was being performed, realizing, too, that your emotions were to degrees influenced by what you heard. Why do I harp on that list of the acts you made at the beginning of the exercise? You would be utterly and unprofessionally derelict in your duty not to acknowledge the excellence of a wire walker or a contortionist, no matter how much the music that accompanied their work left you wanting. Say so. It is also valid to question the musical direction when it clearly seems to have failed an artist.

How much should your overall evaluation be affected by the music? You are watching a performance and you have every right to assign every element of the performance a grade; music is too critical a force to overlook.

Not live: CD recordings accompany many shows. Some sound like old PBS rock-and-roll tributes; others, like a disco out of the 1980s. Some are up to adequate. The point is, do the recordings lend the impression of variety and balance? Whether pre-taped or live, we have every right to expect effective scoring along with proper amplification. If the sound system is muddled, mark it down. There is no excuse in this age of affordable technology for a producer sending static into our ears.

Next, costumes: How appealing. Enchanting? Okay, colorful? No, merely pleasant? Forgettable mishmash? How many distinctive colors and designs can you recall? Believe it or not, a producer does not need a fortune to dress up his cast attractively. Kelly Miller Circus, now operated by John Ringling North II on a tight budget, has put out editions that bore distinctively radiant costumes. The best shows are visually unified.

Lighting: How easy and clear was it to see everything? Did you suffer through light-deprived moments, unable to follow a performer's every move? A clear view of the action, in my view, is always preferable to fancy area lighting. Ringling-Barnum, these frustratingly ill-lit days, employs spotlights in a manner that throws distracting shafts of piercing illumination onto sections of the audience, basically blinding the eyes of unlucky customers. I've winced and fought to see aerial turns through powerful follow spots when I sat directly in their paths. The Felds, and this is my theory, purposely refrain from ever bringing up the house lights in order to avoid exposing thousand of empty chairs to their customers, for, too often these days, that is the case in the major indoor venues.

Introductory announcements: There might have been a ringmaster. Might not have been. Our newer youth-organized companies have tended to shun the traditional man in red. Some shun such gilded oratory altogether. Since I've heretofore addressed this topic in my chapter on how circuses are directed, let that suffice.

And allow us, then, to advance on to arguably the three most critical staging elements in the program: pacing, rhythm, and transitions. Looking back, give me a quick impression: was the show tightly paced? Did everything sail efficiently apace, each act merging smoothly into the next? Or was it a plodding hodgepodge broken up into parts separated by concession pitches and/or puzzling dead spots between some of the turns? By an intrusive announcer asking you at intervals, "Are you enjoying the show so far?!!!!" The best programs move relentlessly forward with pace and assurance. They do not stop.

Entrances and exits: these are the transitions that can glue the individual turns together so that they move steadily forward one after another. A good director will vary the manner of entering and exiting. You do not want to see a show as redundantly stagnant as this: Act performs, takes

Equestrian director Fred Bradna's mantra: "Nothing is so bad in the circus as a pause." COURTESY OF TEGGE CIRCUS ARCHIVES, BARABOO.

a bow and exits. Ringmaster enters ring, announces next act and exits. Next act enters ring, performs and exits. Ringmaster returns to announce next act, and so forth. This amounts in the extreme to the stodgy old European format. A skilled director will diversify transition points. For example, an emerging line of tumblers might be marching up one side of the track while a horse rider, having just completed her turn, is exiting down the other.

So there, you have an overview of the key components that make up a circus program. Now, go write your review!

No, I can't tell you how. That must be up to you. And you will find it in your own voice and your own way. A review can be composed in many voices, from first person to third, academic complete with footnotes, to aggressive. You can say everything you wish to say in so tactful a manner as to leave the reader nearly oblivious to the depth of your delight — or disdain. The risk you take in taking this more circumspect approach is that your convictions, assuming you have any, may fail to register with anybody. Ultra diplomatic prose can raise doubts as to your intent; do you really mean what you seem to be saying or are you maybe a little insecure in your conclusions? This can signal that you are trying both to be critical and yet sympathetic to the plight of the artist or show in question, and that can lead us further to wonder if you might be friends with the subject you are covering so equivocally. Such a review brings into serious question what the critic actually believes, which is the sure road to failure. Nobody will listen to you for long. Most of us regard diplomacy to be part shell game through which the diplomat reveals very little of what she actually is thinking.

There is yet another key issue in play here, and that concerns the bias of comparative analysis. Are you ready to judge the circus you have just seen exclusive of comparing it to other shows or to a set paradigm engraved in your mind? For me, there is little debate. You must be open and ready to take each circus on its *own* terms, up to a point. We will assume those terms essentially consist of circus acts. Here is the problem that will arise when you try grading a circus against a fixed personal belief of how all circuses should be graded: Not only are you refusing to consider elements which vary from the standard you falsely believe to be inviolate, but your critical reviews will soon become irrelevant to all but those who share your notions of what a circus must be.

Under any big top, it is fair to expect a number of traditional acts. Here is where you may find yourself grasping to make a judgment, especially if the animals are missing. Minus their presence, should you give the show under review a lower overall rating? This is your personal call. Although I believe that a circus without animals is incomplete, I have also seen shows that merited four stars. For me, they offered excellent artistry and they managed to convey the true spirit of circus, which is essentially its power to astonish and inspire.

Along the same line of reasoning, when you hold to a set package of traditional circus features, if Circus A does not include a flying trapeze act, should it too be discounted as being not a real circus? Were I to have judged the Pickle Family Circus against the Ringling show, I would have had to downgrade a very charming enterprise that had entertained me on its own more modest terms. Likewise, had I judged the Ringling show against a one-ring Moscow Circus from Russian during the Soviet era, what a nearly impossible undertaking that would have been. Circuses differ markedly from one to another. The primary challenge you face is to judge each as a unique entity. This does not mean that you will give every one a pass. How entertaining was it, whatever it was? That's the more important question, in my view, than how close did it come to matching Circus X or Circus Y.

If you get serious about reviewing, you are bound to come up against a minefield of conflicting forces and personal associations that will work against your efforts to file candid evaluations. How best to insure against such inevitable pressures?

First, *buy your own ticket*, stupid! Do NOT accept a pass or comp from anyone attached to the show. In so doing, you have already compromised your ability to stay true to the mission. Need I explain why? Now, if you are given a press pass by a media employer, be it the *Green River Gazette* or a TV station, such that you yourself had no contact with the show, this is a better option, but it too may come with possible strings attached. Your boss may try influencing you by alluding to a personal relationship with the pass provider, possibly hoping to sway your review and please the source of your cushy VIP chair. The manipulations never end. Beware.

Secondly, you are exhorted to stay away from the backyard. This is that special, somewhat privileged place behind the big top where fans wishing to cut up "jackpots" (gossip) with circus people go. Back there interacting with stars and big shots, you risk falling into quasi friendships with a clown or animal trainer on the hunt for a good write up. You also risk being snubbed by the sexy bombshell who hangs by her teeth, over whom you have been pining, and this could negatively affect how you will cover her in your notice. You could end up writing a review that tosses kudos to your chummy clown-friend and refuses deserved praise for the lady who declined your offer to spend a moment after the show at the Kiss-in-the-Dark Lounge. And you have failed miserably. Repeat: *failed miserably!* Are you starting to think that life in a convent would be easier than this?

Too many circus "reviews" are nothing more than valentines for backyard buddies. Some are, believe it or not, turned out by fans who did not even take the time to sit down and watch the show itself from start to finish, so busy were they trying to hob knob with everybody in the backyard who would talk to them so that, afterwards, they could boast about it to their friends.

Most of the reviews turned out by the fans are invariably upbeat (read the *White Tops* or *Circus Report*), lending a triumphal impression that this year's show was better than last year's, which itself was better than the year before. The smaller tent show owners are ill-served in this manner, for rarely if ever are they reviewed by newspapers or other media outlets, and the only notices they will get are those produced by their adoring acolytes. Indeed, so supportive are the fans, that in one not so distant *White Tops* review of the Cullpeper and Merriweahter show, the writer listed "Peanut Pitch" as one of the acts in the program. Incredibly, here was a circus fans club in effect codifying a blatantly disruptive form of merchandising.

The fans who pen reviews tend to leverage their perceived power and status in order to win backyard visits to big shots and ring stars. Most would rather fashion a rosy report than dare jeopardize their good standing within the circus community. So, if you are really about reviewing rather than lionizing, you should stay seated in the audience, watch the show in its entirety, exit the tent or auditorium and leave the lot at once and go home. And don't look back. At least write your review first and send it off to your publisher or post it online before you think about invading the mobile park scene back of the tents.

I've mentioned conflicts. Your hardest job will be to dodge them altogether. Stay focused on the act itself rather than on the person who performed it, if that person happens to be somebody you are hoping to court — or strangle.

Should you review the work of a spouse or close relative? You should in all instances recuse yourself and state your reasons why, or simply state up front that you will not include in your notice any comments about a certain artist because of a personal relationship. Now, if that person happens to own the show, you are treading on thin ice. You should not be reviewing it at all. The farther away you are from everybody connected to the circus, the more ideally positioned are you to practice the finer art of criticism. Indeed, to give everyone a fair shake free of personal bias or past or current affiliations. In my book, friends should be friends to each other, not critics.

It is not an easy thing to do. You will be going up against a culture of indifference to the very idea of circus reviewing. There are those who believe it odd to critique a circus at all, for they see it more as another cherished American holiday, the main reason, I have concluded, why many shows are today preceding their performances with the National anthem, sometimes including the parading out of an elephant bearing the American flag draped across its back.

Who dares review Easter or Christmas? For many years, the formidable American 3-ring circus was celebrated in this manner by the best press agents whose goal it was to court city editors with rhapsodic prose alluding to the "holiday" angle and to unload free tickets on city desks. Ringling toutmasters led the way, shrewdly helping to insulate the circus against the sort of critical coverage that is regularly directed at virtually all other forms of amusement, from movies to popular music.

Casting a day under the big top as tantamount to a national holiday became a major story slant in press kits. And a grand sacred cow was born. Old industry weeklies from *The Clipper* to *The Billboard* by custom did not issue objective notices. When feisty Sime Silverman founded *Variety* in 1905, he made a big to-do about separating editorial from advertising, and he vowed to review all acts and shows independent of their ads place in his pages. To Ringling Bros. and Barnum & Bailey Combined Shows one year, he sent three scribes, one to cover each of its three rings. That may have been the only time ever in the history of show business when a notice was penned by a triumvirate of critics.

Variety set itself apart from mainstream conventions. *The Billboard*, edited for a time by circus fan and author Tom Parkinson, was essentially an industry supporter, shunning critical reviewing. In my youth, I read its predictably affirmative notices, which, nonetheless, managed to impart a feeling of objective analysis. Rarely did they impart serious reservations. At their most negative, they might hint that the show was not quite up to the one last year, but it was still a very good show. That sort of bland equivocation is rather useless to the serious consumer seeking professional guidance.

When America first witnessed a program encompassing three rings at Barnum & Bailey's Greatest Show on Earth in Madison Square Garden in 1881, two first night notices of the bold new enterprise offer a textbook case of the stark differences between a glow job and a genuine review, a sampling of which:

From *The Clipper's* man, Edward Hoagland, a master at graceful gush, came this: "As a show, from first to last, the new organization was a splendid success...the entire performance on first night was almost without flaw." His write up continues apace in the triumphal vein.

Over at *The New York Dramatic News*, an unnamed critic exercised a free hand at nuanced analysis: "At last, Mr. Barnum's name is attached to the greatest show on earth in reality as well as upon paper...These are ordinary features...Madame Dockril is undoubtedly the most accomplished female rider in the world, but a good deal of her success is, beyond question, due to the sort of artificial bustle which is worked up in her behalf...We did not enjoy this part of the entertainment and we don't believe anyone else did. In the first place, her [Dockril's] horses were not particularly spirited and did not run at all wildly. In the second place it is not a pleasurable spectacle to any but the grossest vision when a woman deliberately undertakes to spread herself over the backs of six horses. The feat is no doubt a difficult one, but it is also more or less disgusting."

So, you can see what a difference a discriminating review can make, and how valuable it can be to history. Remember, your prose, if it is honest, can resonate down through the ages and leave truthful tracks in the sawdust.

The "reviews" that appear in the fan magazines are rarely, if ever, that. For example, the Circus Fans Association of America (CFA) has been unstintingly pro circus from its beginnings back in the 1920s. It is simply not in this organization's DNA to issue critical notices. This means that with every new season, every circus brings out a show that is often deemed "the best ever." These pronouncements are made by the members of a national club whose founding motto was "We fight anything that fights the circus." Evidently that would include adverse coverage.

Now and then, more by accident than institutional design, a big city newspaper will send somebody out to cover a circus, which can be risky. On exceptional occasions that somebody will return with a dissenting, even a mean-spirited write up that does not pay homage to the circus holiday. How ironic that some of the most honest big top reviewing is committed by journalists who may have little interest in or knowledge of the subject, but who can bring a legitimate degree of critical candor to the task. *The San Francisco Chronicle* once blasted James Bros. Circus in one of its early dates, terming it "the biggest hold up since Frank and Jessie harried the Union Pacific in old Missouri." I can't recall ever reading a more caustic review, though it was likely deserved.

"The bareback riders were, for the most part, pathetic."

In recent seasons, *Chronicle* arts critic Steve Wynn has contributed discriminating, arguably spot on reviews of Ringling Bros. So, too, *The San Francisco Examiner's* Leslie Katz. At *The Chicago Tribune*, theatre critic Chris Jones, a rarity among his class in the shrinking Fourth Estate, treats circuses with the same analytical attention.

And then there are those reviews that reek of incest and patronage. Many arrive as warmed over press releases thinly rewritten by small town newspapers that can't afford to craft a review of their own and have no problem in puffing and padding, probably for free tickets or to support a local sponsoring organization.

Believe it or not, the veiled press release parading as a real "review" will now and then infiltrate major news outlets. *Variety* once reviewed a non-existent chimp act at Circus Vargas; a week or so prior to the *Variety* scribe's allegedly sitting down to assess the show, the act had quit owing to a death in the chimp family. Even more mystifying was a *Variety* notice filed in 1986 following the opening of the Big Apple Circus at Damrosch Park in New York, in which nothing less than a full-scale resurrection of a circus god took place. Read this:

> "The Flying Gaonas trapeze troupe is uniformly strong, and performers use every inch of the tent's space for their aerial work, which includes a spectacular triple somersault by Alfredo Codona."

In case you did not know, the great Alfredo ended his life in 1937. How I would love to have been there that night in New York when he flew again!

The Denver Post published what, on the surface, *appeared* to be a review of Ringling-Barnum's *Zing Zang Zoom*. The story opened with a string of adjectives — "Ferocious Bengal tigers and death defying acrobats..." — clichés suggesting the influence of a Ringling press release. Was *that* a reviewer's prose? Upon closer examination, the writer, John Wenzel, appeared almost certainly to have converted press kit materials and an interview with Kenneth Feld into a drum roll for Mr. Feld's show biz holdings "No other circus act comes close to the vibrance, scale and general appeal of a Ringling Bros. show," wrote Wenzel, who did not himself issue a single personal reaction to any of the items he presumably saw at Zing Zang Zoom. Rather, he inflated in glowing terms Mr. Feld's very modest track record as a Broadway producer. He quoted extensively from the Feld "interview," thus allowing the circus boss himself to color and direct the article's affirmative tone. This piece was, plain and simple, a veiled endorsement for Feld Entertainment. Any circus is free to do everything it can to promote itself. The critic is also free, if he or she wishes, to honestly critique the show.

Ernest Albrecht's admirably serious *Spectacle* is a quarterly journal that treats the circus like other art forms are treated. Albrecht's write-ups tread a more collegial path. My only quibble is that some of his contributors are themselves current or ex-circus executives, and so anything they write may bear hidden conflicts of interest. Among the writers, there is Dominique Jando, who served as associate director for the Big Apple Circus for a number of years, and who, from time to time, teaches at the San Francisco Circus School. As knowledgeable as these *Spectacle* contributors may be, what are we to think when they tackle a circus review? Such a nefarious undertaking is tantamount to a Nederlander Organization executive reviewing a new Broadway musical produced by the Shuberts. It does not make sense. Only under the big top.

Here is Jando in the Fall 2007 issue of *Spectacle*, dismissing as "third rate" an American show that presents acts from Russia, in the same article lavishing unequivocal praise on the circuses from Moscow that toured the States during the 1980s. "Glorious," he called them. In Jando's curiously smug comparison, he fails to recognize that some excellent acts have toured the States not just with the Sarasota-based show he was referencing, but with a number of other circuses both small and large. I've seen some that were first rate, like the mother and son team of Olga and Dimitri Timchenko on Circus Chimera who turned in, respectively, captivating big box illusion and hula hoop juggling numbers. Jando also fails to recall or conveniently overlooks a fact of life in Russia: not every act that was sent out to tour with the Moscow Circus companies through the early 1990s was a winner. Not by a long shot. Firm in his bias, Jando concludes, "The Moscow Circus we see here, in the U.S., has definitely nothing to do with the true 'Moscow Circus.' Thank God!"

Spectacle is slightly colored by the editor's advocacy of the newer form of circus that significantly incorporates theatre and ballet. This makes the quarterly a viable voice for counter cultural forces within our newer shows seeking a larger following. Indeed, the circus of the future may more and more come to resemble that which *Spectacle* so generously embraces and is, therefore, prepared to cover with conviction. Then, perhaps, the pages of Albrecht's scholarly periodical will feel more urgent than they do at the moment.

To be a "circus critic" is to face a future more challenging than that faced by critics in any other venue. Why? Because circus art at the moment is in such a turbulent state of flux. Film and theatre sticks to scripting. Plot and character remain its essential ingredients. A circus show, however, can be so many things. Like dance, circus is abstract, fluid. It is body movement capable of being shaped and thrust into numerous directions. So the possibilities for revolution are infinite. How do you approach a widening departure from the current norms, one, for example, that takes the entire show even closer to dance? You might one day find yourself intersecting with ballet critics and wondering.

Then, do you still make a list of the "acts"? And what if your list grows short? What if this approach that I have outlined begins to feel futile? Begins to make you feel hopelessly out of touch? In fact, when do you conclude that what you have just seen is not, in your opinion, a circus at all and therefore not worth reviewing? If this helps you any, after I took in a performance of Cirque du Soleil's superlative *OVO*, I made my list, and that list and its contribution to my review was as valid and helpful a list as ever I'd made. Going by audience reactions to the performances I attend today and by the reviews I am able to find, I can tell you that the public still essentially judges a circus by its acts. Yes, it wants a good show, too.

So far, I have only once come up against the moment of letting go and turning back. And not reviewing. That was after watching a particularly sleazy edition of Circus Oz, to which I have already made mention. At that juncture, I decided that Oz is actually far more a stage show, though not a very well developed one, than a circus. I walked away and I have not gone back.

Someday somewhere, you may be sitting around a ring watching a theatre piece utilizing circus skills, or watching a synthetic marriage of circus and ballet that feels strangely stillborn. You, too, may wish to get up and walk away. Chances are, nobody will try stopping you for it is highly unlikely that anybody will be paying you to do this.

Remember this one thing: You are alone up there, as alone as a high wire walker crossing from one perch to the other who must count on her resolve and skill, faith and courage to complete her journey. And remember this, too: Upon publication of your nakedly independent views, you could come tumbling down off your literary high wire to face the scorn of those who deem your opinions too critical, or too flattering, or too biased, or too out of touch with the present, or too quick to acclaim anything trendy.

Whatever you write up there, the challenge is to reach the opposite side with your integrity intact.

And if the act of writing a circus review of the sort I have championed turns out to be against your constitution, is just too fraught with anxiety and social alienation, if it's not your bag of popcorn then, I suggest it is time to come down from this precarious perch upon which I've placed you with misguided hope, give up your paid-for seat and return to the backyard. And enjoy, as you have every right to enjoy, circus day without critical reservations whatsoever.

And go back to work, pro bono, freelancing as foreign correspondent for the *White Tops*.

17.
Ten Years From Now

"Not one circus will be left in 10 years," predicted one of the most revered press agents who ever lived — Roland Butler.

The year of his popcorn and lemonade pronouncement was 1957. The terse prophecy was passed along to me in a letter by old time fan and gad about Harry "Doc" Chapman. Fan Chapman, born in 1883, one year before the Ringling brothers gave birth to their circus, had been around the lots long enough to talk up Barnum & Bailey's 1914 opera, *Wizard, Prince of Arabia*, as "the best spec that I recall," giving second-best to the Ringlings' 1913 opener, *King Solomon and Queen of Sheba*. I, younger than he by a good half century, had seen the great and marvelous Ringling Bros. and Barnum & Bailey under the world's biggest big top but only once, only two years before. The following season, John Ringling North succumbed to the inevitable forces of progress and change and pronounced the tented circus "as it now exists…a thing of the past."

At the time, North was more correct in projecting an alternative indoor future than was his former embittered flak-in-chief, Mr. Butler, in declaring an imminent end altogether to the entire American circus scene.

Ten years came and went. Circuses came and went too. Most of them stuck around, stayed roughly in the black, trouped on under canvas or over concrete. Buildings and big tops had long flourished side by side as viable venues for the spangled set. And children of all ages continued turning out to take in the hoopla and magic offered in rings from modest to mighty. To marvel at tumblers twirling high and landing erect on each other's stout shoulders. At pretty ballerinas pirouetting daintily atop loping horses.

Ten years came and went, and the Greatest Show on Earth was still playing annually to millions, only now it was hosting their circus appetites under "hard tops," as the pundits dubbed the arenas that had replaced billowing canvas forums. Beleaguered circus king Ringling North was once again pulling in profitable crowds and holding his own against numerous modern amusements competing for the public's favor. Many times since declared dead, finished, passé, the circus somehow keeps resurfacing in some form or another, crassly promoted or brilliantly produced, season after season.

It has not gone away as Mr. Butler predicted it would. No, not by a

The Wuqiao Acrobatic Troupe, from China, perform on "Uniwheels" in the Big Apple Circus's *Dance On!* COURTESY OF BERTRAND GUAY/BIG APPLE CIRCUS.

hundred funny faces. Not by a dozen outlandish parades or a thousand sparkling fanfares.

Ten years coming and going had only proved that this "ageless delight," as Ernest Hemingway once christened it, is, indeed, ageless. So far. The circus springs eternal.

And then another ten years came and went, and another and another — and yet another. Which brings us up to a present tense remarkably different from the one we knew when Mr. Butler tore into his ex-boss, a shaken Mr. North, for radically shaking up the format during the last years under canvas. At Pittsburgh, one era ended. At Pittsburgh, another began.

In the bitter 1956 aftermath of North's controversial decision to abandon the big top for the hard top, the media and public stood sentimentally on the side of cherished traditions. Hardly a soul at the time gave a moment's thought to the plight of performing animals. That was an issue to be taken up another day. And hardly a soul questioned the humanity of allowing a circus aerialist to risk real danger in the pursuit of her art. That, too, was an issue yet to be raised in a future yet to arrive. Daredevils, as once they were fashionably known, were as much a part of circus day as were red and silver trains pulling in at dawn, the hustling of young boys into punk work gangs for a free ticket to the show, the mud and the sawdust and the blaring brass bands.

The idea of turning the show away from peril into a fairly harmless dance and acrobatic spectacle was several ten-more-years to come.

Today, it seems clear, there are fewer and fewer souls drawn to the circus. Fewer souls quite so keen on witnessing courageous trapeze stars taunt the laws of gravity. Fewer souls able to experience unambiguous pleasure over the spectacle of elephants prancing on their hind legs. Oh, to be sure, there are still plenty of takers out there for such fare, but they are less and less willing to endure the endless harassments of the animal rights protestors tossing sneers and "tell-all" flyers in their direction. Going to a circus is not nearly as innocently fun as once it was.

Conversely, there are the loyal holdouts spanning the generations who want their circus straight, who have grown tired of cerebral choreography and vague allusions to story-telling, who long for danger and daring-do, for the unedited roar of wild animals, the shrieks of a crowd being pushed to the edge of its seats in cold stone dread. They long for the "good old days." Ah, what a rosy phrase, used by every generation upon reaching a certain age and starting to compare unfavorably the present to the past. We have all on one wistful occasion or another wished that the music was more like it was way back when. Former press agent Henry Edgar mused, "I can't tell you how many times my friends and I bitched about the old-timers saying, 'That's nothing. You should have been around when the show had three rings of liberty horses and a 20 piece band and a 4-mile street parade,' etc. Now, we're the old-timers telling younger people, 'That's nothing, you should have seen what it was like in the 50s and 60s!' But we've worked to reach our old-timer status, and we deserve it!"

Fifty-five years ago writing in the *White Tops* magazine, Robert Barbour Johnson rued his own sense of loss over traditions he regarded as vital components to a real circus: "Ah, yes, the old-time 'spec' [pre-show opera] had a distinguished history, and it's a pity we've lost it. The Modern Circus, indeed, has lost both ends of its entertainment. The glorious Hippodrome races are gone from the end, and the 'Spec' from the beginning. All people see, nowadays, is the middle!"

'Twas ever thus, this ruing what is no longer in vogue. At the same time, we also enjoy the advancements that, ten years later, can produce exceptional new performing achievements and staging effects. Look what a young Miguel Vazquez achieved in 1982 when he turned a miraculous

Flying for Gold: Trapeze artist Ivo Silva, Jr., with a few quads to his name, keeps the dream alive. COURTESY OF PHILIP WEYLAND.

quadruple somersault on the flying trapeze and kept spinning it over and over for another dozen years. Along, too, will come others similarly determined to steal the spotlights and stop the show. And some of these dreamers will no doubt prove that the present can sometimes be as exciting as the past, if not more so.

Over fifty years after Roland Butler gave the circus just ten more years to final taps, in Atlanta during a 7-day period, *four* major circuses were playing the city simultaneously: Ringling Bros. and Barnum & Bailey, Big Apple, UniverSoul and Cirque du Soleil. *Four*. Would you call that the mark of an entertainment industry on its last legs?

The same year, New York City hosted Ringling, Big Apple, Cirque du Soleil, and a number of small experimental shows, including *Birdhouse*

Factory, a Swiss family circus produced by the famed Dimitirs, and a troupe of acrobats and flyers from Shanghai. For a spell, Gotham had practically turned itself into a world circus festival. Noted Big Apple Circus executive director Gary B. Dunning to *The New York Times*, "We have been succeeding in the most competitive market in the world for 31 years."

There will always be the new young to draw from. As each new generation discovers circus, some will bend to tradition, as did Paul Binder in recreating a Europe style show in Manhattan, and some will turn their backs on it. Oakland-based Circus Bella has taken its early cues from the old Pickle Family Circus. They excel with a cracking good live band and with wry comedy shenanigans, and they wrap everything up with a festive group juggle, as did the once-thriving Pickles. Los Angeles-based Cirque Berzerk pushes the envelope into adult territory, offering hip audiences a bohemian tilt into a "dark seductive underworld." These counter culture groups tend to dazzle the jaded for a time and then fizzle out, sooner than later. Nor do they ever amass large followings.

What next — The X-rated big top? UniverSoul Circus, no stranger to urban sleaze, usually ends its programs with black-centric skits. Some celebrate African-American history. Others admonish audience members, for whom, presumably, such messages apply, to shake off drugs, reckless sex, and spousal abuse. In 2011, the show got down and dirty with a graphic depiction of pimps and strippers, Johns tossing money their way, misogyny and coke, all of it reaching a rough climax when a man sold off his girlfriend to a pimp, who, in turn, slapped her around for refusing to accept her new career calling. She broke free of her slavish addictions and started over, "giving her life to Christ." Never mind a redeeming spiritual endpoint; so outraged by the sordid spectacle was one Atlanta woman, who had taken her 5- and 8-year-old kids to see the show, that she loudly complained to WSB-TV. Other patrons defended the item, some noting the circus had posted a disclaimer up front warning of adult content that might be unsuitable for children under six. But the controversy generated such heat, that at least for a time UniverSoul pulled its portable cat house from the ring.

The size of a typical performance and that of the average crowd it attracts has apparently diminished over the last thirty to forty years. We no longer sit down in mammoth tents. It is rare to see an indoor show fill up most of the seats. For now, we await the next P.T. Barnum who can reinvent an irresistible excuse that will lure the millions back into multi-ring tents of the kind that once drew Americans en masse. A Trump tent perhaps? Will a veiled sex show featuring circus skills do the trick? Cirque Berzerk, a recent visitor to a bankruptcy court, may already be history. A dance troupe specializing in acrobatics? Not for more than a lucky season or two. Circus in its heyday was a populist favorite, and what made it so lusty a draw was the raw authenticity of its connection to the real world. Remember horses and horse riders, lions and tigers, and daring young

The Kenya Boys in *Dance On!* COURTESY OF BERTRAND GUAY/BIG APPLE CIRCUS.

men and women suddenly raising sky high the collective pulse of the crowd? Remember a panoply both glamorous and gutsy, all in the same riveting rush of energy?

Gone?

From Rome to Ringling, Moscow to Montreal, the circus has passed through the hands of a succession of gifted and clever impresarios, or lucky gamblers, responding to customer whims or sensing a new market out there and daring to address it in go-for-broke fashion. Which is the reason why, when you produce a show talented and novel, you still have a good working crack at selling enough tickets to make payroll and prove Mr. Roland Butler wrong once again.

More and more, the challenge seems to be, how do the producers keep their expenses down without resorting to the mediocrity that turns off customers? How long can they survive by replicating grand old traditions? How much novelty must they infuse into the programs in order to satisfy and hold a customer base? The circus industry, such as it is, needs to continually replenish its vanishing older patrons with younger ones, or in time it may well die out.

When Mr. North in 1956 issued his dire verdict on the obsolescence of the big top, he was determined to maintain the size and scope of the three ring program. By transferring it indoors, he was able to do just that by shrinking significantly the cost of keeping an 80-car train on the road to transport 14-acres of canvas and the 1,500 employees needed to make it work. North achieved the goal. Ten years later, ten years after Roland Butler's grim post-mortem, and the nation's most beloved circus was once again back in form and thriving at the ticket counters.

But ten more years keep coming. Fifty seasons following Pittsburgh, came another drastic Ringling conversion, from three rings down to not even one. Although hastened in part by waning crowds, the removal of those three enduring circles, indeed, the most recognizable symbols of a famous American institution, completed what appears to have been the inevitable return, a half century in the making, to a one-ring universe. Some welcomed this more focused format. But some big city newspaper reporters and critics noted a glaring dichotomy in the larger indoor layouts. Minus the rings, the show looked lost and formless. Complained Phil Cornell in the *New York Daily News*, Ringling reduced threatened "to become the lamest show on earth. The new setting has all the charm of a warehouse and tends to swallow up the acts."

Addressing the issue in *The Chicago Sun Times*, Miriam Di Nunzio wrote, "What is good about the [3-ring] format is that the rings serve as the perfect frame for the entertainment, taking acts massive (such as the elephants) or dangerous (such as tigers) and making them quite intimate even in a 20,000 seat arena."

Pity the lonely arena of today when a circus tries impressing itself upon a small gathering of ticketed fans sprinkled across thousands of empty chairs. The new one-ring stars have awakened the public to the appeal of the solo act well staged in a smaller tent of intimate charm. Kenneth Feld, who returned one of his units to canvas for the Coney Island date, may discover that the future lies in the past. Perhaps he, indeed, may reach a point in circus history compelling him to issue a press release stating, "the indoor circus as it now exists is, in my opinion, a thing of the past."

Not only in the United States, but all around the world, circuses struggle to maintain viability. "Circus industry facing threat of extinction," headlined a story in *The Times of India*. Show owner Vinod Kumar blamed lagging attendance on new government laws banning all animal acts from his show, and on the indifference as he saw it of "Gen-Next," the younger set "freaking out in malls and multiplexes." Addressing an issue which I've already raised, asked Kumar, "How can a circus be made meaningful when there are no more lions, tigers or panthers...which used to perform marvelously before the spectators."

In Russia, the agency that oversees some 40 circus companies throughout the country is itself virtually penniless, begging for a little help from the central government.

China is a different animal. And we, the spectator, are lucky. So are the producers. Thousands of handpicked children selected for acrobatic training grow up under the hands of demanding coaches to wow the locals and then the world, if they are lucky, with their inventive edge and spellbinding perfection. And with the Chinese now favoring aerial acts as well, the future for world circus looks much brighter. Even the panda bear has became a part of the act; the Wuhan Circus Troupe includes one of only two performing pandas in the world, according to a write up by Christopher Majaka lauding praise upon the 160-member company:

> "I am always struck by the skillful choreography of the presentations. There is none of the P. T. Barnum style hokum and bravado that for too long was the hallmark of the American circus. It is oriental charm and craft combined with pure circus — dazzling skill and extraordinary feats showing the skill, beauty and ability of the human body — I can't wait to see it again!"

I will stick to a core theme here, worth restating: If there is any one element that sets a circus apart from all other forms of entertainment, certainly it is the performing animal. They give the show earthy vitality, and they give it a certainty that, unlike stage, cinema, TV or ballet, it is real. In the flesh real. Not an illusion but a living breathing spectacle that at any unforeseen moment could fall apart and come tumbling down, or roar off into chaos.

Panda perfect: Little "Gong-Gong" on tour with the Great China Circus in Canada, 1988. COURTESY OF TEGGE CIRCUS ARCHIVES, BARABOO.

As long as there are young people growing up who feel a need to show off, there will be some kind of a circus.

Even the established producing giants face precarious tomorrows. We can only wonder how long Cirque du Soleil will be able to continue attracting large audiences before the pubic decides that it, too, is a yesterday thing and begins drifting elsewhere in search of the next new thing. We can only wonder how long Ringling-Barnum can parade its elephants before a lawsuit somewhere alleging animal abuse yet to reach a state or federal courtroom renders a verdict against the circus, thus banning its touring menagerie from the road.

Cirque du Soleil's Las Vegas shows, during the 2009 economic downturn, were pulling in around 80% capacity, a respectable figure, alright, but they were doing it with discounts. Ringling was charging as little as five-to-ten dollars for promotional tickets. The smaller shows, as usual, were just struggling to make ends meet. And yet, to their credit, they are all still on the road, somehow. John Pugh's Cole Bros. Circus of Stars was rumored to have done so well in 2010, that it came out the following spring with a new tent containing more seats. In today's murky market, that is no small achievement.

Both Kenneth Feld and Guy Laliberte could face momentous turning points at some unexpected turn of events challenging them each to reconsider their respective visions and policies. With Feld, it may be a matter of reinstating the big top and going smaller. How ironic were he to end up operating what could be one of the world's most upscale and respected one-ring tent shows, possibly the classiest classic circus on earth, by returning Ringling to the pedestal of world renown.

For Laliberte, believe it or not, animal acts may bring him a new day, if and when he needs a new day to rejuvenate lagging ticket sales. It is fun trying to imagine what might come of talented bears and monkeys, ponies and goats in the hands of a Cirque director. David Shiner, who staged the engagingly retro *Kooza*, seems the perfect choice to integrate a pack of barking dogs and perhaps a princely pachyderm or two into a program. Guy Laliberte is remarkably flexible in his ability to embrace new and old ideas, so it is not so difficult imagining him actually reinventing his own circus once more, back to its ancient roots in the chariot races of Rome or the galloping gusto of Phillip Astley's horse-riding exhibitions.

Ten years keep on coming. And going. Were you to ask me, in a hundred years from now will there be jugglers and tumblers, roper walkers and clowns, I would answer, of course, no doubt. They will always be with us.

Now, in what sort of programs might these mortals be found? Not so easy to answer. Consider that, once upon a very distant season when you went to a circus, you never saw a flying trapeze act for it did not yet exist. In fact, it did not appear for nearly the first hundred years of the modern-era circus. Which is to illustrate that what you hold dear as "circus" is partly indicative of the time in which you live. What is hard to predict, in fact impossible, is how the various acts will in future years be merged together to create whole performances.

"When I first joined the circus and during my early years," remarked the retired Harold Ronk ruefully in 1998, addressing a gathering of circus fans in Baraboo who had come to honor his legacy as the great Ringling Bros. ringmaster, "I considered myself to be a product of the contemporary modern circus. Now in retirement, perhaps I should reconsider and say I belong to the old fashioned circus."

When you look back across two hundred years of modern circus history, what you see is the evolution more of the show itself than of its individual

Juggler on Market Street, San Francisco, 2005. AUTHOR PHOTO.

parts. Yes, some acts have become more refined, and some in the air that place more emphasis on choreography over tricks are less active. But we still have true daredevils around who take impressive, jaw-dropping risks to keep the program rough and raw, and you hanging by the grip of voluntary trepidation. And how can you subdue an animal beyond its nature? Dogs are still as full of life as were their feisty forbears, elephants, as towering a presence as ever.

The primal power of the circus act must remain at the center of it all if the format in which it is presented, be it old or new, can have any chance with the public. Circuses endure or wither away in a free market place based upon their ability to astound, period. So tomorrow will forever belong to the producers who can craft the shows in which the most unbelievable feats appear. What they achieve together will determine whether tomorrow's wizards on teeterboard and bikes, with clubs in motion or bodies in flight, have a venue in which they can earn a decent livelihood, or whether it will be back to the street corner, the park or the fair from whence they anciently came, hats in hand.

A hundred years from now, some press agent may be giving the circus ten years to live. In the same letter in which Harry Chapman shared with a young teenage fan Roland Butler's prophecy of doom, opined Chapman himself, "I think that maybe the circus could live if it was taken back into the small towns and plenty of ballyhoo is used to tell the folks the circus is in town."

Who knows, maybe a hundred years from now, some ambitious new troupe, having catapulted itself to unprecedented fame and fortune through break-out showmanship, may fast find itself attracting so many people, having to turn away thousands more, that it will be forced by public demand to expand the size of its little tent and, horror of horrors, add more rings!

A thousand years from now, maybe on some distant planet populated by humans from earth seeking maximal pleasures, a sadly reluctant impresario, having to justify an expansionist vision for the following season, will be compelled to issue a press release announcing, "the one ring circus, as it now exists, is, in my opinion, a thing of the past."

Sources

My many references to Soviet circus history and culture are based upon my research in the Soviet Union, in 1979, for my book *Circus Rings Around Russia*.

Quotes from Henry Edgar, Ben Trumble, Patricia White, Paul Horseman, Dick Dykes, and Marcus Bethea, were taken from their respective comments posted on my blog, *showbizdavid.blogspot.com*.

Much of my knowledge in recent years has been gained as a subscriber to *Bandwagon*, published by the Circus Historical Society. Highly recommended.

Chapter 1: Enter, With Luck, the Impresario

Additional insight into Guy Laliberte provided by Jean David in a telephone call to the author, June 30, 2008.

"There Goes Igor," about "Ballet of the Elephants," as reported in *The New Yorker*, May 2, 1942, p. 9.

John Ringling North's handwritten notes to circus staff, 1951, contained in the Ringling-Barnum Archives, Circus World Museum, Baraboo, Wisconsin.

Cliff Vargas under the seats monitoring the performance, as recounted by Ken Dodd.

William Taggart on ticket-selling grift at the Ringling show, in "On the Road with the Big Show in 1953-1954," *Bandwagon*, July-August 2008.

Chapter 2: From Foreign Shores

A wealth of information on the origins of the circus can be gleaned from Wikipedia, about which, suffice it to say, yes, this remarkable on-line encyclopedia is not without errors, but neither are books in general, and Wikipedia has a distinct advantage over traditionally published books in that it allows itself to be constantly updated and revised.

Clyde Beatty contract offer letter to George Hubler, dated February 7, 1952, in author's Collection.

Soviet circus official interviewed by *Amusement Business*, April 3, 1971.

The significance of Bloomington, from "Interviews and Articles on Blooming and the Circus," in *Bandwagon*, July-August 2010; also from Bradna's *The Big Top* — be warned, a great read not without errors.

Chapter 3: Directing the Impossible

Richard Barstow letters and published recollections about his directing Ringling Bros. and Barnum & Bailey can be found in the Richard Barstow Papers at the New York Public Library, Performing Arts Library, Billy Rose section, principally in boxes 2, 3, 4, 5.

Other quotes are from author's interview with Richard Barstow, 1978.

John Ringling on his brother Al, "We Divided the Job — but Stuck Together," in *The American Magazine*, reprinted in *Bandwagon*, March-April, 2010.

My quotes from Fred Bradna are taken from his book, *The Big Top*.

Chapter 4: To Go or Not to Go?

Full page Moscow Circus ad in *The New York Times*, July 10, 1988.

Eddie Howe's letter to James Bros. Circus front office, dated July 3, 1969

Chapter 7: On with the Show!

For an excellent introduction to the technical features of various circus acts from a traditional old European perspective, a must read is Coxe's *A Seat at the Circus*.

Chapter 8: Clowns Are Us

Gerald Nachman against clowning, in *The San Francisco Chronicle*, August 29, 1980.

"Unforgettable Emmett Kelly", by John Culhane, in *The Reader's Digest*, December 1979.

Also recommended, "The Power Clown," *Wall Street Journal*, August 12, 2005.

Chapter 9: Animal Attitudes

"Do Animals Have Emotions?" by Michael Bradbury in *The Seattle Times*, November 1, 2006.

James Bros. Circus review by David Braaten, in *The San Francisco Chronicle*, August 2, 1961.

Bill Ballantine on elephant training and handling, in "Brutes of the Big Top, *True, The Man's Magazine*, May, 1960.

Chapter 13: A Little Big Top Broccoli?

Harold Ronk remembering, "You'll Never Walk Alone," from a tape-recorded address he gave in Baraboo, courtesy of Ken Dodd.

For more on how the Ringling brothers planned and directed their shows, see Jerry Apps' *Ringlingville USA*.

"Mother Offended By Circus Act With Pimps, Strippers," as reported on *wsbtv.com*, February 22, 2011.

Chapter 15: Last Impressions

"Great Day!" lyric written by William Rose and Edward Eliscu, music by Vincent Youmans.

Chapter 16; High Wire Critic

Denver Post story about Ringling Bros. Circus and Kenneth Feld, by John Wenzel, "'Zing Zang Zoom' puts new spark to traditional circus model." Posted October 2, 2009.

About *Play On!* The major 2010 PBS three-part documentary, following a season with the Big Apple Circus, lends scarce evidence of a cohesive staging concept either articulated among the production staff during preparation meetings or given serous attention during rehearsals. In recent years, of the four editions of the Big Apple Circus that I have seen, two in particular standout for their excellence in concept and direction: *Picturesque* (2004-2005) and *Dance On!* (2010-2011).

Dominique Jando, "The Real Moscow Circus Still Shines," in *Spectacle*, Winter 2007.

About circuses rarely getting reviewed in the U.S. by reputable media sources: In contrast to the abysmal record, Cirque du Soleil's shows are regularly covered in most of the major cities where they appear. Indeed, the buildup and first night reviews for a typical show can equal that of a new Broadway musical. On-line research will easily yield numerous critical notices.

Chapter 17: Ten Years From Now

Harry Chapman letter to the author, April 24,1957.

Bibliography and Reference Sources

Antekeier, Kristopher, and Greg Aunapu. *Ringmaster*. New York: E.P. Dutton, 1989

Apps, Jerry. *Ringlingville USA: The Stupendous Story of Seven Siblings and Their Stunning Circus Success*. Madison, Wisconsin: Wisconsin Historical Society Press, 2005

Bradna, Fred, as told to Hartzell Spence. *The Big Top: My Forty Years with the Greatest Show on Earth*. New York: Simon and Schuster, 1952.

Coup, William C. *Sawdust and Spangles: Stories and Secrets of the Circus*. Chicago: H.S. Stone and Co., 1901.

Coxe, Antony Hippisley. *A Seat at the Circus*. Hamden, Connecticut: Archon, 1980.

Fellows, Dexter, and Andrew Freeman. *This Way to the Big Show*. New York: Halcyon House, 1936.

May, Earl Chapin. *The Circus From Rome to Ringling.* New York: Dover, 1963. Highly recommended.

North, Henry Ringling, and Alden Hatch. *Circus Kings.* New York: Doubleday and Company, 1960

Stoddart, Helen. *Rings of Desire: Circus History and Representation.* Manchester and New York: Manchester University Press, 2000.

Taylor, Robert Lewis. *Center Ring: The People of the Circus.* Garden City, N.Y.: Doubleday & Company, Inc., 1956.
A fascinating read; beware of numerous errors.

Magazines and Web Sites

The Circus Historical Society publishes *Bandwagon* magazine and hosts the Circus History Message Board, to which anyone may submit questions. Go to: *http://www.circushistory.org/Query.htm#READ*

Spectacle magazine: *www.spectaclemagazine.com.* Fine coverage, lavishly illustrated, of U.S. and foreign circus scenes.

Cirque du Soleil fan website: *www.cirquetribune.com*

Circus blogs around the world: Go to Ken Young's Circus Links for a list of them all: *www.kenyoung.net/circus,* and look for "circus links" on the main page.

Circus Report (bi-weekly trade and fan journal) *thecircusreport@hotmail.com*

The Milner Library's on-line display of the photography of Sverre O. Braathen: *http://tempest.lib.ilstu.edu/circus/dmsubjects.php*

White Tops magazine (published by the Circus Fans Association of America; actively supportive, non-critical coverage of the American circus scene) *circuselephants@yahoo.com*

Index

"Adam and Eve" 204
Agee, John 28
Alexander, Fay 50, 52
"Alice in Topsy Turvy Land" 207
Allen, Ralph 61
Alzana, Harold 124, 188
Anderson, John Murray 23-24, 66, 238
Angel, Criss 161
"Ariana" 239
Astley, Philip 42, 44, 149-150, 156, 204, 229
Atkinson, Rob 151
Ayak Brothers 29
Bailey, James A. 25, 77
Balanchine, George 19-21, 24
Ballantine, Bill 154-155
"Ballet of the Elephants" 19-20, 24, 66, 206
Barack (the elephant) 242
Barbette 29-30, 59-60, 66-67, 104, 117, 210
Barnum, P. T. 25, 77, 85, 257, 267, 270
Barnum & Bailey Circus 142, 169, 186, 203, 256, 263
Barnum's Funundrum (Ringling Bros.) 241, 250
Barnum's Kaleidoscape (Ringling Bros.) 111
Barracks, Robert A. 49
Barstow, Richard 24, 62, 66-67, 115, 117-118, 124, 207, 236
Beatty, Clyde 48, 53, 55, 153, 221, 229
Believe (Cirque du Soleil) 161
Berosini, Josephine 45, 188
Besalou Baby Elephants 152
Bethea, Marcus 180
Big Apple Circus 45, 53, 79, 80, 86, 99-100, 119, 123, 136, 172, 220, 225, 242, 249, 258-259, 266-267
Billboard, The (newspaper) 256
Binder, Paul 19, 28, 46, 136, 192, 220, 267
Birdhouse Factory (New Pickle Circus) 212, 267

"Birth of a Rainbow" 107
Bloomberg, Mayor Michael 112
Bloomington, Illinois (as circus community) 48-52
Boccia, Arthur 239
Bombayo 121, 242
Boom-A-Ring (Ringling Bros.) 168, 216, 242
Bouglione Circus 53
Bradbury, Michael C. 157-158
Bradna, Ella 67
Bradna, Fred 64-65, 67, 73, 123-124, 128, 222-223
Brown, Debra 70
Brunn, Francis 45, 125, 128, 220, 231
Buck, Frank 117
Burton, Alfred, Jr. 124
Butler, Roland 263-264, 266, 269, 274
Byrd, Geary C. 26, 166
Byrd, Barbara 26, 166, 171-172
Caceres, The Flying 230, 241
Caesar, Julius 40
"Carnaby Street" 236
"Carnival in Spangeland" 60, 210
Caron, Guy 33, 209-210, 220
Carson & Barnes Circus 26-27, 29, 53, 82, 95, 99, 154, 166, 171-172, 179-181
Case, Justin 125, 127, 168
Castle, Hubert 23, 45
Chapman, Harry "Doc" 25, 263, 274
Charming Shanghai Acrobatic Show 71
Chimal, Alex 169
Chimal Family 169
Chimelong Circus 70
Chinese acrobatic training schools 46
Chinese State Circus (in the U.K) 71
Chinese Variety Art 40
Christensen, Jorgan 221

Christensen, Michael 220
Circo Caballero 95
Circumstance (New Pickle Circus) 200
"Circus Ball, The" 206
Circus Bella 42, 242, 267
Circus Chimera 96-97, 99, 167, 169, 259
Circus Fans Association of America (CFA) 257
Circus Flaminius 40
Circus Knie 161
Circus Krone 230
Circus Maxentius 41
Circus Maximus 40-41, 43, 65, 149-150, 185-186, 227
Circus Neronis 40
Circus Osario 84, 171, 181, 244
Circus Oz 213-214, 260
Circus Report (magazine) 255
Circus Ring of Fame (in Sarasota, FL) 27
Circus Vargas 28, 79-80, 82, 95, 98, 120, 122, 163-164, 180-181, 230, 242-243, 258
Cirque Berserk 267-268
Cirque du Soleil 19, 31-32, 34, 45, 53, 55, 61, 69, 71-72, 74, 79, 85-86, 91, 107-109, 120-121, 149, 160-161, 172, 185, 193-194, 198-200, 209-210, 212, 214-216, 219, 223, 232, 239, 243-245, 250, 260, 266, 271-271
Cirque Tribune (Cirque du Soleil fan website) 121
Cirquesita 212
Clarke, Ernest 230
Clarkonians, The Flying 52
"Cleopatra" 203
Clipper, (newspaper) 256-257
Cliz Biz 158
Clown College (Ringling Bros. Circus) 81, 140-141
Clyde Beatty-Cole Bros. Circus 28, 103 (See also Cole Bros. Circus of Stars)
Codona, Alfredo 45, 65, 121, 221, 258
Cohan, George M. 64
Cole Bros. Circus (circa 1940s) 21, 117
Cole Bros. Circus of Stars 28, 110, 152, 229, 250, 272
Colleano, Con 123, 231
"Columbus Discovering America" 203
Combs, Ryan 141, 165, 171, 203
Comeau, Antoinette (see Antoinette Concello)
Concello, Antoinette 50
Concello, Arthur 23, 50, 175, 177

Copeland, Steve 141, 165, 171, 203
Cornell, Phil 269
Corteo (Cirque du Soleil) 32, 121, 193, 210
Costello, Dan 77
Coulrophobia (fear of clowns) 140-141
Coup, William 77
Court, Alfred 45
Coxe, Anthony Hippisley 59, 209
Cranes, The Flying 230
Crash Moreau 159
Cristiani, Norman Davenport 27
Cristianis, the 221
Cucciola 127, 153
Cuchulainn (juggler) 42
Culpepper Merriweather Circus 171, 255
Curtis, Tony 50
Curtis, C. D. 50-51
Dagenham Pipers 30
Dailey Bros. Circus 27
Dance On! (Big Apple Circus) 220
Davenport, Ben 27
David, Mark 48
David, Jean 85-86
De Mille, Cecil B. 23
Del Oro, Pinito 45, 128, 189
"Democrats and Republicans" 235
DeSanto, Greg 141
Di Nunzio, Miriam 269-270
Dion, Celine 34
Dobritch International Circus 118
Dockril, Madame 257
Dodd, Kenneth 103-104, 169
Dominguez, Angel Quiros 74
Dominguez, Angel Villarejo 74
Dominguez, Roberto Quiros 74
Dominguez, Vincente Quiros 74
Downie Bros. Circus 106-107
Dragone, Franco 32-34, 69-70
Dralion (Cirque du Soleil) 121
Dufresnoy, Guillaume 220
Dunning, Gary B. 267
DuPre, Calvin "Casual Cal" 95
"Durbar of Dehli, The" 203
Dykes, Dick 84, 164
Eastwood, Wally 55
Edgar, Henry 265
Edwards, Justin 31
ERA Intersection of Time 70-71, 243-244
Espana, Desi 212

Espanias, The Flying 52
Evans, Merle 121, 208
Feld, Kenneth 25-26, 32, 46, 72-73, 87-88, 109-112, 118, 152, 214-215, 239-242, 251, 256, 258, 270, 272
Feld, Irvin 73, 81, 132, 140-141
Feld, Nicole 215
Feng, Guo 70-71, 249
Flying Acrobatics Show (Beijing) 70-72, 249
Foreman, Harry 50
Franconi's Hippodrome 204
Fumagalli and Daris 134, 136
Gaona, Tito 128, 222, 235
Gaonas, The Flying 52, 234, 258
Garden, Dick 27
Gatto, Anthony 55-56, 74, 221-222, 231-232
Geddes, Norman Bel 24, 66, 91
Gleason, Jackie 136
"Glorious Fourth, The" 206, 238
Gold, Rose 45, 186
Golden Dragon Acrobats (touring company) 192, 225
Golovko, Vilen 209
Gongli, Zhang 219, 225
"Good Old Times, The" 206
Graham, Lew 65
Gramma Phi Circus (at Illinois State University) 49
Grandma (see Barry Lubin)
Greatest Show on Earth, The (film) 23
Greene brothers 48
Griebling, Otto 131-134, 136, 138, 146
Grossman, Sammy 23
H.S.H. Princess Stephanie (of Monaco) 150
Hagenbeck Wallace Circus 145
Hanneford, Poodles 127-128
Hanneford, Nellie 127
Hanneford family 67
Hemingway, Ernest 264
Herbert, Dorothy 186, 221
Herman, Danny 239
Hoagland, Edward 257
"Hoop Dee Doo" 67
Hope, Bob 23
Horseman, Paul 167
Howe, Eddie 81, 86
Howe's Great London Circus 145
Hoyle, Geoff (see Mr. Sniff)
Hubler, George 53, 55

If I Ran a Circus (Dr. Seuss tale) 34
Illuscination (Ringling Bros.) 112
International Clown Hall of Fame 141
Irwin, Bill 135
Iverson, Jonathan Lee 241
Jacobs, Dolly 117
Jacobs, Terrell 156
Jacobs, Lou 23, 134, 136, 143
James. Bros. Circus 81-82, 156, 257
Jando, Dominique 259
"Joan of Arc" 202-203, 205
John Lawson Circus 140
Johnson, Jane 21
Johnson, Robert Barbour 203-205, 265
Jones, Chris 258
Jordan International Shrine Circus (2005) 100, 108
Jordan, Lena 230
Judkins, James 169
Julian, Victor 153
"Jungle Drums" 206, 239
Karandash 137
Kastsaros, Doug 239
Katz, Leslie 258
Kaye, Paul V. 118
Keller, Professor George J. 152
Kellner, Sid 81-82
Kelly Miller Circus 79, 127, 141, 154, 158, 165, 171, 203, 251
Kelly, F. Beverly 106
Kelly, Emmett 144-146
King Bros. Circus 105-106, 115
King, Floyd 106
"King Solomon and Queen of Sheba" 263
Kline, Tiny 183, 186
Kooza (Cirque du Soleil) 55, 61, 74, 193, 210, 219-220, 245, 272
Kumar, Vinod 270
La Maire, Charles 117
La Mars, The Flying 50
La Norma 128, 186, 188, 223
Laliberte, Guy 19-20, 31-34, 160-161, 193-194, 211, 221, 272
Larible, David 139, 167
Leitzel, Lillian 45, 127-128, 186, 189, 222
Lenin, Vladimir 68
Leotard, Jules 229-230
Liao, Yi 39
Lipkowska, Gena 153

Lipton, Scott 214
Loaiza, Carlos Enrique Martin 74
Logan, Fred 48
Loyal, Justino 123
Lubin, Barry 80, 136
Lunacharsky, Anatoly 68
MacDonald, Peggy 48, 152
MacDonald, Mack 48, 152
Majaka, Christopher 270
Martel, Veronica 23
May, Earl Chapin 64-65, 187
McClain, Walter 20-21
McCoy, Casey 158
McCray, Ted 128, 180-181
McKinley, Phillip William 73
Meng, Guiming 136, 225
Miller, Dory 29
Millman, Bird 184, 186, 221
Min, Tian Run 71, 226-227
Mister Mistin 28
Monte Carlo Circus Festival 56, 150
"Monte Carlo Aerial Ballet" 104
Monteril, Alexandre 214
Moore, Bob 48, 159
Moore, David 143
Moore, Sonny 48, 159
Moore's Mongrel Misfits 48, 159
Morris, Doug 23
Moscow Circus (Russian touring company) 69, 86, 254, 259
Moscow Circus of Stars (Sarasota-based company) 100, 259
Moscow New Circus 47, 137, 208
Mosher, Willie 28
Moss, John III 203
Mr. Sniff 132, 135
Nachman, Gerald 185
"Nepal" 117
Nerger, Judit 250
Nerger, Juergen 250
Nerveless Nocks 62
New Pickle Circus 200, 212
Nine Ward Bell Flyers, the 50, 52, 60, 210, 243
Nixon, Richard M. 45
Noble, Frank 49
North, John Ringling 19-25, 28, 32, 43, 45, 50, 53, 61, 66, 68, 70, 91, 99, 108-109, 117, 120, 123, 128, 145, 159, 175-176, 189, 205-206, 208, 225, 238-239, 263-264, 269

North, John Ringling II 171, 208, 251
"Old Vienna" 206
Opal (the elephant) 48, 151-152
OVO (Cirque du Soleil) 260
Palacios, The Flying 52
Pallenberg Wonder Bears 117
Parkinson, Tom 256
Pauli, Matthew 136
PETA (People for Ethical Treatment of Animals) 151-152, 157-158, 200, 223, 229
Pickle Family Circus 42, 119, 134-135, 161, 242, 254, 267
Picturesque (Big Apple Circus) 123
"Pilgrimage of Mecca, The" 203
Pisoni, Larry 119
Play On! (Big Apple Circus) 249
Poema, Adrian, Jr. 127
Polack Irving J. 29
Polack Bros. Circus 29, 30-31, 50, 59-60, 101, 104, 151-152, 159, 210, 220, 232, 243
Poulin, Michel-Thomas 85
Pugh, John 28, 152, 272
Quiroga, Nelson 28
Quiroga, Katya 28
Quiros, Vincente 74
Rada, Mirena 123
"Rainbow Around the World" 24, 61, 239
Rice, Dan 141
Rickets, Bill 203
Ringling Bros. and Barnum & Bailey Circus 25-26, 44-46, 50, 53, 65, 72, 73, 79-80, 83-84, 86-88, 97, 100, 107, 112, 115-116, 118, 121, 124, 140, 156, 158, 168, 177, 180, 194, 202, 204, 214-216, 221, 230, 235-242, 251, 254, 266, 271-272
Ringling, Albert 63, 64-65, 205
Ringling, Charles 205
Ringling John 64, 67, 143, 205
Ringling Otto 93
Ringling, Robert 175
Rivels, Charlie 138
Rizzi, Pasqualina (see Cucciola)
Robbins, Lindy 239
"Rock! Ringling Rock and Roll!" 206
"Rocket to the Moon"
Ronk, Harold 65, 115, 122-123, 208, 235-236, 272
Rooney, David 209-210
"Ruslan and Liudmila" 202

INDEX

Russian State Circuses (today) 47, 270
Russian circuses (see Soviet Union as circus producer)
Saltimbanco (Cirque du Soleil) 185
San Francisco Circus Center and School 259
Sanchez, Flouber 74
Sapata, Jimmy Ibarra 74
Schubert, Leda 21
Segeras, The Flying 52
Sells-Floto Circus 50, 65, 107
Shamsheeva, Svetlana 43
Shanghai Swingers trapeze act 194, 223
Shenyang Acrobatic Troupe 45-46
Shiner, David 74, 272
Shrine Temples (as circus producers) 26, 29, 140, 159, 175, 176, 177, 179, 181
Silbon, Eddie 230
Silva, Ivo, Jr. 230
Silverman, Sime 256
Smith, Bernard 50
Smith, Steve 249
Sonin, Alexei 48
Soules, Gerard 48
Soviet Union as circus producer (Soyuzgostsirk) 32, 47, 67-69, 190, 250
Soviet Union circus school 46
Sparks Bros. Circus 122
Spectacle magazine 259
Spinner, Kate 212
Springer, Arthur 123
Steel, Tony 230
Stern, Louis 29, 30, 31
Stoddart, Helen 186
Stravinsky, Igor 19-20, 24
Sullivan, Henry 206
Tabaares, The Flying 230
Taggart, William 27
Tian, Cong 225
Tiebor, Roland 152
Timchenko, Dimitri 167, 259
Timchenko, Olga 259
Topastras high wire troupe 229
Traces (New Pickle Circus) 212
Trapeze (film) 50, 53
Trumble, Ben 179
Tulchinee 42
"Twas the Night Before Christmas" 206
Tzekovi High Wire Troupe 190
Uncle Heavy's Pork Chop Revue 156

UniverSoul Circus 45, 95, 99, 121, 172, 194, 266-267
Unus 23, 28, 45, 224-225
Valdo, Pat 23, 61
Varekai (Cirque du Soleil) 32, 74, 210
Vargas, Clifford 19-20, 24-25, 28-29
Variety 256, 258
Vazquez, Miguel 52, 128, 230-231, 266
Vazquez, The Flying 230
Voise, Harold 53
Walker, Cedric 95
Wallace Bros. Circus 94
Wallenda, Karl 43
Wallendas, the 45, 123, 222-223, 229, 231
Walt Disney 206
Ward, Eddie, Jr. 50
Ward, Harold 50
Ward-Bell Flyers (see Nine Ward Bell Flyers)
Wards, The Flying 49
Watson, Minor 53
We Reinvent the Circus (Cirque du Soleil) 33, 74, 198, 243, 245
Wei, Wu 46
"Welcome to the Fair" 208
Wenzel, John 258
White Tops (magazine) 255, 261
White, Patricia 157
White, Miles 67, 238-239
Williams, Mark Gebel 153
Williams, Gunther Gebel 128, 222
"Winter Wonderland" 236
Wintuk (Cirque du Soleil) 161, 200, 214
Wirth, May 186, 221, 231
"Wizard, Prince of Arabia" 263
Worth Circus 50
Wuhan Circus Troupe 270
Wynn, Steve 258
Yaarab Shrine Circus & Carnival 177
Yilao, Xiong 39
YMCA Circus (Bloomington, Illinois) 50-51
"You'll Never Walk Alone" 208
Yuan, Boyi 103
Yunnan Flyers 194
Zachinni, Hugo 45, 65, 221
Zapashny, Mstislav 47
Zarkana (Cirque du Soleil) 209-210
Zerbini, Sylvia 125
Zerbini, Tarzan 127
Zhao Family 74

Zhenya's Dogs 208
Zi, Lan 39
Zing Zang Zoom (Ringling Bros.) 258
Zoppe, Alberto 45, 127

Bear Manor Media

Classic Cinema.
Timeless TV.
Retro Radio.

WWW.BEARMANORMEDIA.COM

www.ingramcontent.com/pod-product-compliance
Lightning Source LLC
Chambersburg PA
CBHW060556230426
43670CB00011B/1840